Architecture
of Resistance

Architecture of Resistance investigates the relationship between architecture, politics and power, and how these factors interplay in light of the Palestinian/Israeli conflict. It takes Palestine as the key ground of spatial exploration, looking at the spaces between people, boundary lines, documents and maps in a search for the meaning of architecture of resistance. Stemming from the need for an alternative discourse that can nourish the Palestinian spaces of imagination, the author reinterprets the land from a new perspective, by stripping it of the dominant power of lines to expose the hidden dynamic topography born out of everyday Palestine. It applies a hybrid approach of research through design and visual documentary, through text, illustrations, mapping techniques and collages, to capture the absent local narrative as an essential component of spatial investigation.

Yara Sharif is a practicing architect and an academic, she is a lecturer at the University of Westminster and at Oxford Brookes University and is a partner at Golzari-NG Architects London, an award-winning practice that has developed a reputation of working on sustainable community projects with specific interest in issues of cultural identity and responsive design. Her work generally stretches internationally where she mainly looks at design as a means to facilitate and empower forgotten communities, while also interrogating the relationship between politics and architecture. Sharif has co-founded Palestine Regeneration Team (PART); a design-led research group that aims to search for creative and responsive spatial practices in Palestine. Her research by design was granted the 2013 commendation award – RIBA's President Award for Research for Outstanding PhD Thesis. Her built projects have won a number of awards. She was granted the 2016 RIBA President Award for Research (commendation) in the cities and communities category.

Design Research in Architecture

Series Editors:

Professor Murray Fraser
Bartlett School of Architecture, UCL, UK,

Professor Jonathan Hill
Bartlett School of Architecture, UCL, UK

Professor Jane Rendell
Bartlett School of Architecture, UCL, UK

and

Professor Teddy Cruz
Department of Architecture, University of California at San Diego, USA

Bridging a range of positions between practice and academia, this Routledge series seeks to present the best proponents of architectural design research from around the world. Each author combines innovative historical and theoretical research with creative propositions as a symbiotic interplay. In offering a variety of key exemplars, the book series situates itself at the forefront of design research investigation in architecture.

Other titles in the series

Marcel Duchamp and the Architecture of Desire
Penelope Haralambidou
ISBN 978 1 4094 4345 2

Digital Poetics
An Open Theory of Design-Research in Architecture
Marjan Colletti
ISBN 978 1 4094 4523 4

Transitions: Concepts + Drawings + Buildings
Christine Hawley
ISBN 978 1 4724 0909 6

The Architecture Chronicle
Diary of an Architectural Practice
Jan Kattein
ISBN 978 1 4094 5186 0

Expanding Disciplinarity in Architectural Practice
Designing from the Room to the City
Tom Holbrook
ISBN 978 1 4724 8173 3

'In this subtle, compassionate, and clear-eyed book, Yara Sharif offers architecture as both a tactic of physical resistance and a contesting form of knowledge and possibility – a critical mnemonic for a culture under erasure. Her profound mappings of Palestine beautifully harmonize space and life and, with courageous modesty, advance creativity and improvisation in defense of a beleaguered, precious, normality'.

Michael Sorkin, Distinguished Professor of Architecture, City College of New York, President and Founder of Terreform, and Principal of Michael Sorkin Studio

Architecture of Resistance

Cultivating Moments of Possibility
within the Palestinian/Israeli Conflict

Yara Sharif

*Golzari-NG Architects, Palestine
Regeneration Team (PART) and
the University of Westminster*

Routledge
Taylor & Francis Group

LONDON AND NEW YORK

First published 2017
by Routledge
2 Park Square, Milton Park, Abingdon, Oxon OX14 4RN

and by Routledge
711 Third Avenue, New York, NY 10017

Routledge is an imprint of the Taylor & Francis Group, an informa business

British Library Cataloguing in Publication Data
A catalogue record for this book is available from the British Library

Library of Congress Cataloging in Publication Data
A catalog record for this book is available from the Library of Congress

ISBN: 9781138694293 (hbk)
ISBN: 9781472447883 (pbk)
ISBN: 9781315524290 (ebk)

Typeset in Avenir and Baskerville
by Servis Filmsetting Ltd, Stockport, Cheshire

Printed in the United Kingdom
by Henry Ling Limited

Contents

List of Illustrations

All illustrations are by author unless stated otherwise below.

Colour Plates

Preface

A decade ago, when trying to shape my identity and role as a Palestinian architect, I became no longer able to live with the subtle acceptance of the 'norm' that existed in Palestine. I needed to zoom out in search for a breathing space beyond the constraints of the Israeli occupation. I needed to search for a broader narrative where everyday life would be bigger than the city of Ramallah, where adventures might involve more than journeys across checkpoints, and where dreams could go beyond merely those of sneaking into Jerusalem (which, after all, is only 15 minutes away from my family home). I eventually made it, but not in the way I had intended. I discovered that I could not reach Jerusalem, nor could I cross the Kalandia checkpoint. Yet somehow, someway, I managed to get out of the entrapment. Now faced with a confused identity, I realized that I have spent the past ten years of my time actually searching for my Palestine.

Between zooming in and out, I am still struck to realize that my Palestine, seen from an inside lens, is very different to that from outside. From an outsider's perspective the signs all clearly seem to be there: the Separation Wall, the contested map, the confusing landscape, the uncertainty of where Palestinian space starts or ends. When viewed from the inside, however, it is not that these signs are less obvious, it is just that we Palestinians have to live with them in every single detail of our daily life. This is probably the aspect that those from outside cannot see, since it might be too small to observe, or maybe too surreal to absorb. The sense of invisibility, subversion and in-between-ness that comes with an everyday life of surviving under occupation, time, immobility, as well as the sheer sense of chaos that this brings with it, form exactly what this book is about. Having spent ten years living in and out of Palestine, it has enabled me to see the spatial possibilities that lie in those little details and small spaces of everyday survival and resistance.

The projects in this book explore these spatial possibilities through drawings, maps, narratives and designs. What they reveal is that there is a degree of irony and power that lies within Palestinians that can subvert spaces of oppression such that they are changed into spaces of play and creativity in which social life can be recuperated. This hidden dynamic topography, born out of extreme political conditions in Palestine, may help to draw the lines for what could be seen as architecture of resistance in such a context.

Acknowledgements

This book is a collection of the different thoughts and ideas provoked by my journeys when I used to live and work in Palestine, and which were later transformed into projects when doing my PhD by Design at the University of Westminster. Throughout my journey many people have been instrumental in helping me bringing this book into light.

First and foremost I want to thank Professor Murray Fraser, now a close colleague and previously my primary doctoral supervisor at Westminster University. Without his support, time, and careful reading of my thoughts while I was doing the research for my PhD by Design, this book would not have been possible. Professor Jane Rendell, another of the co-editors of the 'Design Research in Architecture' series, along with Professor Jeremy Till, were helpful examiners for my doctoral thesis.

I'm also enormously indebted to Dr Nasser Golzari, my partner and friend. I thank him for the fruitful discussions and his critical thinking, which challenged me and pushed me whenever it was needed. I thank him for his patience, especially when it meant missing so many working days in trying to get this book completed.

Both Murray and Nasser have accompanied me since the start of my postgraduate studies, all the way through. Our thoughts, ideas and approach towards architecture have now been directed through the Palestine Regeneration Team (PART), a design-led research group we have jointly set up as a mean to explore emerging spatial possibilities in Palestine through both live and speculative projects.

I would like to thank all the residents in Palestine who allowed me to become part of their daily lives, especially the 'invisible' women, van drivers, vendors and workers who taught me how to see things through their eyes. Their company has enriched the research and made it possible with a lot of adventurous journeys to remember and talk about. Ala, Amjad and Muneer provided great humour while driving across the fields and hills, making those dead-ends more bearable and indeed possible to enjoy. I thank them for introducing me to new and endless means of resistance that makes life worth living for.

I've been fortunate in my great friends in Palestine – Sahar, Eyad and Dana – who I want to thank for the unique time we spent and the mad journeys we initiated out of curiosity, all of which ended up as the core of my work. I would like to thank Majdi Hadid for the fantastic photographs we took together, and the amazing drives we had across the Palestinian landscape, which led us to discover unforgettable locations, including those where we got lost in the middle of military areas or Israeli settlements, and struggled to find our way out.

Suad Amiry is a person for whom my gratitude does not suffice; she has always been the reflection of my thoughts. I'm grateful for her constant support, especially the invisible one. Thanks to her also for allowing me to remain an active part of Riwaq's family, of which I owe a lot and so wish to honour. Suad – as a friend, committed architect and inspirational novelist – cannot be thanked enough for reminding us of how essential it is to keep our sense of humanity and humour even in such a terrible situation.

Of course much of my work is based on interviews and discussions with different scholars, architects, planners, politicians, academics and others that I met in Palestine or here in the UK. Among these figures are Salim Tamari, Reema Hammami, Leyla Shahid, Luisa Morgnaitni and Nazmi Jubeh who all in one way or another added something to my work, whether consciously or unconsciously. I appreciate their valuable knowledge, which has been extremely insightful.

I should also mention that I owe a lot to my beloved family who have patiently endured my moods and offered me the unconditional love that kept me going throughout the difficult times. Thank you to my mother and father.

Last, but by no means least, if it was not for Palestine, its troubled landscape and the unique daily experience that I have lived – and still live – through, then I would never have been intrigued enough to direct all the confused identity inside me towards this book. And for that I'm so grateful and proud to be born Palestinian.

INTRODUCTION

In the history of colonial invasions maps are always first drawn by the victors, since maps are instruments of conquest. Geography is therefore the art of war but can also be the art of resistance if there is a counter-map and a counter-strategy.

Edward Said, 1994

Coming from a place that is so divided by geo-political conflict, it is crucial to define one's role as an architect. Choosing an ideology of practice in such circumstances is not a technical activity: rather, it becomes an 'ethical' approach as well as a political statement.

This book forms part of a research by design journey that I started between 2005–2011 while I was trying to shape my identity as a Palestinian architect. Working against the Israeli project of marginalisation, I was aware that the impact of the Israeli policies of hardening the border zone does not only bring fragmentation and destruction to the physical space, but also aims at destroying the space of imagination; Stemming from such realities, I felt the urgency to rethink architecture in Palestine, to find a new ideology which can overcome the highly orchestrated matrix of Israeli occupation. In my design-based research, I started looking at the spaces between people, lines, documents and maps for the meaning of architecture of resistance; searching for potential spaces of possibilities that can empower the fragmented society and bridge the gap between their divided spaces.

Looking back at all that has been discussed, proposed and imposed in relation to the Palestinian/Israeli conflict, it might seem that there is nothing more left to be said. We are now faced with two lopsided 'entities' superimposed on one another; neither can be integrated, nor they can be separated.

The outcome of the various political agreements, summits and talks from the Oslo Peace Agreement[1] to the 'Road Map' to the Camp David Agreement has laid bare the failure of any prospect to find a 'just peace'. Rather, all these do is to leave Palestinians with endless maps, lines, boundaries and designated areas that mean nothing apart from separating and fragmenting their social and physical space. The urban morphology of the land is being pushed to its extreme condition. As a result, Palestine today is left with an absent mental map, no longer making sense of where its spaces start, or end.

The need for an alternative discourse, especially with the unbalanced economic and political status, has thus been the focus of my work in the aim to explore spatial possibilities. I have tried to re-read the land from a new perspective by stripping it of the dominant power of lines – including any imagined ones – to expose the hidden dynamic topography born from social conditions. The outcome is hopefully to provoke a deeper and more critical kind of architectural thinking that in its explicit engagement with political and social realities, as Fraser suggests, 'moves on from Koolhaas'[2] towards a truly embedded critical architecture and design practice.

Looking at the dialogue of daily resistance also shows that within the current Israeli policies of hardening the border zones, the quest for a counter space is carving out new cultural and urban realities against the forces of power. Perhaps the most outstanding outcomes of this reality are the everyday forms of Palestinian spatial resistance, which is recasting the geo-political map of Palestine by displaying creative tools that architecture and planning have so far failed to match. The emergence of small-scale Palestinian networks seems to be able to overcome

I.1 The Separation Wall in Kalandia, 2005–2006. Photograph by Majdi Hadid.

and adapt to the situation, and as a result they can redefine the meaning of the built environment around them. These collective and informal networks/events are now also drawing their own lines for a new kind of thinking within architecture. Ostensibly, their task is to subvert spaces of pure oppression and change them into spaces of play and creativity so that social life can be recuperated.

THE ABSENCE OF THE PALESTINIAN NARRATIVE

The literature on the Palestinian/Israeli conflict is dauntingly vast. However, when it comes to the issue of colonisation and its relationship to the daily production of space, more often it is a one-sided image, focusing mostly on critiques of Israeli strategies and the manifestation of power. The mainstream literature on the conflict in Palestine/Israel has tended to ignore the social narratives involved in using and changing urban space by the Palestinian community, which is what I will instead try to focus on.[3]

Indeed, the notion of 'locality' seems to be absent in the majority of work addressing Palestinian/ Israeli conflict, especially that of western scholars, and instead the focus is mainly on the forces of occupation/occupier. The outcome is therefore incomplete, in the sense that it does not show a true account of the socio/spatial relationships that have been created. Through such studies, the dominant group – in this case, the Israeli Army – is again rendered more visible through their artefacts

I.3   Amari Refugee Camp in Ramallah,
2005. Photograph by Majdi Hadid.

of occupation, while those who in fact have to occupy the resulting space with their ordinary lives are alienated from the description of the context, and hence rendered almost non-existent. The focus is more on addressing the 'oppressor', while the inclusion of the lived realities of Palestinians and their spatial conditions is hardly mentioned.

Christopher Harker's work on cultural and political geography has brought this aspect into the surface through his very recent research into Palestine, which probably comes closest to the premise of my work. Harker, in '*revisiting verticality*', tries to explore the recent shifting topology of Palestinian everyday life from horizontal to vertical living in the city of Ramallah.[4] Harker also critiques the fractional understanding of the politics in the Occupied Palestinian Territories which leaves Palestinian people as passive subjects in that Israel makes history while Palestinians can only react to it.

Rema Hammami's work have also provided an excellent entry point for unwrapping certain social patterns, especially since she is one of the very few Palestinians who have carried out relevant research to discover the socio-economic impact of checkpoints on Palestinian daily life. Her work – especially the one exploring the economy of checkpoints – comes really close to the premise of my work, backing it up with many observations I have mapped or traced.[5]

Hammami, Amiry, Taraki, Jad and other Palestinian feminist writers offer a truer insight into the Palestinian context by viewing it explicitly from within. They have managed to bring in the local voice of

I.4 Selling fruits and vegetables
on an alternative route to Nablus,
2003. Photograph by Majdi Hadid.

ordinary people, notably the socially and politically excluded groups of low-paid workers, unemployed, women, etc. Their work, offered me a point of departure for this book, and indeed provided significant inspiration for the methodological orientation of my study, especially in exploring the relationship between the personal and the political, for which – in places – I have combined theory with personal voice.

The idea of narrative has therefore become a visible, and indeed essential, component when exploring design possibilities. I have tried to capture and represent the sense of daily life as it is experienced by Palestinians, specifically by unfolding the relationship between time and space. Narrative and subjective experience in this context became both a spatial condition and a conscious strategy to examine relationship between identity, place, the personal and the political all of which surface strongly in the chapters that follow.

The time period for the research takes us back to 1993–95 when the Oslo Peace Agreement took place. The Oslo Agreement marks a turning point in history and geopolitical changes in the present and future Palestinian/Israeli territories. In effect it has redrawn the map of Palestine and reshaped the political as well as the social narrative. As will be shown in the first chapter, the Oslo Agreement basically shifted the struggle and confrontation from within cities and villages out to the borders and margins, leaving the invisible forms of power to operate inside these spaces. Therefore, I intend to concentrate more on tracing the post-Oslo period, especially examining the gap that distances the actual reality installed by the Oslo Agreement from the image portrayed by the media in its wake.

In parallel, the socio-political and spatial character of Palestine from 2000 onward marks another turning point in which I will shed a light on. It is when Israel intensified its artefacts of segregation as represented by checkpoints, roadblocks and the Separation Wall. This has resulted in a mass collision between the rural and the urban, the centre and the periphery, the structured and the chaotic, which in effect has produced different forms of spatial resistance as well as adaptation tactics by Palestinians.

THE PRACTICE OF RESEARCH BY DESIGN

Since this book forms part of a research project through design, the relationship between text/theory and design/drawings is crucial, and indeed each complements the other. It can be seen as a process of intellectual conversation given that it facilitates ideas to emerge and yet also suggests innovative, and at times spontaneous and unexpected, outcomes. Therefore, the structure and visual layout of the book is also intended to reflect the three interdependent components of textual analysis, analytical mapping, and design propositions. In this sense, mapping operates between writing and drawing, and indeed intersects with both manners of working. I regard it as the key link in the research since it is how I navigate through the process to document, represent, question, and suggest new possibilities.

SOCIAL AND SPATIAL MAPPING: MAPS, COLLAGES AND MORE

Mapping as a technique is not only seen as a matter of documenting and describing the surface of the globe, but also a way of reconstructing a scene that is being lived through and indeed an imagined one yet to come. Here it needs to be seen both as a visual record of reality and collected narratives as well as my own thoughts on these. In this way, mapping can be

an image, a line drawing, a collage, or a combination of all these. At times the process of mapping acts as a form of documentation that captures the different kinds of social attitudes and spatial patterns which are emerging and developing in Palestine/Israel; at other times, it brings forward otherwise abstract forms that are more responsive and sensitive to the specific context, with its need for invisibility and subversion. Indeed, mapping offers the best means for recording and memorising, while also respecting the social context. Quite simply, it facilitates a space for observations that could not have been written or read within text alone.

As much as mapping triggers thought through visual forms, it also suggests aspects which need to be researched further. It poses questions to be answered and often leaves certain moments unresolved and in need of future exploration. Indeed, the precise moment that mapping goes beyond pure documentation it opens up promising and imaginative routes into the unknown. The process reveals points which are often neglected, unseen, or missed. Therefore, the outputs of mapping, especially which combined with deliberate collages, are perhaps the most liberating and open-ended part of this book, since they can always be revisited and drawn. This is why the maps produced for this study must be seen as part of an ongoing process of change, expansion and revision.

The collages as an illustrative form of mapping are intended to generate the process of thinking.

fragmentation, but can also be recaptured as 'bridges' that connect invisible networks, space of livelihood, or collective spaces to dream. Some of the collages are meant to break all boundaries, deliberately escaping from current reality to offer imaginative moments that then surface in my subsequent design proposals. In other words, the collages are employed to reflect, interpret, frame, analyse, question, propose, exaggerate and dream. For that reason I consider them as the initiation of design process where I go beyond documentation; it is my starting point for the conversation with design.[6]

Similarly, the use of maps as a medium of communication in this book has two key purposes. The first is to investigate the links between space and politics; in this case they mainly expose the shrinking and erasing the Palestinian land, and the expansion of Israeli-controlled territory. In this sense they are mainly analytical, and assist the factual data presented in the text where needed. The other purpose is to offer new insights and new possibilities. The aim is to read beyond what is there, to come up with new matrixes of 'resistance' that might operate without the limitation of boundaries. In doing so, my maps primarily emphasize spatial gaps rather than given boundaries, either by subverting existing boundary lines, or by inventing new layers. The uniqueness of these maps lies with the fact that they are very experimental, welcoming the insertions of new layers that explore what has been lost and what has been kept. In the process of reviewing the map, I have tried to draw it from below, rather than the conventional 'top-down' view, with its complex social layers of invisibility and subversion. Both allow for moments to emerge that can break and penetrate through boundaries – while remaining invisible.

I.6 Early sketches while reading the fragmented map.

Mostly they are employed to capture social and spatial moments – which go beyond the text – that demonstrate the multiple spaces and social networks inhabited by Palestinians. Collages are a way to rethink the passive way in which some writers perceive contested space, and can therefore be used to imagine new possibilities. As a result, Israeli checkpoints, or the 'Separation Wall', are no longer perceived merely as spaces of division and

I.7   A sketch from my own diary showing my journey from Ramallah to Jerusalem, 2002.

Maps, as a medium for representation and exploration, are thus very crucial for this book/research. Here I can return to Edward Said's quote at the start of this chapter, in which he calls for the Palestinians to offer alternative maps and alternative strategies to resist. This is indeed urgent for Palestinians as their maps have always been replaced by those in power (Britain, Israel, etc.). This in return has resulted in lines that 'distort' and sometimes erase the powerless, the Palestinian people, who have been only represented from the coloniser's perspective. My aim here is to initiate alternative maps of possibility that do not see Palestine, and Palestinians, as a passive audience. Rather, these alternative maps hope to put their authors in a position of greater power, and as such they act as a crucial tactic for creating new spaces of possibility.

NARRATIVE

In order to structure my writing, and to complement the techniques of maps and collages, sections of narrative text are introduced at times to bring in new voices and capture the sense of everyday life. They are seen as a conversational process to express a 'situated truth' and an attempt to understand the invisible dynamics of space. Narratives in this sense are not egotistic, but rather are 'a form of being self-reflective, aware and politically conscious', as Rendell describes it.[7] The intentional use of narrative is an attempt to bring in alternative voices to resist the authoritative stance that secretly denies the possibility of multiple realities.

The accumulation of narratives also explores the idea of whether a connection can be made between the different layers of social spaces. While the subjective stance of a personal story may be seen as 'upsetting the objective tone of academic writing', as pointed out by Rendell[8], my aim is to argue that the narratives that I am documenting constitute an 'embodied objectivity'. Their objective strength lies in the fact that they offer the partial, situated perspectives of Palestinians and it is exactly because of their specificity, their subjective positioning, that these stories give us crucial information about experiencing daily life under conflict.

DESIGN PROCESS

The whole process of navigating through text/narrative, mapping and design undoubtedly provoked and at times challenged my design proposals, by

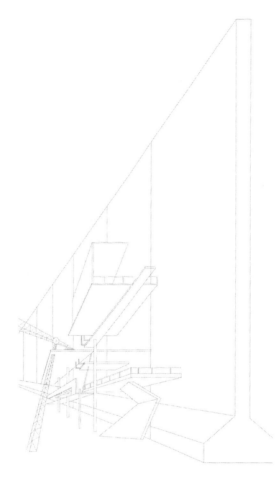

networks on the ground (these are mainly expressed through line drawings and collages). The third form has a slightly different spirit. It is a real manifestation of these findings through 'live' projects in terms of 'situated' architectural and urban interventions for an exact client in Palestine that celebrate networks which have been formed away from the confrontation and physical boundaries with Israel.

Even though in the design process I have tried to uncover the invisible fragments of occupation and overlay them onto the map. I don't in my work impose an alternative map. Nor have I wanted to legitimize the Israeli fantasy of separation with more lines drawn from the Palestinian side, as this will only deepen the mindset of occupation and alienate the land even more from its people. Rather, the act of mapping current social conditions has strongly set up the material for my designed spaces. They are seen as means of 'organic' spatial stitching to negotiate spaces on the surface of the Palestinian land, as well as below and above it.

All of my design approaches share the common ground of awareness of the role of ordinary narratives, and the constant questioning through the designs of how much structure is needed before it inhabits people's freedom of choice and gets in their way. Finding the right balance between creativity, emergence and design, and assuring that the ordinary is celebrated and 'made special and the special made accessible' – as Hamdi puts it[9] – is the challenge for this study.

Where there is power, there is resistance.[10]

Michael Focault, 1990

creating new matrixes of possibility. Consequently, three different forms of design need to be seen as the constituent parts of the process. The first is the act of social and spatial mapping: i.e. plotting existing patterns and reconstructing scenes that have been lived through (via maps, images and collages capturing moments of individual and collective change in the occupied land). The second form is speculative design, or what I call 'moments of possibility', which imagine potential yet to come and their relevance to the informal

I.8   An imaginary moment of reclaiming the Separation Wall.

The areas of confrontation and surveillance were the starting point of my journey. However, being local myself, I was aware that these points – despite their intensity – do not represent all of the urban changes happening on the ground. In fact, these embody only part of the story, as most of the other locations appear neutral and abstract on the surface, yet are concealed with intense tactics led by locals and informal users who have established their own maps, sites and spots. Therefore, the constant site visits, informal discussions, observations and the integration with these emerging groups as part of everyday life are what directed me towards the rest of the collective matrix. These 'extended' sites, away from the physical borderlines, were far more crucial and fundamental for creating different spatial forms of resistance, since they form the backbone where tactics can be tested out and appropriated to respond to people's needs.

I therefore can't say that the design proposals are site-specific in the normative sense. The combination of its clandestine nature and the fluidity and constant change of boundaries and resulting adaptation tactics have encouraged my interventions instead to become 'moment' and 'event' specific. My journey was spread all along the map to capture the key moments of spatial possibility, wherever a new tactic was needed.

It is import to note that this work is not meant to survey or reveal where these informal networks are specifically located, or where spatial resistance is, or could take place — especially given that most of these points are ephemeral in their nature and change with conditions, and above all need to stay invisible. The moments chosen are only meant to reflect certain characteristics currently shaping the land with potentials that can be further explored.

NAVIGATING THROUGH THE BOOK

The layout for this book needs to be seen as another aspect of the design led research that combines written text with visual images, shaping the book as a graphic artefact. Each component is seen as a necessary part of a whole.

The images, for example, are not purely illustrative. They also contribute to the process of documentation; hence they are communicative yet analytical, revealing patterns of everyday life that are often missed or hidden. The collages should be seen as the starting points for my design proposal. They contain a possibility of crossing, hiding, concealing, or creating. They are meant to bring closer awareness of moments of everyday life in its chaos and liveliness, such as waiting at checkpoints or being involved in some form of mobility. Between zooming in and zooming out, a space is left for the reader to imagine, question and break boundaries.

In the case of maps, two languages are employed; one which documents Israeli dominance and its defined boundaries, and another which is liberated from boundaries to show possibilities. Some of the maps have been prepared to capture the social angle and the human scale in shaping the lines. They are also seen as a territorial representation of what might creative space be. Therefore these maps take a slightly different character in that are liberated from confined borders or given historical lines such as after the 1948 and 1967 wars. This is very consciously done, since all the complex maps previously drawn have also distorted the mental map of Palestine. Therefore I see my interpretative maps as a form of liberating the mind from given boundaries.

My starting point is thus to strip the act of mapping away from 'authoritative power', to see how far one can go instead. Some maps are specifically intended as cut-outs; they are never seen completely, and are always in the process of development. I regard them as a starting point for others to finish. Emptiness and the white background of the paper is never a natural condition on the map of possibility. Instead it is a moment waiting to happen, and an invisible space concealed with other agendas (either Israeli strategies of control and/or tactics being born by Palestinians). White space in this sense takes over the whole page, or at times both pages, while at others it even consists of a combining and overlapping of images or text.[11]

The book is structured into five chapters. The first chapter provides a short 'journey across the vanishing landscape' to introduce Palestine, its troubled landscape, and sets the scene for some of the key historical moments that have contributed to shaping the Palestinian/Israeli map, starting from the 1948 War until recently.

'The Art of Resistance' is very much born out of my own journeys and experiences all across Palestine, capturing informal agencies on the ground with an emphasis on their different ways of shaping spaces through resistance. Building on Bayat's theories of 'quiet encroachment', I have tried to show how organic and spontaneous these informal agencies are; they are only driven by the necessity to adapt and survive, rather than being a conscious act of resistance. I will also show how individual attempts are gradually being 'moleculed' in Bayat's terms to become collective energies. Not only they have managed to cross borderlines, but they have also inhabited them, reclaimed them, and thus reoccupied the occupied. This second chapter therefore sets the basis for my argument in other chapters where I

celebrate the informal networks and introduce design tools to sustain and empower them.

Birzeit chapter might seem totally different in its nature and visual language since it focuses on the regeneration of the centre of a historic town in Palestine called Birzeit. However, the chapter also attempts via a 'live' project, to find alternative ways to enact spatial change within the current Palestinian/Israeli conflict. Building on my social mapping and site investigations, I will provide an insight into how, by using limited resources one can still cultivate possibilities for change by tapping informal networks. Throughout the Birzeit project I try to test whether one can bring back the local community into the front lines by giving them active roles other than just being passive audience. Working in old historic centres has also been intentionally selected as a way to explore areas of potentiality in Palestine, which are currently left on the margins to decline and fade away, despite their obvious cultural and social value.[12]

The design interventions in this chapter are intended to bring forward a different way of architecture, one that moves away from the conventional practice of making buildings into design proposals which are more related to local everyday practices, beliefs and habits. In this part of the research and design, my role as an architect is positioned in the background as a facilitator, and instead local agents are the key forces involved in making their own spaces. Therefore, the design interventions in the third chapter are subtler, quieter and sometimes almost invisible in nature.

The two highly speculative design chapters – titled 'Underground' and 'Air' – place an emphasis on the need to step above and underneath the exhausted surface of Palestine to look for possibilities. Both

I.9 Re-reading the West Bank through its margins.

chapters share Henri Lefebvre's quest for a counter-space and re-imagine the 'play and creativity' of the ordinary while inhabiting and recasting space. I have tried to show how social and economic innovation can be born from need. While doing that, I also realised how rooted the Israeli invisible occupation really is, eating away slowly and quietly at the Palestinian landscape and cultural identity to allow for domination by Israeli values.

The 'Underground' chapter therefore sheds light on water supply, sewage and archaeology, and looks at how with parallel strategies controlled from the surface by Israel, these services are being captured, directed, and secured. A particular emphasis is placed on stone and specifically the issue of stone quarries in the West Bank. The impact on the landscape has not yet been fully addressed by scholars due to the largely concealed nature of these quarries, and thus my aim is to make visible this fractured part of the land. In this chapter I have also tried to show how the Israeli occupation strategies underground collide with the tactics of Palestinian resistance, which I comment on through designs with subversive and playful forms of reclamation for space and identity.

The 'Air' chapter, on the other hand, examines the issue of airspace, the electromagnetic spectrum, the struggle of Israel to dominate the skies, and the challenges they faced as a result. Not only is this due to the constant Israeli fear of possible air strikes from imagined enemies, ironically more worrying for the Israeli armed forces is their fear from birds given that Palestine/Israel is one of the busiest corridors of bird migration in the world. Again, the 'Air' chapter uncovers another degree of weakness that Israel is concealing, and another prospect for a subversive map to be drawn by Palestinians (with the airspace being another 'space of possibility' shared with birds).

It is important to note that both the 'Underground' and 'Air' chapters end with suggested 'moments of possibility'. These projects are deliberately characterised by a different design language in comparison to those in the third chapter. My approach here is concealed by subversive and at times ironic forms of contestation and reclamation, and this spirit influences the character of the design proposals that I arrive at the end of both of these chapters.

Finally, in the concluding section, while 'seeing less and less of the other', I will reflect upon my journey through the Palestinian socio-political map, and what might be done in future.

NOTES

1 The Oslo Peace Agreement is the name for the main peace agreement between Palestinian and Israelis, which started in 1993 and concluded in 1995. The Oslo Peace Agreement was supposed to set up a framework for improving Palestinian/Israeli relations. However, it was used instead by Israel as a tool to redefine the type, scope and practice of 'zoning' methods for controlling Palestinian areas.

2 Fraser, M. (2007) 'Beyond Koolhaas', in Rendell, J., Hill, J., Fraser, M. and Dorrian, M. (eds), *Critical Architecture*. London: Routledge, pp. 32–9.

3 Palestinian refugee camps are an exception to this rule, being an unresolved matter that is always under negotiation and one of the most visible consequences of Israeli occupation.

4 Harker tries to uncover the socio-cultural effects of post-Oslo apartment growth on the geographies of everyday life in the Ramallah-al Beirah conurbation, through a focus on changing family/neighbour spaces and mobilities. See http://backdoorbroadcasting.net/2010/12/christopher-harker---the-politics-of-verticality-revisited/ [accessed 26 November 2011].

5 Hammami, R. (2006) *Human Agency at the Frontiers of Global Inequality*; Hammami, R. (2004) 'On the Importance of Thugs: The Moral Economy of a Checkpoint', *MERIP Middle East Report*, Vol. 34, pp. 26–34.

6 Different principles of collage have therefore been used to combine the visual elements in this thesis, and to demonstrate the capacity of these spaces to host informal practices that give a meaning to space. Superimposition was strongly used, whereby certain elements – which I found limiting – were kept in the background while exposing those which might offer greater possibilities. It is seen as a method of stitching that brings up new spatial dimensions to the context, and indeed to start the design process.

To draw the viewer's attention to certain moments/elements so as to emphasize their similarities or differences, juxtaposition within collages was also used at times – mainly within the second chapter – to represent informal daily networks and the acts of waiting, crossing and uncrossing, in which all seem to share common artifacts of resistance. For instance, images were cropped or removed from their context at times, to stress the fact that they are not actually that site-specific. Rather, it's the overall network that counts, or the object itself, whether it is a van, cart, worker, etc.

7 Jane Rendell, letter on the subject of 'Art Writing', *Art Monthly*, no. 272 (December–January, 2003/4), p. 15.

8 Rendell, J. (1998) 'Doing it, (Un)Doing it, (Over)Doing it Yourself: Rhetorics of Architectural Abuse', in Hill, J. (ed.), *Occupying Architecture*. London: Routledge.

9 Hamdi, op. cit., p. xvii.

10 Foucault, M. (1990) *The History of Sexuality: An Introduction*. New York: Vintage Books, p. 95.

11 Going back to the subject and question of mapping, and how much this can be altered without disturbing the objective stance of the research, my argument here is that maps can never actually be neutral as they will always be influenced by their makers. Hence the key aspect is to assure that maps are made to reflect and express an objective reality, however unpalatable, and that is where I believe my research stands.

12 As will be explained later in Chapter 1, the historic centres in Palestine are mostly located in villages or areas which are either partially controlled by the Palestinian administrative authority, or else are located in areas under full Israeli administrative control.

A JOURNEY ACROSS THE VANISHING LANDSCAPE: MAKING SENSE OF MY TERRITORY

Since there are many different ways to tell the story of the Palestine/Israel conflict, and the disturbed landscape that it has created, mine is going to be expressed through my own journeys – through the act of living there, trying to make sense of my troubled internal territory as much as the external one. In this chapter I will briefly highlight the key points which have deformed and are still shaping the urban fabric and the map – especially the 1993 Oslo Peace Agreement – with special emphasis on zoning and land use, as well as the new reality created by the politics of power and control. The tale will be told largely through daily narratives; however, my focus will be mainly on the West Bank where I live, as the Gaza Strip and the rest of the map have been out of reach since 1998, due to the Israeli strategies of dividing the Palestinian communities into disconnected cantons. This makes it difficult to trace the daily changes in the urban and social character of Palestine as a whole.

Unlike Meron Benvenisti, 'who had wandered in a land with six dimensions: three for the Palestinians and three for the Israelis',[1] I never had to wonder who was the guest and who was the local. It was my early childhood when I realized the surrealist map we have inherited, formed and deformed by occupation, settlements, our daily life and the will to survive. The six dimensions are endless today; borders became even more irrelevant with the erection of the infamous Apartheid Wall as they run inside as well as along the edges of the West Bank. The cold wind of change is flattening the landscape on the surface, and invisibly shaping it underneath and above, which makes it difficult to understand or even begin to draw it on the map.

For the purpose of introducing Palestine and its troubled landscape, I will start with this imaginary example[2]: London is divided into a couple of community cantons, crisscrossed and separated by main roads (like Camden Road, Marylebone Road, or Oxford Street), which are under the control of an imaginary 'other'. Central London areas are controlled by the 'other' because of their strategic location near to the Thames, or their economic importance. Their electricity, water and gas resources are therefore under the full control of this 'other' force. Moreover, and to secure free movement for their illegal presence, the 'others' have constructed a new network of roads and underground points to be used exclusively by their people. ID cards and car plates with different

1.1   Shortcut to avoid the checkpoint near Kalandia by Majdi Hadid.

colours are also issued to identify those living within the cantons and the excluded Londoners living around. Consequently, if the excluded Londoners living around this area want to move to any of the artificially created cantons – to go to work or university for instance – they need to get special permission, all in the name of security. In summary, movement, goods, services and people, are all constrained and restricted by the 'other' dominating agency.

When people decide that they are not satisfied with their sad situation, and begin to protest against the 'imaginary other', they are accused of threatening their security. As a result, no more permits are issued to allow them to move from one canton to another. Furthermore, all major streets are blocked by checkpoints, gates and concrete walls; all the exits and entrances into and out of Central London are closed; and all the busses, railway and underground stations are also controlled, so people can cross only in certain times of the day.

Do you think that people living in London under such conditions would stay in the centre after all? Do you think that their livelihood will be affected? What would you do? Would you use the roads of the 'other' if you can? Would you sneak in to the area of the 'other' to reach your work if you found that your permit is refused, or would you just give up and leave London? Do you think the image of London would be different? If such things happened, wouldn't you think that London is under occupation?[3] This imaginary example enlightens some of the hardships that Londoners could undergo if they were in contact with the overwhelming daily reality of people in Palestine living under the Israeli occupation.[4]

THE EDGE OF THE CITY

'I cannot get you into Nablus, but I can get you to Burin from where you can walk to the town just up the hill some thirty minutes or so'. Yes, yes, of course, we know, we have been on the road, or more accurately off the road, since eight in the morning. It is already three hours now. We started our trip by walking across Birzeit checkpoint mound, and then Al Jawwal dirt mounds and Dora Al-Qare.[5]

Introducing Palestine and its urban identity to those who do know it has become increasingly associated with issues of time and restricted mobility since 2001 until today. Being conscious of one's surroundings is now related to how many roadblocks and checkpoints we as Palestinians have to go through and how many alternative routes we can create across the confused landscape. While living under Israeli occupation, one can't evade all signs pointing towards a vanishing landscape. With rapidly shifting facts on the ground, a new face for the land is being shaped by vast elastic changes, which increasingly make it very difficult for anyone to follow.

DISTORTED BEGINNING

My first encounter with the distorted landscape of Palestine and the existence of the 'other' that is Israel started when I was six years old. My father was put in jail for few years and we had to move to different cities chasing my father from one prison to the other. For a child there was some sort of pleasure in all this, as it was the only time we ever managed to see the 'other' side. Going through the Israeli areas was striking; rich, clean, and full of cars, colours and life. People looked relaxed, speaking a different language. I always felt I was traveling very far outside Palestine; I always thought it was actually America.

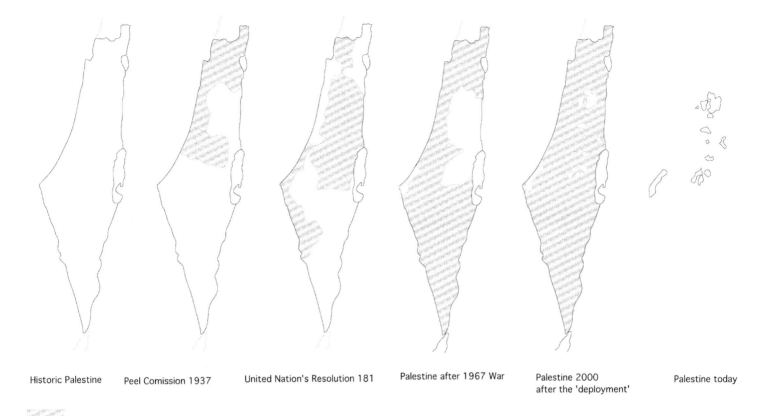

Historic Palestine   Peel Comission 1937   United Nation's Resolution 181   Palestine after 1967 War   Palestine 2000 after the 'deployment'   Palestine today

Areas captured by Israel

1.2   Maps of Palestine shrinking.

Entering the prison itself was never a great experience. Located on the outskirts in the middle of nowhere, the tension was high and those who looked relaxed outside were now being so aggressive and violent towards us. I spent four years of my life visiting the same prison, standing at the same point. Only then did I know where my limits as a citizen start, and where they end. The bars got wider until we couldn't move outside Ramallah or visit my father anymore – the prison became our own house.

From my own diary

For a six-year-old child, the Palestinian map seemed to be frozen in time. Before 1948, the country was still associated with the Mediterranean Sea: the mountains, the olive tree terraces, the big cities of Jerusalem, Ramallah, Nablus, Hebron, Jaffa, Acre, and the hundreds of villages around. I was of course too young to realize that the 1948 had brought an end to the British Mandate,[6] which was then replaced with the newly born 'Israeli State' – leaving the Palestinians with a hollow map, of marginal lands, which were recommended weakly by the United Nations as a 'Proposed Arab State'.[7]

1948 'AND MAKING THE DESERT BLOOM'

The 1948 war was a painful landmark in the history of Palestine.[8] It is known as *Nakba* or 'the catastrophe'; as it was also the beginning of the Palestinian Diaspora crisis. The British Mandate had come to an end when Britain decided to withdraw in order for the Zionist movement to take place, and Israel was to be initiated as a national entity on the Palestinian land. This sharp edge, divided Palestine into before and after. Prior to 1948, Palestine was a series of big cities surrounded by small villages located on top of the hills, set into a rich agricultural landscape. However, by the end of 1948, approximately 418 villages had been systematically erased and more than two thirds of the entire indigenous population was forced into exile in refugee camps.[9] The demolition of these villages was a central component of the Israeli occupation to replace Palestine with an Israeli state, which extends to reach the Nile on the west, to the Euphrates on the east.[10]

> The present map of Palestine was drawn by the British Mandate. The Jewish people have another map which our youth and adults should strive to fulfill – from the Nile to the Euphrates.
>
> Ben Gurion, 1973[11]

Israel's intention was to erase people and their history, as well as allowing for the construction of houses for new Jewish immigrants who had come to the 'promised land'. The destruction was not only of Palestinian houses, but also their landscape and the olive terraces; anything that couldn't be integrated within the new state was simply eliminated. As Joseph Weitz, a Zionist leader who was responsible for Jewish colonization at the time, noted in his diaries:

> Between ourselves it must be clear that there is no room for both people together in this country ... there is no other way than to transfer the Arabs from here to the neighboring countries, to transfer all of them; not one village, not one tribe, should be left.[12]

The war on the indigenous Palestinians did not end there; it actually started with an ongoing Zionist agenda to wipe Palestine away from the face of the map and replace it with 'Greater Israel'. This led later to the 1967 war with Egypt and other nations, which was another key historical moment in Palestinian history.

Thus, 1967 marks the Arab/Israeli War. It is known as the 'Six-Day War' as it ended quickly, and it redrew again the Palestinian and Arab map after Israel attacked Egypt, Jordan, and Syria. The war ended six days later with a complete Israeli victory. They then occupied the rest of Palestine (the West Bank, Gaza and East Jerusalem) as well as some parts of Egypt and Syria. As a result, even more refugees were forced into exile and all of Palestine was effectively under the occupation of Israel.

For Palestinians occupation has, since 1967, introduced a new meaning and familiarity with our landscape. Despite the agony of Israel occupying the whole country, many Palestinian refugees – in the West Bank – also recall this as a time when they were able to revisit their homes after previously being forced apart in 1948. The occupation erased

the 'Green Line' that drew the border of West Bank, to contain all Palestinians within a bigger entity. Those who had kept the keys and land certificates for their pre-1948 lands could revisit them. But they found their houses had been demolished, or else taken over and inhabited by the new Jewish immigrants.

Being simultaneously included and excluded, the battle between Palestinians and Israelis has since been about the land; it is a battlefield of who gets to draw what division line. This accumulation of oppression and land confiscation erupted in the first Palestinian mass popular uprising in 1987, known as the *Intifada* in Arabic, which means, 'shaking off'.

The energy that came out of mass civil Palestinian resistance against the Israeli occupation – boycotting Israeli goods, refusing to pay taxes to Israel, establishing their own mobile medical clinics, providing social services, organizing strikes and demonstrations, etc. – has had its own profound effect. As a result, calls for peace started, which later came to prominence internationally through the Oslo Peace Agreement in 1993.

THE OSLO PEACE AGREEMENT AND AFTER

The 1993 Oslo Peace Agreement was the main political outcome (if not really an achievement) of the *First Intifada*. Officially it is called the Declaration of Principles on Interim Self-Government Arrangements. It stands as a key point in shaping Palestinians' life, history and landscape, as it was supposed to set up a framework for Palestinian/Israeli relations. Many Palestinians also supported the agreement at the time, considering it to be an uplifting stage. However, other early Palestinian critics of the Oslo Agreement saw it as leading to a continuation of occupation – either in

the form of spatial apartheid, as described by Edward Said, or as 'occupation by remote control', according to Meron Benvenisti.

The Oslo Agreement has since in effect enforced a new map onto Palestinians; it has been ruthlessly used by the Israeli Government to create points of connection and separation, a tool to define the type, scope and 'zoning' of control between areas.[13] The agreement had three stages of negotiations that were agreed upon by both Palestinian Liberation Organization (PLO)[14] and the Israeli side. The first stage in 1993 was the 'Declaration of Principles' that will govern future relationship, and negotiations. It agreed on the creation of a Palestinian Authority (PA) to represent the Palestinian people, and granted confined autonomy in Gaza and Jericho as part of the transition of power that would continue in later stages. The second phase was in 1995, when both parties agreed on the details for further redeployments of Israeli soldiers from the main cities and town in the West Bank and Gaza Strip. It also identified land zoning and mechanisms of control over territories in West Bank, Gaza and Hebron (as a special case). The third phase was supposed to take place between 1996–99. It was the most important as it related to the 'permanent status' negotiation, covering the thorny issues of Jerusalem, Jewish settlements, return of Palestinian refugees, and control over natural resources as the crucial points. This third phase of course never came to light due to the change of Israeli Government, now being run by those who voted against the Oslo Agreement in the first place.

According to the terms of agreement, the West Bank was divided into three zones labeled as Areas A, B and C.

1.3   Jaffa's historic fabric with its Mediterranean architectural style. Courtesy of Riwaq Photo Archive.

Area A

Area A & B

Palestinian
Built-up areas

Area C

1.4   Map division according to the Oslo
Peace Agreement.

There was complete Palestinian Authority control in Area A, complete Israeli control over Area C, and 'joint responsibilities' in Area B, which was intended to provide civilian Palestinian rule alongside Israeli security control. In terms of the West Bank and the Gaza strip today, Area A includes six of its major cities or urban areas – excluding East Jerusalem – these now being under the jurisdiction and control of the Palestinian Authority (PA), while key issues of external security, water, provision, airspace, exits and entrances still remain under the control of Israel. While Area A covers only 18 percent of the West Bank, Area B covers effectively the Palestinian villages and rural areas, which includes about 22 percent of the West Bank. Again, the PA assumes responsibility here for public order and civil affairs, while the Israelis are still in overall control. Thus in Area B the PA has no real control or sovereignty over the land. Area C is made up of Israeli settlements and major roads, including a network of bypass roads for the purpose of connecting the Israeli settlements with each other and with Israel, and all of which falls under full Israeli control. This in effect captures approximately 60 percent of the rest of the West Bank and the Gaza strip.[15]

The city of Hebron in the West Bank is a very special case, having ultra right-wing Israeli settlers occupying the historic centre, where the main Palestinian residential area used to be. Hence, the city has been divided into H1 and H2 Areas. This plan is enforced to allow Israeli settlers to move freely within the historic centre under full control of the main roads and transportation system. Thus, since 2001 Hebron is known to Palestinians as the 'ghost town'. With the support of Israeli government only around 400–500 Israeli settlers occupy the central historic district of a larger city of 160,000 Palestinian residents. This has resulted in closing over 1,000 Palestinian residential units (over 42 percent of the total number of homes),

1.5a   Surda checkpoint. Photograph by
Majdi Hadid.

1.5b   Kalandia checkpoint before the
erection of the wall.

1.5c Signs at the entrance of all Palestinian Area A to alert Israelis. Photograph by Majdi Hadid.

1.5d Palestinian road blocked in Ramallah western villages to allow for Israeli by-pass road connecting the settlements all the way to Tel Aviv. Photograph by Majdi Hadid.

1.5e Map showing the enforced military checkpoints, 2005.

- ⬤ Checkpoints
- ▲ Earth Bounds
- ◉ Temporary checkpoints
- ✕ Gates
- ▪ Road Blocks

the vegetable market and main streets inside the historic centre, so as to guarantee security and free movement of the Israeli settlers. After the *Second Intifada* in 2001, over 60 percent of these houses and 70 percent of the businesses aimed at Palestinians in Hebron were abandoned due to attacks by Jewish settlers or closures by the Israeli military forces, in addition to seizing control of all the water resources.[16]

The Gaza Strip has a similar case of land division. However, it was not only the land in this case; the Mediterranean Sea here has also been divided into three areas. Two of them are restricted for Israeli navy activities, while the third area has full Israeli control with few kilometres open to Palestinian fishermen to use, who have to get special license to use their boats in the sea.

BREAKING THE PROMISE

In summary, what the Palestinians have been given as a result of the Oslo Peace Agreement are defined borders of disconnected cantons, which are surrounded by Israeli settlements, roadblocks and bypass roads – weaving above and under to linking the illegal settlements to Israeli areas. All are located within urban areas in the West Bank and Gaza Strip. According to Amnesty International, by 1999– which was the time to implement the third phase – the disconnected cantons created has divided the West

Everybody has to move, run and grab as many hilltops as they can to enlarge the settlements because everything we take now will stay ours . . . Everything we don't grab will go to them.

Ariel Sharon, 1998[18]

The number of the new Israeli settlers in the West Bank, according to a statistical report by the Palestinian Central Bureau of Statistics, reached 483,453 in 2007 against 2.2 million Palestinians in the area. According to B'etselem (an Israeli human rights organization), while Israeli settlements currently constitute less than 2 percent of the West Bank, including East Jerusalem, they control 41.9 percent of the territory and its natural resources.[19] Settlement expansion with new housing units is still doubling, especially around Jerusalem.

1.6   Illegal Israeli settlements.

1.7   Map showing the illegal Israeli settlements in the West Bank, 2005.

● Settlements in the West Bank

Bank into 227 separate areas with the majority of these areas being less than 2 square kilometres in size. The Gaza Strip, on the other hand, 'was divided into three enclaves surrounded by an electric fence'.[17]

The division plan implemented by Israel is unfortunately still under execution today, and if anything things are getting worse, as only the terms that might benefit the Israeli strategy of control and division is occurring, which on the ground means, extra 'security' measures, more checkpoints and border-control lines and foremost increased number of illegal Israeli settlements and associated bypass roads. During and after the Oslo Peace Agreement, these new Israeli settlements have expanded at a tremendous rate; roughly about 50 percent of them are concentrated around the city of Jerusalem as the centre of the Israeli occupation plan. All of the settlements are aimed at incorporating Jerusalem and indeed much of the West Bank and Gaza Strip into Israel. Settlements have since been used as a key tool to break any prospect for peace negotiations looming in the air. As Sharon puts it:

Unfortunately, the Palestinian side has accepted the terms of the Oslo Peace Agreement despite its oppression without trying to find any alternatives of empowerment. Not only the agreement came at a time where the Palestinians were at their weakest stage in terms of power-relation, but I believe they were also ignorant of the hidden long-term strategies behind the agreement, especially that most of the maps and plans negotiated were prepared by the Israeli side. Hence, all the invisible agendas of separation and oppression strategies through planning, were not picked up by the PA. As a result, the Palestinian people ended up being the losers. Edward Said pointed out the danger of maps being created by the Oslo Agreement in its early stages, and he constantly asked for alternative plans by the Palestinian side to avoid the threat of the occupier.

In the history of colonial invasion maps are always first drawn by the victors, since maps are instruments of

1.8   A section across the land. Between
       excluding parts and including others.

conquest. Geography is therefore the art of war but can also be the art of resistance if there is a counter-map and a counter-strategy.[20]

A NEW CHARACTER IS SHAPING UP: READING
A TERRITORY BETWEEN WAR AND PEACE
AFTER OSLO: A NEW CULTURE OF URBAN SPACES

The situation after the 1993 Oslo Peace Agreement has thus created more obstacles and sources of conflict within the allocated Palestinian territory on the West Bank and Gaza Strip. Now the bypass roads circumvent Palestinian villages, towns and cities in order to link the various Israeli settlements to each other, deliberately excluding Palestinian areas. This situation has created a physical and spatial disintegration of major urban areas in the West Bank and also the Gaza Strip. In addition to reinforcing fragmentation, bypass roads limit the scope of future development and expansion of Palestinian cities and towns. Under the new security arrangements, buildings are not allowed to be constructed on either side of roads up to a distance of 75 metres from the centre of those roads.[21] If we take village of Jaba' between Ramallah and Jerusalem as an example: the Oslo Agreement has divided the 3,000 or so residents of the village into Area B and C. This literally means that some of their houses are split into two parts; for example, the living room and the kitchen lie within Israeli jurisdiction, while the other part is within shared territories. Adding to this complexity, the Israeli bypass road running across the village to connect the settlements around Ramallah with Jerusalem, – known as Road 60 – has also by de facto created a 75 metres buffer zone, in which no building extension or development is allowed. The rest – which is the majority of their lands – are mainly agricultural lands, either located now within Area C, or confiscated by Illegal Israeli settlers, or even belong to the village yet, are enclaved within the boundaries of the Israeli settlement Geva-Binyamin, which is constantly expanding to encircle what is remaining. Furthermore, after the erection of the Separation Wall, thousands of donums are now located on the other side out of their reach.

On the other hand, the Palestinian built-up areas (Area A) have been facing a building 'revival'. Since the agreement has only delineated Area A to be the built-up areas in the big city centres, all now have the chance to build whereas before the creation on the Palestinian Authority they could not do so. Even though the economy boomed after 1995, building construction has also resulted in mass destruction to the Palestinian urban fabric. Not only Israel is to be blamed, but so too the Palestinian lack of planning control has resulted in approving chaotic building construction within Area A, in a desperate attempt to make up for the economic recession that happened before, and get the maximum of the 22 percent or so, they have control on.

Hence, a new spirit of the Palestinian city has been expressed after the Oslo Agreement as Taraki has framed it:

> it represents a collision between a 'postcolonial' nation in the process of making, one in which the Palestinian Authority has some self-autonomy away from Israeli military occupation, mixed with ideas of nationalism and international influences.[22]

This has created new social practices, lifestyles and architectural identity. A city like Ramallah, for example, has become far more accessible than Jerusalem, which is forbidden for most Palestinians. This has resulted in new urban attitudes reflecting the desires and needs in the city for new kind of public representation. This in turn has created even more fragmentation between Palestinian social groups itself because 'imported' capitalist ideologies were in effect recreated in their 'own' cities. This can be clearly seen in Ramallah neighborhoods of Al-Tireh or Al-Masyoun as well as in Nablus, with substantial mansions and high-rise buildings existing side-by-side with refugee camps.

Due to the scarcity of urban land, these high-rise buildings have taken over the skyline of the major Palestinian cities; the local authorities could not hope to enforce strict regulations especially after the great pressure that Palestine had gone through before and after the Oslo Agreement. Setbacks to blocks are at a minimum, and the number of floors built was so often clearly over the limit allowed. To create more land, adjacent mountains were flattened and the olive trees were cut down; the reality is that historic Palestinian centres started losing their integration within the landscape as tall concrete buildings took over with their red brick roofs.

Life soon became unbearable in Palestinian cities in the West Bank; quiet neighbourhoods became construction sites, mounds of building rubble became the main feature of the urban landscape, with no green colour, no fresh air and of course not enough water – especially after Israel limited the right for Palestinians to dig wells, and copious water was stored in the Israeli wells for their settlers to use for their agricultural lands and swimming pools.

The Oslo Agreement has therefore only accumulated oppression and inequality under the mask of peace, given that built-up areas for Palestinians were very limited; settlements, checkpoints, roadblocks, and bypass roads were increased, characterizing the Palestinian urban fabric. A journey that otherwise would only need 15 minutes now started to take three hours, until over time the destination became impossible to reach. All of this tension and social pressure resulted in the *Second Intifada* in late 2000, under which life has been turned upside down until today. As Edward Said noted:

> The Intifada we are witnessing today is not against peace; it is against the very text and maps of the Oslo Agreements with all the oppression and inequality factors they contain and against the planners of the 'peace process' on both sides.[23]

At the height of the *Second Intifada*, the urban violence of the Israeli occupation reached its extreme in 2006 with the decision to start construction of the Apartheid/Separation Wall, despite a clear ruling of the International Court of Justice in The Hague, confirming the illegality of the wall. The wall was not even designed to follow the border between the Armistice Line and the West Bank, but to encircle the 'settlement blocks' and annex them to Israel – in the process penetrating the land held by the Palestinians like a series of daggers. The construction of this wall is still taking place today, radically altering the physical, spatial and socio-economic realities of the land.

THE INVISIBLE OCCUPATION

The combination of the Oslo Agreement, the expansion of Israeli settlements, the bypass roads, and the building of the Separation Wall, has

1.9   Neighbourhoods are split into fragments by the Separation Wall, access in and out is usually restricted by iron gates and at limited times during the day. Photographs by Majdi Hadid.

created even greater fragmentation and distortion to the Palestinian landscape. Not only are such measures dividing Palestine from Israel; they are actually dividing Palestine from Palestine, cities from villages, people from reaching work or from going to their schools and universities. The danger of the Israeli occupation does not stop there; it lays more in the invisible occupation strategies with their destructive and ongoing changes. It is hence a danger from below and above as much as what can be seen on the surface.

The opening up of some of the main Palestinian cities to the world economy has caused yet another form of fragmentation on the social level. Luxurious buildings introducing the values of globalization and easy living now exists in a state in which citizenship and civil rights are still deprived, including clearly the right for proper urban planning.

The outlying villages of the West Bank have if anything suffered even more, especially by being categorized as 'Area B' and at times 'Area C'. In

1.10 Map showing the extent of the Separation Wall in 2005.

addition to scarcity of built-up areas, it is very difficult to obtain building permission from Israel (in Area B, where Israel controls building permits). On top of that, their lack of control over the agricultural land, water and natural resources. The economic imbalances between the Palestinian city and village, 'our' territory and 'theirs', was intensified with deliberate mass destruction to Palestinian infrastructure all over the West Bank and Gaza Strip, creating more poverty, unemployment and the desire for extra space.

The economic situation in Palestinian areas keeps worsening. According to B'tselem's statistics (The Israeli Information Centre for Human Rights in the Occupied Territories), the average level of unemployment in each West Bank Palestinian village exceeds 38.1 percent in 2002, while it reached 48 percent in the Gaza Strip.[24] The villagers who used to work as builders in Israel have lost their jobs, and those who had depended on exporting their agricultural products to the other side of the wall, or abroad, have ended up unemployed and looking for alternatives to survive. This new situation has contributed towards the change in the nature of these villages. Agriculture is replaced with small businesses to try to respond to the difficulties of reaching the main cities. The identity of the public space had also to be changed to adapt to the new lifestyles that needed to be adapted. Consequently, illegal two-storey live/work units at the edge of the historic centres started to emerge; greenhouses were replaced by concrete sheds for small industries like car repairs and steel processing. The edges of the village have become one of the main source of livelihood, with car boots often filled up with vegetables, office furniture and home products to serve to Palestinian commuters on their long journeys to and from their workplaces.

MOBILITY AND IMMOBILITY

Since 1994, after increasingly strict restrictions were imposed between the West Bank, the Gaza Strip and Israel, movement has become impossible. There is no visible line to identify Palestinian territory from the Israeli one, except wherever there is a checkpoint we know that we can't go any further. This was the only indication of Palestinian territorial borders which was not only dividing Palestinian areas from Israeli ones; in fact the restrictions were inside West Bank separating villages, cities, and people from each other's. Restrictions on movement of Palestinians have become a very powerful invisible tool of occupation that penetrates through to reach every village, house and family. It has thus affected social as well as economic situations.

Israeli occupation has thus created social and religious differences through mobility. Division has been intensified with the different types of ID cards enforced under Israeli control: Jerusalem residents have their own blue colour ID card that allows them to enter Jerusalem, other Israeli areas as well as West Bank, whereas Palestinian West Bankers have their own orange ID cards – today green – that only allow them to travel within the West Bank area, which after 2000 was also more or less impossible. Green ID cards were used to mark out those having a political record in Israeli prisons – which automatically means restriction of movement and a long wait on checkpoint. Gaza, on the other side has its own red ID cards that do not allow its residents to move anywhere, while diplomats and Palestinian Authority administrators have their own red VIP

1.11 Israeli checkpoint at the entrance to Nablus. Photograph by Majdi Hadid.

passports which means they can travel relatively easily.

In summary, the colour and religion which mark one's ID card has become a clear indicator of who you are and to which social class you belong. It determines which road one can use or which checkpoint one can enter. It has made mobility a privilege, not a right, especially available to those who have the money or political status. To express this in simple daily practice, being a Muslim from the West Bank, I have to travel on the 'lower level roads' with the 'ordinary people' whereas my work colleague, being a Christian with foreign citizenship, or holding a VIP card, can go on top and sometimes in same roads as the Israelis to reach the same destination.

Likewise, the Gaza Strip has become completely out of bounds, not only for Palestinians from the West Bank; today Gaza – one of the most high densely populated spots on earth – is an open air prison with no accessibility. Back in 1998, when I was still studying at the university, students from Gaza had no choice but to stay in the West Bank, and if an urgent matter required them for whatever reason to visit Gaza City, which is only 40 minutes away, they had to travel east to Jordan and fly from Amman to Cairo, and then drive through Sinai desert to enter the Gaza Strip from the Rafah border. My mother, being born in Gaza, had to go through this agony for a few years to visit her parents there: she was the only daughter out of ten who ever managed to visit my grandmother after getting exceptional

1.12 Map showing the trapped villages between the Separation Wall and the Green Line, 2005.

permission to do so in 2000. It was ironic, because my grandmother thought bringing up ten children would be a future investment and provide collective support for her when she got old. However, the new Israeli map and her children's different identity cards did not allow her dreams to come true; each has now a different legal status depending on where they live.[25] Sadly my grandmother passed away in 2006, and nobody managed to attend her funeral, neither by going through Jordan or via Egypt. The funeral had to be arranged by her neighbours and since then Gaza no longer remembers her, while we as her family cannot visit her grave.

The Israeli restrictions have only got worse in the past few years with the infamous aforementioned Separation Wall. Today, over 10,000 residents from the West Bank are 'trapped' within the folds of the wall and the 'green line'. Residents of these 'trapped' Palestinian villages can leave only through gates that open twice a day, at 7 am in the morning, and 7 pm in the evening. It is like a prison sentence.[26] Qalqilyah to the north is now caught up in such a bottleneck; it has its 45 percent of its land and 19 percent of its wells out of reach. The fruit and vegetables that the farmers and inhabitants grow can no longer be distributed to the rest of the West Bank; so they ended up feeding the surplus to the only giraffe and monkey left in the little, and indeed only, zoo in the West Bank.

The Palestinian economy has recently declined severely due to these border closures that were not only limited to villages or cities surrounding the Separation Wall, but all over West Bank, as no export or import of any products is possible anymore. Everyday life and habits have had to change to adapt to the fragmented built-up areas; now it was the case

that many Palestinians could not reach their schools or universities, so they either moved to live close by or gave up on education to look instead for new sources of income.

Recent statistics reflect how the general attitude of most West Bank Palestinian residents lately has changed more towards the idea of settling down, with the minimum amount of movement possible, as people seek the least amount of confrontation with daily delays and implicit pain. People now tend to stay at home, or remain in their own villages; hence, the spatial vagueness of the current situation is resulting in isolating people not only physically but socially as well.

THE POLITICS OF ROADS

Before the Oslo Agreement it was more obvious where the Palestinian territory was located, given that the 'green line' created by the 1948 settlement, have identified clearly Israeli from Palestinian areas. After the *Second Intifada* in late 2000, and the accumulation of further political complications, the West Bank is now left with a big question mark and real confusion where its territory starts or ends. With the Israeli attempts to divide Palestinian from Israeli areas, with what are in effect new mazes excluding 'us' and including 'them', it has become very easy to get lost on the way or end up in an Israeli settlement entrance or a checkpoint. It is even easier for an Israeli settler to end up in a Palestinian neighbourhood, losing his or her way between the new bypass roads. As much as this has been an obstacle for the Palestinian after the Oslo Agreement, it is lately becoming also a source of potential, as people familiarized themselves with new different alternative routes where by they can connect to other parts of the West

1.13 Old Palestinian roads. Photograph by Majdi Hadid.

1.14 Beir Nabala: new matrix of roads constructed by Israel after the Oslo Agreement with Israeli roads above the Palestinian ones to minimise connection points.

Bank or even sneak through into Israeli areas to seek employment.

The size, nature, street furniture and overall quality of each road in the West Bank today are also now fair indicators of whether we are actually in a Palestinian or Israeli area. The yellow street lights and convenient wide highways bypassing Palestinian neighbourhoods without distracting Israeli drivers, plentiful benches and bus stops with breathtaking views, and lots of security police, soldiers and armed settlers, are all indicators of being on an Israeli road. In contrast, Palestinian roads suffer from under-investment. Residents still have to rely on existing old road systems – some which dates back to the Roman period – whose non-hierarchal nature relies so much on familiarity with the surroundings, especially since the old road signs with Arabic and Hebrew do not make any sense to Palestinians anymore.

This new complicated system of roads in the West Bank, as much as it created division and confusion, it has also actually created more overlapping points between both parties, especially of Palestinians with Israeli settlers. Area B today includes Palestinian villages, Israeli settlements and the network of bypass roads built exclusively for the purpose of connecting Israeli settlements with each other and with Israel; hence, it is impossible for any party to move within such complicated lines without some meeting points. This in fact offers 'spaces of opportunity', as more leftover spaces have emerged as a result, and are now used by Palestinians as transitional areas.

To counteract this, a new road system has been introduced in the past three years by Israel to minimize these points of overlap wherever possible. The horizontal lines of roads became

1.15   Concrete blocks located in between villages to mark 'Area B' and identify the start of 'Area C' land. Photograph by Majdi Hadid.

three-dimensional; as a result Israelis get to drive on top, while Palestinians have to use roads underneath or even travel in tunnels.[27] This is creating a brand new landscape of roads and walls within the West Bank area, which is also shaped up by the new alternative routes that Palestinians are unofficially using.[28]

THE WIND OF CHANGE

THE VILLAGE

The Palestinian villages were always associated with poetic narratives due to their magical nature and easy integration within the rocky landscape. A cluster of small houses made of lime and stone with their gentle roofs or domes blended naturally with the rolling hills surrounding them, overlooking the valleys below. However, the typical Palestinian village today is facing a sharp contrast between old and new patterns of living. Scattered around the historic fabric, there are now houses and even high-rise buildings and recently built from concrete or limestone blocks, with flat roofs crowned with television antennae and satellite receivers. Neither the building style nor the visual image reflect any link to past history or culture. These houses are also sprawling and connecting the scattered villages together, as well as joining up with the Palestinian towns and major cities.[29]

The first real changes in the appearance of these villages started to take place after 1920, during the period of the British Mandate in Palestine. This was the result of social and economic transformation, which greatly affected Palestinian settlement patterns and daily life, especially the reality of wage labour, which was drawing increasing number of villagers away from agriculture. During the British Mandate many villagers sought employment as labourers in the city centres or as employees in schools or the police force; then later in the 1970s, large numbers of Palestinians began to find employment in Israeli farms, factories and construction projects.[30] This too contributed towards the marginalization of Palestinian agriculture, or the social trends towards nuclear families in opposition to the extended family groups, which the spatial formation of historic villages had been all about.

As noted, today the majority of villages in the central highlands of Palestine, the area known as West Bank, have even more 'urban characteristics' in terms of their spatial formation compared to those in the coastal zone or villages in historic Palestine. As Amiry noted, this past tradition was largely due to the accumulation of wealth during Turkish rule in the nineteenth century, when the concept of 'throne villages' occurred. Rural sheikhs enjoyed an independent status, which gave them the opportunity to build more sophisticated houses, reflecting the centre of power and prestige of these rural landlords who had been appointed to collect taxes on behalf of the Ottoman Empire. These feudal leaders usually borrowed their architectural style and the urban features from the nearby cities and placed them into the villages.[31]

It is only in the past 15 years that Palestinians themselves have participated in destroying what is left of their cultural identity. Whoever has enough money and land to build a house on the outskirts of the village took the opportunity; whoever lived inside the historic centres would either erase and rebuild, or simply build vertically with concrete skeletons to be filled up with stone and extra storeys when opportunity allows. Historic centres in Palestinian areas were the most affected in the

1.16   Map showing bypass roads in the West Bank, 2005.

1.17   Traditional Palestinian village of Lifta. Courtesy of Riwaq Photo Archive.

1.18   The stone terraces and watchtowers characterising rural Palestine. Photograph by John Tordeh. Courtesy of Riwaq Photo Archive.

1.19   Part of the cultural landscape in Palestine. Photograph by Mia Grondahl. Courtesy of Riwaq Photo Archive.

Bypass roads in the West Bank in 2005

Checkpoints, earth mounds and road blocks

Roads

Separation Wall

into a car parking-space while starting on new buildings.

Choosing historic centres as alternative and potential sites was easy because they were mostly abandoned (apart from the very poor who had no other alternative for where to live). They were hence seen as a dead leftover space with huge potential for redevelopment. The complexity of ownership in these historic centres was another difficult issue to resolve, and this also made it simpler to erase history and start from scratch.

The changes in the villages were massive and fast. As the value of land went up, due to the limited amount of built-up areas, investment in building and land ownership became both a career and a skill. Smart operators would know where and when to buy and sell, or to build and demolish. A town like Birzeit has witnessed this change from the Oslo Agreement onwards; when Ramallah found it had no more vacant land for construction, building investment moved out towards the Birzeit, Abu Kash and Surda areas as well as the Betunia and Al Bireh neighbourhoods.

The Separation Wall and other Israeli closures have contributed even more towards the changes in a town like Birzeit. Because of the major university there, students simply moved from Ramallah and neighbouring cities and villages to Birzeit to avoid the problem of limited mobility and travel delays. This has encouraged more residential buildings to be built in the town, and new services have sprang up at the edge of the town and in the surrounding villages.

Today, the historic centres are witnessing a dangerous phenomenon. Not only are the television antennae and satellite dishes taking over, but the villagers are replicating the settlements surrounding

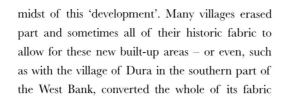

midst of this 'development'. Many villages erased part and sometimes all of their historic fabric to allow for these new built-up areas – or even, such as with the village of Dura in the southern part of the West Bank, converted the whole of its fabric them, probably as a pattern of 'modernity'. In a curious act of cultural imitation, the box-like houses now being built for Palestinians, with their new red brick roofs, are blatantly copied from dwellings in the Israeli settlements around, while meanwhile those Israelis come to steal at night the precious Palestinian architectural elements from the historic centres.

It is against this difficult climate that Riwaq: The Centre for Architectural Conservation, as well as other NGOs, have taken the initiative to protect and revitalize the historic fabric of the old Palestinian villages in the West Bank, and to work on community awareness campaigns there.

Even though the work that Riwaq and other agencies are doing is now protecting many of the historic centres in West Bank villages, the programme and the actual building designs are still in deed of a comprehensive ecological as well as socially sustainable approaches. This is mainly due to the urgency of taking action within such a short time span and with such minimal resources, especially because of the lack of survey maps of the areas involved.

It is a painful fact that, on the West Bank, its villages and historic centres are not part of the governmental strategy. The Palestinian Ministry of Local Government does not even consider historic centres to be a valid source of economic development; rather, they are simply awkward leftover spaces that can be maintained or destroyed within the larger PA master plans.

Riwaq has thus been working on a law for protecting historic centres, which has now been passed to the PA for ratification. Meanwhile, new planning strategies and projects are thankfully for the first time being conducted with a more holistic approach towards the issues of regeneration. Birzeit is one of the first testing sites; in that town a new strategy of empowerment is taking place, along with experimental design interventions with which I am involved, and hence which will be discussed later in this book.

RAMALLAH: CONFLICT OF MODERNITY

Lately, Ramallah's reputation of being the Palestinian city of culture and modernity is increasingly taking over its urban form. Hence, a new character of the city is shaping up, one that raises many questions, as well as debates and fears about the act of forgetting the collective Palestinian dream of regaining Jerusalem as the political and cultural capital of Palestine.

Even though Ramallah is known as being the passageway to cities in the north of the West Bank – such as Nablus, Nazareth and Damascus – it was never recorded by historians as being a true cosmopolitan city, as was the case with Jerusalem or Haifa or Jaffa in the 1920s. Nor was it really seen as a well-established inland city like Nablus or Hebron. Indeed, up until the end of the nineteenth century, Ramallah in contrast to these other cities was still a village. Its architecture was not any different to other hillside villages, reflecting a peasant lifestyle that relied on agriculture as its main income.[32]

The winds of change however started in the mid-nineteenth century when a number of public buildings emerged in Ramallah, reflecting the presence of foreign churches in a village largely then of Greek Orthodox Christians. In addition, its location was very close to Jerusalem. According to Taraki, the expansion of Ramallah into a genuine town really started in the early-twentieth century, when Palestinian immigration to America increased and these emigrants started changing the face of

1.20 Ramallah city centre.

the town by sending back money for new investments. This soon turned Ramallah into a commercial centre for that region. The British Mandate period also attracted new kinds of immigrants to Ramallah, especially after local agriculture was largely abandoned and citizens from other cities and villages around started looking for alternative careers.[33]

After the 1948 *Nakba*, Ramallah became known as 'the city of refugees'. Mostly they were the middle-class Christian refugees who had migrated from the coastal cities and became involved in commerce. According to Taraki, unlike other peasant refugees who were isolated in the new refugee camps, these social groups were well integrated within the fabric of the town itself. In the 1950s Ramallah turned into a hybrid town hosting further new arrivals, especially students who came to join the Christian Quaker-run Friends School, of which few even came from neighbouring Arab countries.[34]

With the 'Americanized' citizens who still come and visit Ramallah each summer, the city has changed radically to become more diverse, open and relatively more tolerant in relation to other cities around – certainly when it comes to mixing of men and women, and in terms of general social relations. As a result, Ramallah quickly became a magnet for those wishing to escape the oppression of the occupation and the social constrains in other West Bank villages and towns. This was especially noticeable and strong by the mid-1990s further to the Oslo Agreement, when Ramallah became the headquarters for the Palestinian Authority, it also became a cultural hub for intellectuals and activists and Palestinian returnees, many of whom returned back from exile to work for the Palestinian Authority.[35]

During the Oslo Peace Process, the political prominence and the urban development of Ramallah reached its extreme with the optimistic

36

URBAN CHANGES

These financial investments have converted the city of Ramallah today into a cultural capital. But on the other hand it has also spread far beyond the capacity of the city and its surrounding neighborhoods; the construction boom – or what Anani expressed as 'magnified economization'[36] – has taken over without any proper planning. Hills were leveled and apartment blocks are now going up so quickly that the place seems ever to grow before your eyes.

The city has also ended up with thousands of vacant residential units due to the high rents. Most of the houses or villas built were aimed at those working for private companies and non-governmental institutions who can afford to pay the rent, while in contrast there are hundreds, if not thousands, of employees and newly married Palestinian couples struggling to find affordable houses – ending up in them leaving to go to the surrounding towns and villages, or to rent 'low quality' houses in the outskirts of Ramallah.[37]

A further factor in the 'prominence' of Ramallah today is also related to the intensification of Israeli policies of siege and encirclement, especially for those Palestinians trying to get into Jerusalem. This has left Ramallah as a breathing point to penetrate through the Palestine/Israel borders. The siege has encouraged internal immigration from surrounding cities and villages towards Ramallah; employees and students who find mobility a major obstacle, started looking for cheap rented flats to accommodate them temporarily in the city. When the Israeli closures did not come to an end, renting and selling of these flats became formalized, as people were forced to look for long-term alternatives to adapt to the ongoing situation.

1.21 Walking towards the dead end of Kalandia.

1.22 A journey through the 'Valley of Death'. One of the very few alternative routes left to connect the north of the West Bank with Bethlehem and the south.

political atmosphere surrounding. This encouraged a spirit of construction investment and business opportunity aimed at developing Ramallah into a major cosmopolitan city.

1.23 New apartment blocks in Ramallah/Betunia, 2005–2006. Photograph by Yazid Anani.

This new situation in Ramallah is resulting in the arrival of different social groups, which are now shaping the character of the city in their search for a livelihood, but it is also excluding many others from being integrated within the urban culture or even the political arena. Although the influx of people into Ramallah on a daily basis was in fact much greater prior to 2002, before the erection of the Separating Wall and all those other Israeli barriers and checkpoints, the city still today gets its fair share of shoppers and traders. New waves of unemployed labourers from the surrounding villages and the northern cities of Nablus, Jenin and Tulkarem arrive, regularly in Ramallah. Those who can't work in Israel anymore come to seek job opportunities inside Ramallah, while others wait for opportunities to sneak into Israel through the villages of Nilean and Bilean, or into Jerusalem through Beir Nabala. These groups have managed to create their own meeting points, communities and even social networks. They use the urban street as their living room and search for opportunities of survival and livelihood, either near the vegetable market, or else by driving their vans around the city centre, or parking at what is known in Arabic as *mojama el-sayarat*, or simply just hanging around in the main city square known as *Al Manara*, which on its own is developing unique social and cultural practices.[38]

Ramallah is now the primary urban centre in West Bank; it is still constantly hosting new visitors, capturing the imagination of students, politicians, intellectuals and activists as well as unemployed labourers. As much as it is offering new opportunities, it is also preventing other cities around from taking their share. The city is socially and economically excluding others from taking equal part. If anything Ramallah is now distorting the image of the 'collective political project' which is being lost with the emergence of these new-capitalist schemes. This has opened various debates amongst Palestinians as to whether this stream of development in Ramallah should be redirected, stopped or even erased.

The Palestinian Pavilion at the 2008 Venice Biennale took this matter to its extreme through a project by two Bethlehem-based architects called 'Ramallah Syndrome'. The project questions the paradox of 'normality' while living in a bubble like Ramallah, which is completely isolated culturally and socially from the outer sphere. The project very much incorporates the idea of decentralizing Ramallah, and alleviating the fear of those living outside the city from being excluded from any future plans or involvement in Palestinian urban growth. Emily Jacir

and Yazid Anani also addressed the subject with their recent artwork 'Al Riyadh'. The work involves a series of public interventions that explore the rapid transformation of the urban fabric of Ramallah in isolation from the Palestinian community as a whole. The work exaggerates the development of high-rise building through billboards located in strategic locations in the heart of the city advertising fictional developments yet to come. This in return has raised a lot of debate and questions, by the locals and even rage and anger by the municipality, which asked for removing the artwork as a matter of urgency. As Anani and Tamari ironically describes it:

Al-Riyadh Tower is a proposition to destroy the old vegetable market and replace it with a modern Dubai style tower, promoting a clean business environment and spaces for foreign trade exchange while, replacing the intimacy, heritage, and memory of the place. The other billboard promotes a gated community emulating the proliferation of housing projects around Ramallah, with walled perimeters, surveillance cameras, and private security personnel; projects that threaten to wipe out the historic center of Ramallah and replace its architectural heritage with a housing project that looks similar to that of Israeli settlements.[39]

1.24   Fake billboards for the Al Riyadh project by Emily Jacir and Yazid Anani. Posters by Emily Jacir and Yazid Anani.

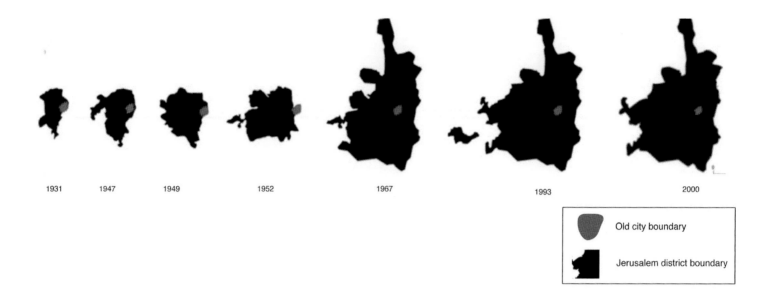

1931   1947   1949   1952   1967   1993   2000

Old city boundary

Jerusalem district boundary

JERUSALEM: BUBBLES OF ENCLAVES AND EXCLAVES

Jerusalem has of course developed different meanings along the years; it's the capital, the target, the dream and the witness of identity.

For a West Banker today, Jerusalem is the unseen, the 'other' side that one can hardly approach without jumping over the wall or sneaking through the sewage tunnels. For a Jerusalemite, it represents the struggle to keep their blue ID card and the right to live there under the pressure of squeezing all the 'Arabs' out of the Jerusalem map.

My brother could not marry his girlfriend who has a Jerusalem ID, as her family was not willing to sacrifice their daughter's ID card for love, just in case the Israelis came to know that she would not actually be living in Jerusalem anymore. This left them struggling for two years meeting at the edge of nowhere at the checkpoint between Ramallah and Jerusalem, just to keep their relationship going.

1.25   Expansion of Jerusalem district.

FAKE JERUSALEM

Over time, however, my brother and his girlfriend lost hope. The conflict over Jerusalem has penetrated under the wall to reach into the surrounding landscape and urban fabric. The map of 'Greater Jerusalem'[40] was increasingly excluding Arab areas and including others. It was also getting bigger in the area until it reached Ramallah's neighbourhoods from the north, Hebron on the south, and the Jordan Valley to the east. Even though they realized the risk they were taking, my brother and his girlfriend decided to live in Kofor Akab; a village allocated to Jerusalem municipality boundaries, even though it is outside the wall and adjacent to Ramallah. The village now houses most of the working-class Palestinian Jerusalemites who happen to be working in Ramallah and want to avoid checkpoints and ID confiscation.

Unlike Jerusalem and its ancient city centre, Kofor Akab is a clear indicator of Palestinians' status. A high density of building construction contains as much as possible the desperate workers and newly married couples. These structures are now creeping towards the main Jerusalem/Ramallah road, leaving no space for any public amenities, green spaces, car parking or even building setbacks. Kofor Akab is a time-bomb, or a magnet pulling all those Palestinians inside Jerusalem out. It is the only area where building construction for Palestinians is allowed by the Jerusalem municipality without any regulation or prior permission, and the result is near-chaos.

The prospect of Jerusalem as a future capital for the Palestinians is vanishing slowly, Palestinians are not allowed any building permits within the old city boundaries and the surrounding neighbourhoods. Their only building activities can take place illegally at night, usually waiting for the Israeli bulldozers to come in the morning and wipe them away.

Urban and political conflict in the city has transformed it into extreme spatial configuration of exclusion and inclusion. The Palestinian villages and neighbourhoods of Jerusalem have become densely knit, crowded and uncontrollable. Families invest in cement structures to extend and improve their daily lives wherever possible. As Khamaisi describes it: 'The conflict between life and occupation, lack of public institutions is forcing Palestinian neighbourhoods into urbanization without urbanity'.[41]

PLAYING WITH LINES

The winds of change in the West Bank are still blowing hard, and what was taking place a year ago can change in a day due to the political, social and economic changes imposed by Israeli occupation. Ramallah, unlike other cities like Hebron and Nablus, did not have any social groups with historic roots that contributed to its urban development in a way that excluded others, or was without conflict. As Taraki summarized it: 'Ramallah belonged to no one and thus is for everyone'.[42] Jerusalem in the middle of this situation is struggling to survive while other cities around it are changing daily with deep resistance and great discrepancies between institutional and political fabrications.

Despite such harsh realities of occupation, the Israeli Army checkpoint isn't just a physical divide between two warring peoples; it's now becoming a ritual space in which Palestinians reconstruct their relationship on a daily basis. Checkpoints become the market, the meeting place, the stage, the living room, the lover's corner and the place of heartbreaking memoirs. Playing with lines on the map has thus created new lines. Palestine is no longer the city and the village – it is also the in-between, the dead spaces and the margins, in which people perform wait, remember and resist. It's the new routes that its people create, the tunnels we dig under the wall, and the sewage pipes we walk through everyday just to reach our university.

This chapter is a brief introduction to the Palestinian/Israeli situation today, and a reflection to the political conflict and its effect on the map and the landscape. The following chapter will be zooming into some of the cities, villages and leftover spaces trying to read these sites through narrative cards. I will be showing how the lines are being transformed by the everyday behaviours to try to create spaces of possibility.

empowering the yellows' network

1.26   A reflection of a new spatial
character formed on the margins.

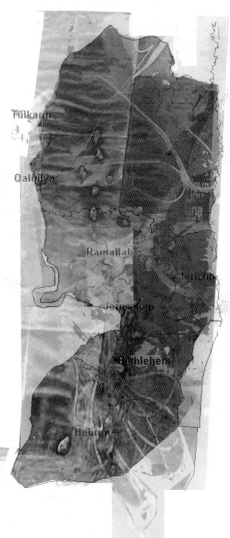

Tulkarm

Qalqilya

Ramallah

Jericho

Jerusalem

Bethlehem

Hebron

NOTES

1 Benvenisti, M. (2000) *Sacred Landscape: The Buried History of the Holy Land since 1948*. Berkeley: University of California Press, p.1.

2 This is inspired by Muhawi's scenario described in his MA thesis. Muhawi, F. (2001) 'The Politics of Land Use and Zoning Under the Oslo Accords', MA thesis, State University of Buffalo.

3 See the short film 'No Way Through' by Directors Monro, A. and Monon, S. Available at Anon. 'Imagine if London was Occupied by Israel', *YouTube*. See: http://www.youtube.com/watch?v=dYamviV7ZSY [accessed 7 June 2011].

4 London is perhaps not that different from Palestine in terms of the existence of inequality, power relations and hidden control of space – it just might be more visible in Palestine. However, the mesh of tension caused by the forces of globalised power is creating new layers other than the surface structures of money flow; globalization today is creating a network of societies that are left behind, struggling to overcome the hidden forces of power.

5 Amiry, S. (2002) 'Getting There', in Amiry, S. and Hadid, M., *Earthquake in April*. Ramallah and Jerusalem: Riwaq and Institute of Jerusalem studies, pp. xii–xiix.

6 In 1922, Britain was granted the Mandate for Palestine to facilitate the establishment of the Jewish State; this resulted after the issue of the so-called Balfour Declaration in 1917, in the form of a letter in which the British promised to assist the Jews in creating their homeland.

7 The United Nations Partition Plan for Palestine was a recommendation approved by the UN General Assembly in 1947 to terminate the British Mandate of Palestine, and facilitate the creation of two states, one Jewish and one Arab. The partition plan came at a time where the land acquired by Jews in Palestine was less than 1/10 of the total land area of Palestine.

8 A slogan used by the Zionists, presenting themselves as 'making the desert bloom'.

9 See Khalidi, W. (1992) *All That Remains: The Palestinian Villages Occupied and Depopulated by Israel in 1948*. Washington, DC: Institute for Palestine Studies.

10 The Israeli currency coins show the map of Israel expanding to reach Egypt in the west and Iraq to the east.

11 A famous slogan initiated by the first Israeli Prime minister, David Ben Gurion. See 'Zionist Quotes', *Scribd*, 15 November 1998. Available at: http://www.scribd.com/doc/6200102/zionist-quotes [accessed 18 November 2008].

12 Weitz, J. (1940), ibid.

13 For further details on the Oslo Agreement, its phases and implications see Muhawi, op. cit.

14 The PLO was founded in 1964 as the only representative for the Palestinians then, and called for the right of return for Palestinians and for self-determination. It's Chairman was Yasser Arafat, who later became the President of the Palestinian Authority.

15 Shalev, N. and Cohen-Lifshitz, A. (2008) *The Prohibited Zone: Israeli Planning Policies in the Palestinian Villages in Area C*. Jerusalem: BIMKOM. Available at: http://sandbox.rebuildingalliance.org/wp-content/uploads/2011/04/23ProhibitedZone.pdf [accessed 8 June 2011].

16 Harel, A. 'Palestinians Abandon 1,000 Hebron Homes under IDF, Settler Pressure', *Jerusalemites*. Available at: http://www.jerusalemites.org/reports/87.htm [accessed 20 November 2008].

17 Quoted from Roy, S. (2002) 'Why Peace Failed: An Oslo Autopsy', *Current History*, Vol. 100 (651), pp. 11–27.

18 The Israeli Foreign Minister, Ariel Sharon, addressing a meeting of militants from the extreme right-wing Tsomet Party, Agence France Presse. See Sharon, A. 'Zionist Quotes', *Scribd*, 15 November 1998. Available at: http://www.scribd.com/doc/6200102/zionist-quotes [accessed 18 November 2008].

19 Lobe, J. 'Israeli Settlements Control Nearly Half of West Bank', *CommonDreams.org*, 14 May 2002. Available at: http://www.commondreams.org/headlines02/0514–04.htm [accessed 22 November 2008].

20 Said, E. (1994) *The Politics of Dispossession: The Struggle for Palestinian Self-determination, 1969–1994*. London: Chatto & Windus.

21 Muhawi, op. cit.

22 Taraki, L. (2006) *Living Palestine: Family Survival, Resistance, and Mobility Under Occupation*. Syracuse, NY: Syracuse University Press.

23 Said, E. (2000) *The End of the Peace Process: Oslo and After*. New York: Pantheon Books, p. 111.

24 Anon. 'Statistics on Unemployment and Poverty', *B'tselem*. Available at: http://webcache.googleusercontent.com/search?q=cache:-sUjodPNUT8J:www.btselem.org/english/freedom_of_movement/unemployment_statistics.asp+unemployment+in+palestine+btselem&cd=1&hl=en&ct=clnk&gl=uk&client=safari&source=www.google.co.uk [accessed 8 June 2011].

25 Residents born in the Gaza Strip now require special permission to enter Gaza if they don't live there.

26 Frykberg, M. 'Trapped Between the Wall and the Green Line', *IPS*, 26 February 2009. Available at: http://webcache.googleusercontent.com/search?q=cache:AbVfwMyEghAJ:ipsnews.net/news.asp%3Fidnews%3D45896+what+is+the+percentage+of+land+trapped+between+the+separation+wall+and+the+green+line&cd=1&hl=en&ct=clnk&gl=uk&client=safari&source=www.google.co.uk [accessed 8 June 2011].

27 The website guide prepared by the Israeli Consulate in Britain for travellers to Palestine/Israel, is a good example of the confusing landscape and the need for familiarity to use roads. It tries to indicate for visitors where to go on Israeli roads and where not to go, and as such is a telling document.

28 For further information on the Israeli politics of roads, see Weizman, E. (2003) 'The Politics of Verticality: The West Bank as an Architectural Construction', in Franke, A., *Territories: Islands, Camps and Other States of Utopia*. Berlin: Institute for Contemporary Art; Weizman, E., '10. Roads, Over and Under', *Open Democracy*, 30 April 2002. Available at: http://www.opendemocracy.net/ecology-politicsverticality/article_809.jsp [accessed 8 June 2011].

29 Amiry, S., and Tamari, V. (1989) *The Palestinian Village Home*. London: British Museum Publications, p. 7.

30 Ibid.

31 Amiry, S. (2003) *Throne Villages Architecture: Palestinian Rural Mansions*. Ramallah: Riwaq [Arabic text].

32 Jubeh, N. and Bshara, K. (2002) *Ramallah: Architecture and History*. Ramallah and Jerusalem: Riwaq, and Institute of Jerusalem Studies [Arabic text].

33 Taraki, op. cit.

34 Taraki, op. cit., p. 22.

35 Ibid.

36 See 'Interview with Yazid Anani by Shuriq Harb', *ArtTerritories*, 7 September 2010. Available at: http://webcache.googleusercontent.com/search?q=cache:krLo_OHvTtUJ:www.artterritories.net/%3Fpage_id%3D889+ramallah+for+rent+ngos+only+artterritories&cd=1&hl=en&ct=clnk&gl=uk&client=safari&source=www.google.co.uk [accessed 9 June 2011].

37 Ironically, it even became a common feature to see signs on vacant luxurious blocks or mansions saying 'for rent: NGOs only'.

38 See Shibli, A. (2006) 'Al-Manara Square: Monumental Architecture and Power', *Jerusalem Quarterly*, Vol. 26 (Spring), pp. 52–64.

39 Anani, Y. and Tamari, V. (2010) 'Ramallah – The Fairest of Them All?' *Nafas*, August 2010. Available at: http://universes-in-universe.org/eng/nafas/articles/2010/ramallah [accessed 2 June 2010].

40 This plan aims at expanding the borders of Jerusalem as much as possible into West Bank territory. Currently there are around a quarter of a million Jewish settlers living in Jerusalem settlements, even though all of these settlements are deemed illegal under international law given that they are built in occupied territory.

41 Khamaisi, R. (2006) 'Villages Under Siege', in Misselwitz, P. and Rieniets, T. (eds), *City of Collision: Jerusalem and the Principles of Conflict Urbanism*. Basel: Birkhäuser, p. 121.

42 Taraki, op. cit., p. 24.

THE ART
OF RESISTANCE[1]

The *First Intifada* drew its apparent victory from mass civil resistance and collective disobedience against Israeli occupation – by boycotting Israeli products, converting homes into 'underground' schools, refusing to pay taxes to Israel, installing mobile medical clinics, etc. – and this has left its own profound effect on the political and social structure of Palestinian society. As Karkar noted, it was the 'lower social strata' that took the responsibility for leading the *Intifada* through what was then called the United National Command.[2] These united resistance groups consciously avoided any calls for military action in order not to alienate ordinary Palestinian people. However, the collective role-played by the local community and its leadership in the *First Intifada* has gradually disappeared over time due to the different political layers that have been enforced upon them. Some put the blame on the failure of the 1993–1995 Oslo Peace Agreement to fulfill the needs of Palestinians, while others have blamed it on a lack of effective leadership and collective ideology within the newly established Palestinian Authority (PA). In any case, the result has been a growing feeling of frustration amongst a Palestinian community which has been not only trapped in disconnected areas by the policy of Israeli occupation, but has also been left behind by Palestinian politics. As Hammami and other critics have noted, the loose structures of overwhelming military resistance by the PA has replaced the previous role of community groups, and thus has left the Palestinian people as a passive audience in the background.[3]

Within the current situation of widespread frustration and political conflict in the West Bank, the necessity to look for alternatives to rebuild the community and empower their role is becoming ever more crucial. Looking at problems from 'below' rather than 'above' is opening up new possibilities, especially when examining the everyday life of 'ordinary' Palestinians. Today a series of small-scale events are contributing towards the social and spatial formation of the West Bank and can be seen perhaps as a new face for the 'lost' ideal of community resistance. Even though these new everyday practice might not be based on a 'conscious' political agenda or leadership, nonetheless they are transferring and developing individual attempts into collective forms of power that are able to create solid facts on ground, despite the obvious tensions being enforced on both sides of the West Bank borders.

THE ART OF RESISTANCE: ANYWHERE AND EVERYWHERE

Distance and time have become irrelevant phenomena in Palestine over the last 15 years or so. Immobility is a key tool in Israeli occupation: waiting to cross a checkpoint, walking through 'no-drive' zones, or spending hours finding a way out to reach work or school, all have become a central feature of Palestinian life. A journey that normally takes an hour is now taking up to four hours, if not a whole day. Palestine has become more associated with the checkpoints enforced on its citizens and the alternative routes that one needs to look for, or indeed creates, in order to reach one's destinations. Traveling now is more about the yellow Ford Transit vans, the two-wheel-drive carriages, the street vendors along the way, and the stories that one needs to make up in order to be able to cross from one point to another.

'The orders are to let no one through today', the Israeli soldier was shouting while I was dragging my suitcases and myself through the dusty checkpoint. I had to find my way out to Nablus. At the edge of the road, the drivers were shouting their destinations: 'Tora-Bora, Wadi-al-nar, Elmoarajat, Tom and Jerry'. Mine, however, is the 'Tora-Bora' route. It might sound like Afghanistan; but it is actually the new route to get to the city of Nablus with its series of rocky landscape and dramatic topography while crossing through the agricultural routes and stone quarries along the way.

The above experience reflects my everyday life in the West Bank, specifically between 2000–2005 when I used to travel to university, and later to my work as an architect on site. Each day and each journey has in this sense left its profound impact on shaping a different mental map of Palestine/Israel. For all Palestinians today, the space is still not making any sense. In fact, today might even be worse than ever with the stalemate in peace talks and the intensification of illegal Israeli settlements which Prime Minister Benjamin Netanyahu calls, chillingly, 'facts on the ground'.[4] Yet, at every point when power is exercised to its maximum by stripping Palestinians of their right to choose – as Dovey expresses it[5] – a new journey is also born across nowhere and everywhere.

Despite the difficulties and sheer despair experienced by Palestinians living under Israeli occupation, an enforced short drive or walk along some fields is in truth equally as enjoyable as it troubles the mind. It feels like one is running away from the madness of the occupation – instead of facing it – in every path we create or every checkpoint we avoid. These new alternative routes across Palestinian rural areas have become associated with memories and narratives: *Wadi-al-nar*, or what is known as the 'Valley of Fire', the impossible 'Roller-Coaster' route where you can hardly climb up the hill, the 'Tom & Jerry' route with its cat-and-mouse relationship, and many others, started out as individual attempts to proceed with one's journey but have ended up as a form of collective experience representing most Palestinians in the West Bank today. These are the 'non-places' being made by everyday life into very real places.

In the face of such challenges, Palestinians have managed to negotiate borderlines by introducing new social roles and possibilities whenever the need to find alternative routes has emerged. The landscape has since become jammed with a plethora of Ford Transit vans – or the *Fords*, as every Palestinian familiarly refers to them – found at the edge of main roads and even in the middle of nowhere, waiting to pick up the desperate faces who haven't managed to cross the Israeli checkpoints. Most of these vans are unlicensed or leftover supplies passed to the Palestinian Authority who had found them to be mechanically unreliable.[6] They thus proved easy and relatively cheap for Palestinians to buy with no registration fee. And as a result, Ford vans have turned into the main public transport system that Palestinians count on, and working out the various alternative routes offers a new source of income for young drivers within a situation of limited job opportunities.

Operating in-between the West Bank cities and villages gives these Ford van drivers a new-found source of power and authority; they have transformed themselves fairly quickly into an active network through which they can trade reports about

Israeli checkpoints amongst themselves, or search for promising routes along the hills and valleys, or pick up and swap passengers, or above all organize the traffic flows in order to assure the security of their careers.

Hamammi, in her writings on the Surda checkpoint, has referred to the role and importance of the Ford van drivers as a network given the absence of other structures:

> In Palestine the absence of mass organizations, networks of informal sector workers have stepped into the gap. Thus the unlikely symbols of the new steadfastness are not national institutions, but rather the sub-proletariat of Ford van drivers whose semi criminal bravado is summed up by the ubiquitous Nike 'no fear' stickers emblazoned on their rear windshields . . . the same thuggishness has become a crucial force for everyday resistance and organizing at checkpoints – not just to deal with the crowds and traffic jams but also deal with the thuggishness of soldiers.[7]

In the case of busy checkpoints like Kalandia, Jawwal, Surda and Huwwara, the Ford drivers have realized that they need to work out some sort of organization between themselves. This is mainly to control the traffic and chaos created on each side of checkpoints where passengers get picked up and dropped off. However, it is also necessary to secure and control their business by preventing any driver from 'stealing turns' – as they call it – while the others are stuck in the traffic jam.[8] Consequently, at each end a representative is selected to organize the van community and allocate passengers. In the case of Surda checkpoint for example – which lasted over three years from 2001–2003 – a van driver called Ziad from the town of Birzeit was appointed to look after the business. He was offered by the drivers 6 shekels per car to organize the crowd, which was considered to be far better income than just driving his own van. Later, when the checkpoint started to get busier and the Ford vans were easier to obtain, more drivers from other destinations joined in. Consequently, the task became far more challenging for Ziad, especially after the Jawwal Checkpoint was sealed and all its drivers moved towards Surda to fish for work. Jawwal was mainly controlled by the Jalazon refugee camp community living close by, and its residents are known to be tough and hard to deal with. Therefore, the governor of Ramallah appointed two other representatives to help with the job of controlling the Ford taxis, but both had no real social weight or backing within the Jalazon drivers, and thus they proved to be ineffective. As Hammami wrote about the subject:

> the same hard-nosed culture of resistance that has made refugee camps the front line of each Intifada, produces the collective ability to fight and win turf wars with neighbouring communities.[9]

As a result, the Ramallah governor had to interfere again; he therefore set a quota between drivers from

2.2 Surda Checkpoint, 2003.
Photographs by Tom Kay.

2.3 Ramallah vans waiting their turn
in the queue.

each village and appointed Abu Alabed from Jalazon – the former organizer of Jawwal Checkpoint – to be in charge alongside Ziad. Even though the majority of drivers in Surda Checkpoint came from the neighbouring town of Birzeit, the governor could not help but give the majority of turns to the Jalazon camp, as he knew that they would be able to bring the necessary 'muscle' – as Hammami puts it – if needed be in case of any disruptions. Ziad was also more than happy with the calculated decision, since he knew his job would not have been sustained without the right backing from social committees.[10]

As the main form of transportation, and for many Palestinians the very place in which one spends the most time, the flotilla of Ford vans now offer a much more important social role than simply confronting and passing Israeli roadblocks or barriers. Their drivers have managed to create new spatial qualities while trying to fulfill the needs of passengers streaming through the dusty roads. With the collective journeys including different sectors of society, it means that these groups have time to share their political views and become involved in creating new stories. The Transit van has slowly been turned into a living room, a supermarket, a stage, and a mobile theatre where everybody can have their say. While joining Kareem on the way to Hebron, for instance, he thought out loud about expanding his business plans if the checkpoint remain closed. Being highly experienced in traversing the Ramallah/ Hebron route – not only does he offer tea and coffee every morning, as do many other drivers around – but with the complexities and dislocations created by the shifting border lines, he has decided to accommodate those stuck in-between checkpoints by offering his own van as a temporary overnight residence if need be:

> 'An ambulance is not any better. It will be the best business in the coming few years', Kareem told me. 'I will try also to get another van for females as well. I am sure that in five years time everybody will be imitating me'.

Even though this phenomenon of the Ford vans has been intensified around 2003 at Surda and Kalandia Checkpoints, these being the main transportation hubs connecting the north with the south and the west of the West Bank – one can see it taking different forms and functions all across the map, especially in-between cities where the Palestinian Authority has minor responsibility, if any. On the way to Nabi Saleh village, for example, the vans stretch all across the side roads in Areas B and C selling fruit and vegetables by those who could not reach the main urban centres. Towards the village of Ein Areek, the vans are mostly specialized in terms of selling furniture and building equipment, which might be more relevant given its proximity to the industrial area of Ramallah. Near the village of Jaba', the Ford vans are located at the crossroads dividing Areas B with C, and sell stone cut from the six or so local quarries dominating its landscape. In winter, however, when the routes across the agricultural fields get flooded with rainwater, the vans find themselves stuck at the bottom of the valleys in the middle of nowhere. Hence, another new responsibility has been given to the heavy vehicles like tractors and caterpillars which wait to pull any stuck vehicles up the hills.

It was my bad (or maybe good) luck back in 2002 to drive through the informal route of Kufur Ni'me which leads to the western villages around Ramallah. The entire valley had been transformed into a big lake with floating cars, including mine, until Abu Ali's tractor from Ras Karkar village came to rescue us. The 15 shekels I paid then was not the issue; it's the embarrassment of being pulled with a tractor, hoping I didn't encounter anyone I know. I knew I had to get out whatever it took, especially since any minute an Israeli jeep could arrive, start shooting and the experience of the cat-and-mouse chase would end absolutely. I thought then that it was a one-off experience that I would not like to share, but few days later, some friends were proudly broadcasting their adventurous trip through the Qana valley. There they had to pay 50 shekels to get a caterpillar from the village of Deir Istya to pull their minibus up the hill. Within few weeks, the one tractor

ARTIFACTS OF RESISTANCE

With the ongoing system of segregation created by Israeli occupation, a whole culture has thus started to develop around the checkpoints and informal routes. Individual 'experiments' in negotiating space are turning over time into a collective act; the street vendors who have joined the pattern of the commuters along the checkpoints and 'no-drive' zone have also taken over the left-over spaces. Hence, a whole series of canteens selling sandwiches, fruit, drinks, ice cream, coffee and even clothes and furniture has come to fill the urban voids. Porters also have joined in with their wooden three-wheel carts being used to earn their living in the most difficult areas – especially between the two ends of checkpoints where no cars are allowed. Not

2.4 Huwwara Checkpoint, 2003.

2.5 'Tom and Jerry' route, with the bottom of the valley flooded with water in winter, 2002. Courtesy of Riwaq Photo Archive.

became two, and the hitherto voluntary service, turned into a new business throughout the winter season serving what was named the 'Tom & Jerry' route.

2.6 Finding our way to Nablus through valleys and no-drive zones, 2001. Courtesy of Riwaq Photo Archive.

Kalandia Checkpoint, for example, gained its unofficial name of 'the duty free', since one could buy anything in the 'no-drive' zone at very cheap prices. This network has gradually turned into a rather good source of income, and thus has accumulated more porters who have now started to organize themselves to assure their businesses in face of competition from other three-wheel wooden carts. Even though these porters appear and disappear depending on the sudden changes in political conditions and borderlines, it is nonetheless common to see them all over the West Bank. The peripheral streets in the historic urban centres of Hebron and Nablus are good indicators of the accumulating amount of porters just waiting to pop out.

It is happening not only on the urban margins. A city like Ramallah is now constructing an attitude towards the intensification of Israeli border controls and the consequent frustration in Palestinian economic activities. Ramallah's vegetable market today hosts the waves of porters who had previously gone to work at the nearby Kalandia Checkpoint, but were later banned from there by Israeli forces after the checkpoint was transformed into a permanent border with its 8-metre-high wall. So in 2006, those who had left the market in Ramallah to work at Kalandia came back to Ramallah with their three-wheel carts (and their relatives) in the search for new job opportunities. Amjad, who had originally left Halhoul village near Hebron to seek work in Ramallah with his cousins, is now based in the main street at the entrance of the market so as to avoid the high license fee charged for stalls in the actual vegetable market itself. They are thus playing a devious cat-and-mouse game with Israeli soldiers at

only do they carry goods, but they also take elderly people, children, women and unwell patients across checkpoints at Kalandia, Surda, Huwwara, Burin, and elsewhere.

53

Off the road

2.7 Artifacts of resistance emerging at the margins.

the checkpoints and with officials from the Palestinian Authority inside the West Bank cities.

Two-wheel donkey-driven 'taxis' – in effect, the simplest type of carts – have also appeared more recently to carry Palestinian people and their luggage on secret journeys around checkpoints and in 'no-drive' zones where wheels are only allowed by the soldiers if not motorized. Even though they have so far been limited to specific areas in the West Bank – especially in the north around Nablus and Qalqilyah – these so-called *al-bisat elsihry*, or 'magic carpets', have turned into a source of hope that can seemingly 'fly' over any perceived obstacle. With their imaginative stories of heroic figures, their drivers have made the impossible easy to reach in the village of Burin. Signs such as 'no fear', '*Azeza*', 'the Mercedes is at the other end', are all written nicely on the bright yellow plastic covers of the donkey carts, with colourful decorations to attract the few 'shy' pedestrians who might otherwise rather prefer to walk. With a piece of carpet laid on the carts for

sitting on, and a big blue 'evil eye' or prayer beads hanging up to bless the route, now one can not avoid such experiences – giving up on twenty-first century vehicles completely – if one has no choice.

There were around 600 other Israeli checkpoints, roadblocks and different kinds of obstructions estimated by the United Nations office of the Commissioner of the Humanitarian Affairs (UNCHA) between 2000–2003, causing a massive decline in the Palestinian economy and a chronic increase of unemployment that was described by the World Bank as 'amongst the worst in modern history'.[11] Each one of these points has instead become a lure for the unemployed in a certain way. These unnoticed people have challenged, negotiated and restructured the dead spots such that they become central in their daily life; filling them with porters, cart drivers, donkey-driven taxis, vans, small taxis, peddlers and unemployed people all trying to make a living from the thousands of Palestinian commuters passing through.

2.8   The 'magic carpet' at Burin, 2001.
       Courtesy of Riwaq Photo Archive.

2.9   Group of commuters in Burin, 2001.
       Courtesy of Riwaq Photo Archive.

The constant movement along the West Bank borderlines implies continuous changes in the routes being taken, and in the minds of their users as well; as mentioned, the village of Burin has suddenly been placed on the map, while the importance of other major cities has been eroded by the Separation Wall. What dissolves at a given point simply pops up at another location. Today (2012), the Huwwara Checkpoint near Nablus is repeating what was seen in Kalandia about five years ago, with the same features of everyday life dominating the margins, whereas Kalandia Checkpoint no longer infact holds its famous 'duty-free' reputation (following the erection of the Separation Wall, Israeli soldiers banned any

commuters or vendors in that area). Today, no more than four or five canteens stand there offering basic drinks and food, with the vendors mainly from the refugee camp nearby.

What is outstanding in this new-found border culture are the collective networks of communities that work together just to survive and resist. Van drivers, refugee camp residents, commuters, porters and vendors each have a role, whether as a host, or a guide, or an organizer. They all share responsibilities in order to ensure the sustainability of daily practices in these emerging places. Each one of them tries to form alliances against what they call 'outsiders', counting to a substantial degree on tight knits families, friends and blood relatives getting together.

> The checkpoint took men from the margins and allowed them a role that was fundamentally and publicly important for the entire society's survival.[12]

The formation of these collective communities has also managed to stretch the associated social spaces far beyond checkpoints and borderlines to reach other destinations. Taking the Kalandia Checkpoint as an example, when the traffic jam started to create mass chaos for cars and commuters, the famous stone quarry near Kalandia took part in facilitating a spill-over space for the cars to park. The owner donated gravel as well as bulldozers to level the rubble mounds around the checkpoint. Later, when it became impossible to walk through the 'no-drive' zone at Kalandia, people started using the quarry as a crossing route to get to Jerusalem. Ever since then, the route has been named humorously as 'Tora Bora'. It served commuters for few years before the Separation Wall was constructed in 2005–2006. The residents of Kalandia and the Kalandia refugee camp never hesitated to take part. Of course, many were initially working in the 'duty-free' market, but they also used to host overnight any commuters stuck at the checkpoints. Different incidents are still remembered by the residents of the refugee camps, like a lady giving birth when her ambulance was delayed at checkpoint and could not reach the hospital, in time, or housing a few workers from Hebron when their village was under Israeli curfew. Of course, all are proud to look after commuters during the fasting month of Ramadan, offering water and dates to ensure no-one is left

hungry while trying to get home in the rush hour; likewise the residents of Al Ram town were feeding those stuck at the Jerusalem end of the checkpoint.

Bayat in his book, *Street Politics*, reflects on these newfound clusters of networks and their role in shaping street culture through a dialectic of individual and collective actions. He describes them as being 'passive networks' representing individuals who share a certain status:

> The instantaneous communication among atomized individuals which is established by the tacit recognition of their common identity and is mediated through space . . . A woman who enters a male-dominated party instantly notices another female among the men; vendors in a street notice each other even though they may never speak to each other . . . all represent atomized individuals who, at a certain level, have a similar status and an identity of interests among themselseves.[13]

Above all, Bayat notes that despite the fact that these people represent 'individual actors', still all ensure instant cooperation once they feel a threat to their well-being, They also tend to protect their gains by acting cautiously and invisibly if need be.

> marked by quiet, atomised and prolonged mobilization with episodic collective action – an open and fleeting struggle without clear leadership, ideology, or structured organisation, one that produces significant gains of the actors.[14]

He goes to explain how these groups do not carry out their activities as a conscious political strategy; rather such activities are 'spontaneous individual attempts, driven by the force of necessity, to survive and live a dignified life away from the pressure or

2.10 Donkey-driven cart at Surda Checkpoint, 2003. Myself, Dana and Sahar on the way to Jericho.

2.11 Donkey-driven cart in Burin, 2001. Courtesy of Riwaq Photo Archive.

2.12 Vendor at Kalandia Checkpoint, 2006.

2.13 'No-drive' zone at Surda Checkpoint, 2001–2003.

2.14 'No-drive' zone near Kalandia Checkpoint, 2002.

2.15 Mazare Al-Nobani, myself on a donkey, 2002.

2.16   Alternative route to reach Nablus, 2001.

2.17   Beir Nabala route, or 'women's route', to cross into Jerusalem, 2003.

2.18   Three-wheel carts emerging at Surda Checkpoint, 2003.

2.19 Helping a patient to cross the no-drive zone at Surda Checkpoint, 2003.

the eyes of the state'. Furthermore, Bayat refers to them as:

> groups in flux: they are the structurally atomised individuals who operate outside the formal institutions ... These groups tend to fulfil their needs by themselves ... In short their politics is not to protest but to redress (equalise); it is a struggle for immediate outcomes largely through individual direct action.[15]

RABBIT HOLES AND BLURRY BOUNDARIES

As noted previously, the West Bank today includes Palestinian villages, Israeli settlements and a network of bypass roads built exclusively for the purpose of connecting the Israeli settlements with each other and back to Israel. Hence, it is impossible for any ordinary Palestinian to move within such complicated lines without meeting unwelcome surveillance points. For the untrained eye, one sees so little apart from the roads, dust and occasional settlements; however, Alaa' and his friends refer to their hidden spaces as 'rabbit holes' which operate only because of their invisible power. These concealed points of whispers and secret movement are activated at night by local workers and young men who gather there to look for job opportunities after the Israeli blockade has left them unemployed.[16] At the beginning of each week, usually at two or three o'clock in the morning, these groups gather at agreed points and sneak through together to different areas across the West Bank, hopefully to reach the other side of the wall, where the rest of the team will be waiting. Needing to move secretly between the two very different sides, where even the reception of mobile phones gets confused between Israeli and Palestinian networks, these 'rabbit holes' manage to create new

methods of communication between people, assuring their invisibility and subversion. However, because the borderlines are so 'elastic', these points soon end up being ephemeral given that they only emerge with the emergence of condition. While constantly moving and multiplying, the moment they get exposed they have to dissolve to allow for new tactics to be born. As Michel de Certeau puts it:

> The place of a tactic belongs to the other. A tactic insinuates itself into the other's place, fragmentarily, without taking it over in its entirety . . . . The 'proper' is a victory of space over time . . . because it does not have a place, a tactic depends on time – it is always on the watch for opportunities that must be seized 'on the wing'. Whatever it wins, it does not keep. It must constantly manipulate events in order to turn them into 'opportunities'.[17]

I was lucky to join with Alaa' and his friends in one of their 'rabbit journeys' on a Saturday night, starting from the village of Ibwein to the west of Ramallah. Of all the moments of fear and 'silent agitation' the ones that left their imprint on me the most are the collective tactics that I had to grasp in order to escape the surveillance surrounding us – either to avoid the deadly sniper who might spot us at any minute from a distance, or the occasional underground detectors planted across the olive groves to capture the quiet footsteps of any workers at night. If the unlucky 'ghosts' happened to step on them, bright flashlights would automatically be set off from underground, followed by the soldiers' live bullets. The strategy was in this sense a non-strategy; at times, we would all just run chaotically in different directions to mislead the underground detectors; at other times, one or two of us would lead the way to

2.20 The Separation Wall near Kalandia, 2009.

reveal the position of the detectors and ensure the safety of the rest of the group.

In all situations, however, what brings all Palestinian workers together is their persistence and desperation in the effort to make a living and survive. And what gets them to pursue their own journey are their collective actions to manipulate the system to their advantage. All seem to share the search and formation of agencies and collective networks that Florian Kossak[18] has described as being aware of the relationship between individual action and the bigger picture, and of knowingly exploiting and working with cause and effect. Kossak expanded on the importance of knowing the 'system' and how one can intervene, transgress and exploit it to one's advantage. He also stresses the power and transformative potential of connections between subjects, disciplines and people as key ingredients to understand and formulate the term known as 'agency'.

After a few hours of negotiating the dark olive groves and rocky paths down the Palestinian hills, my journey ended early at the sewage pipe which I wasn't meant to cross through.[19] I nonetheless did so, and

managed to become one of the few 'female rabbits' ever to cross these amazing shadowed landscapes under the darkness of night. Despite my frustration and disappointment, I knew that even though some people can't make it to the end of the hidden pipe, like myself, still whenever the opportunity reappears, such journeys would start over and over again. Such daily experiences take place in every village and every olive grove, wherever the possibility exists to find a hole to penetrate through.

Suad Amiry, who has taken the lead in joining these subversive groups, has reflected on her own experience with what she terms the 'night hunters':

> I froze, listened and fearfully examined all that surrounded me: suddenly there were hundreds and hundreds of dark silhouettes. There were ghosts there, there were ghosts everywhere. Some appeared from behind ghostly olive trees, some where still winding along narrow paths . . . some were fast in motion, some were slow, some hovered in large groups, some in small, some in pairs, some alone . . . I stood there and wondered: was it a carnival of existence or a carnival for survival? Was it a dance for life or a masquerade of death? . . . Once I got rid of my fears and the black spot in my heart, I figured out what it was: an innocent Saturday evening chase for a living.[20]

Invisibility, silence and subversion thus guarantee the sustainability of these invisible networks. They contribute towards a new geography of 'resistance' wherein the sense of absence introduces new potentials; every object and context – even if it's a sewage pipe, a plastic bag, or a blue 'evil eye – becomes a possibility to survive, or a tactic to resist. The exercise of the 'invisible power' – which requires, as Barnes argues, ignorance from one side

and knowledge from the other[21] – becomes crucial to sustain and negotiate one's own space in Palestine.

This condition can also be seen in recent events in the Gaza Strip, which by being turned by Israeli forces into effectively an open-air prison had no other alternative for survival but to go underground. Gazans mastering of the subsurface – as a result of Israeli control over their land surface, airspace and sea – is another example repeating in a way or another Vietnamese experience during the war with the USA and their infamous 'Cu Chi' tunnels. Back in 2008, the underground corridors were becoming the main source of livelihood for Gazans, and involve smuggling household goods all the way through to smuggling scooters, refrigerators, cows, petrol and cement to rebuild the demolished land. The smuggling industry was prospering so fast that even those who were not born into the business of trading and smuggling could work as labourers digging tunnels; or otherwise if people had some money to invest – such as our 80-year-old neighbour, Im Rami – they could start their businesses by buying shares in newly constructed tunnels. According to Im Rami, each tunnel costs around $75,000; given that she could only afford $20,000, the agreement was to take 30 percent from anything or any person traveling through her route – after of course paying the necessary taxes to the government run by Hamas.[22]

Furthermore, creativity has far exceeded need in some cases. According to the local newspaper *Alquds*,[23] 'VIP tunnels' were the latest 'achievement' – that is, before the recent Israeli military onslaught in December 2008 when Gaza and its community were all but wiped away – in that they happen to be wide and high enough so that one doesn't need to

2.21 Sewage tunnels connecting to Jerusalem.

2.22   Mapping a journey of a night hunter.

bend or crawl while using them. In order to smuggle wealthy people walking upright, the VIP tunnel also offers phone lines, electricity and the luxury of sitting areas, coupled with proper ventilation systems along the way.

STILLS FROM A SOFTER SIDE OF OCCUPATION

> These margins are ugly and beautiful; they laugh and cry, full of energy yet remain calm. They are without sound while they speak. They stabilize still, they exist through instability.[24]

The frustration and oppression that came with the building of the Separation Wall and military checkpoints is also accompanied with a softer side that makes life more bearable while crossing through Israeli borders. With the new urban realities, each traveler tries to capture a moment of hope to lift them up through the difficult times. For me, the checkpoint has to be seen as a space of imagination and inclusion more than anything else. If anything, it seems like a two-way cinema screen with the audience and the actors on every side. Unemployed people lay against the wall waiting to be picked up for possible building work. Some just come to socialize, others are busy advertising their skills on the wall,[25] while those who spent the night trying to sneak through are trying to catch a bit of sleep during daytime. The rest of the local people are aimless, eating nuts while watching the commuters, as if they were in their own living room or theatre. Indeed, it has to be seen as a theatre; what else can one call a moment when an unpredictable wedding suddenly takes place at a point on the checkpoint?[26]

Unlike the Separation Wall, here commuters have a slightly different angle. While collectively waiting to cross in the midst of dust and barbed wires, each one stitches their own potential space within the sights and smells of the new urban markets – such as with a toy to enjoy, a sandwich to eat, or even a pair of shoes or glasses to try on. Others create graffiti on the wall, hoping they can heal the scars of the occupation through a new imaginative space. At Bethlehem's checkpoint, people even get to sit in Banksy's drawn living room with the two big sofas enjoying the landscape on the other side. Others watch his little girl while searching the defeated soldier with his face against the wall, his rifle on the ground. Few others sneak to climb his ladder hoping to avoid the long hours of wait, while schoolchildren watch the flying girl and her black balloons in the hope they can clutch to her to avoid the torture of their actual journey.

Palestinians today, as well as visitors from all over the world, are taking part in the process to transform the Separation Wall and its surrounding non-places into a new means of resistance. Despite the contradictory nature of dividing the old apartheid wall also becomes one of the most exclusive social spaces on the planet. As Amiry writes:

> I was about to lose hope in mankind when I heard soft whispers. I looked behind and saw little girls and boys right next to Banksy's wall. I looked out of the window carved into the wall and saw alpine landscape. I also saw workers running through the big holes cracked in the wall; a little boy stood on the other side of the wall whispering to the workers, 'Come this way, Come this way'. . . . Yet, another little boy sat under the snake-like ladder, offering his tiny hand to hundreds and hundreds of workers. Like olive tree hikers, they went step by step up the painted rope ladder until they got to the top of the wall. I could see their bodies twist as they climbed up to the other side of the wall. Had it not been for my imagination and for the cosy living room of Banksy's canvas wall, I wouldn't have been able to gather the energy and morale required to carry on with my trip.[27]

In the Gaza Strip, it is as if one is located in a different world. The 45-minute drive to Gaza is impossible today. The Strip, with its population of 1.8 million, has been trapped for years in what is today called one of the biggest open air prisons in the world. To get around the blockade, Mohamad Barghouthi has had to create his own imaginative world. During the Israeli military offensive in December 2008, Mohamad lost some of the animals he happened to owe in his little zoo, out of hunger. All that remained were the monkeys, one tigress, which he smuggled through tunnels at some point, and a few rabbits and birds. While trying to replace the lost zebras Mohamad realised that it would cost him around $40,000 to smuggle one in via the tunnels. Instead, with masking tape and a judicious use hair dye, his two white donkeys were suddenly

turned into zebras.[28] The popular new zebras have since drawn visitors to the zoo from all over Gaza, and each busload of children is now paying an entry fee of $15 to see the new faces. In an interview with the Reuters news agency Barghouthi said:

> The first time we used paint but it didn't look good. The children don't know, so they call them zebras and they are happy to see something new.[29]

Luckily, the little ones don't know the difference between a real and a fake zebra – but who cares if it serves to bring joy? Consequently, Khaled Hourani, a Palestinian artist from Ramallah, adopted zebras as the new theme of his artworks, producing a new series of postcards from Palestine entitled the Zebra Copy Card.

THE INVISIBLE HITCHHIKERS

All I wanted was to go for a swim in the Dead Sea before I made my way back to London the next day. Sahar, Dana and Luke joined in; all of them were exhausted from a hot summer day and could not wait to be in the water. We got into a famous yellow Ford van on the Ramallah-Jericho route, and half-way through the van drivers in the opposite direction were flashing their lights. Apparently, a 'flying checkpoint'[30] was blocking the entrance, just a few metres before reaching the seaside. Our driver was not interested in taking a new route, nor did he want to risk crossing the checkpoint. So we were instantly dumped in the usual 'non-place' at the junction where the roads for the Palestinians face those of the Israelis; hopefully another adventurous driver would pick us up. From there, at the entrance to Jericho, our journey really started.

'Put your scarves on', Dana whispered while leading the way towards the opposite side of the road. 'What headscarf?'

2.23 The Zebra copy card.
Artwork by Khaled Hourani.

I asked. With confidence, she wrapped hers around, just like the Israeli settlers do, and headed towards the hitchhiking spots known in Hebrew as 'trempiyada' (טרמפיאדה). My heart started sinking; for the first time in my life I was heading towards Israeli settlers instead of running away from them. 'Dana, this is insane', I cried. 'Don't worry, Yara, not only it is free, no checkpoint will stop us; we can go all the way to Eilat beach if you like'. Despite my shock and fear, I sensed from Dana's confidence a lifestyle she was so accustomed to. I defied my dear friend Suad's words rumbling in my heart – 'nothing to lose but your life' – and thought to myself instead, 'why not let's give it a try?'

I remained quiet, trying to think what needs to be done to pass as an Israeli settler? Other than myself, no one else seemed to care if we ever got caught. Why should they? Sahar has a Jerusalem ID, Luke is American, and Dana is so blonde that she can hardly be recognized as a Palestinian – especially with the distorted stereotyped image that settlers have about Palestinian looks and image. The main problem is really in terms of how I look. I disguised my face as much as I could. Unsuccessfully I tried to wrap the scarf around my head, while watching the crowd pointing with their fingers to the cars.

Ten minutes of waiting, and nothing still is coming through. Only the spoken Hebrew of the settlers around me is echoing in my ears. It took me a while to feel anywhere near confident; instead, I kept examining myself to make sure I looked convincing. I knew that hitchhiking is a common thing in Israel, but how on earth should I, as a Palestinian, know how it works? 'Just press the button', Dana suggested after a long wait. Apparently, it is a way to alert Israeli drivers while waiting on traffic lights that they get ready to pick up their fellow settlers on the way. 'Don't worry, Yara, we'll be fast; no settler would want to be at the entrance of Jericho at this time of the day', Dana whispered with a cheeky smile.

A few minutes later, and we were all squeezed at the back of a car driving across the highway. Dana starts with her

American accent: 'Can we get as close as possible to the Dead Sea, please'. The car driver replied: 'Dead Sea? Sure it's on my way, I live in Mitzpe Shalom. Where from are you?' While Luke tried to join the conversation, Sahar and I stared at one another realizing what we got ourselves into. Mitzpe Shalom is well known for its right-wing settlers who would not hesitate to do anything if they recognize our real identity. Luke's loud voice interrupted my scary thoughts: 'We're from Ohio, but we're here to look around'.

Yes, it was true – I really started to look around, nervously examining the car, its objects and any possible signs that might help us in case we got kidnapped, attacked or had to run away. Of the whole car, I could only spot the tiny stickers on the rear window. All I could read with my broken Hebrew was: 'They are handing over the Dead Sea too', and 'Hebron, ours and forever'.

I happened to remember the Hebron sticker very well; Ruba my friend would use them in her car to pass through checkpoints with less hassle. Apparently, such cynical tricks have worked so well that Palestinian taxi drivers have also been using them inside Jerusalem for some time. With such stickers, not only do they get one through checkpoints fast, but they also increase the chances of taxi drivers picking up customers who might otherwise not want to get into a Palestinian cab.

The map beneath the sticker also looked very familiar to me. I had once worked on the regeneration of the historic centre of Hebron for a whole year, and visited every single house and walked through its maze of alleyways. I was hosted at Maha's house for three days under curfew just so that the Israeli settlers could walk free. Who knows, our driver could have been one of them?

At that point, I felt the poster was really there to remind me that, Hebron is indeed OURS – not his – just as the Dead Sea is also ours. If it takes an Israeli settler to drive me through my own map, then let it be, why not to enjoy it, if eventually I will be able to cross all boundaries?

With a few jokes here and there, we were soon about to reach our destination. A shiver ran down my spine; this one however was of happiness, not of fear. For some reason, I felt that I was no longer chained; neither the driver, nor the settlements around, could occupy us anymore. At that moment, it was me who was occupying him. Just before he drove off, I asked: 'Where is the best spot to get dropped at Beersheva?[31] My friend Dana wants to visit Adamama Farm'.

I didn't join the final leg of the trip to Beersheva, but definitely it was worth the effort. From Ramallah, Dana told me she had made it through to the village of Beit Sahour, down to Hebron, reaching her first hitchhiking point near to the Israeli settlement of Kiryat Arba (known to host one of the most extremist right-wing groups in Israel). From there she made her way to Beersheva and finally to Adamaa Farm. 'I smelled the scents of Gaza and the Mediterranean few minutes away, before I made my way back hitchhiking through Jaffa, Jerusalem and finally Kalandia checkpoint'. It was Dana's only way to explore what she has been missing in her whole 30 years of life.[32]

Indeed, if it weren't for Dana's sense of humour, or the car stickers and the whole hitchhiking adventure, my own mental map would not have been stretched so far. The journey itself did not really matter; more important were the boundaries we broke with our new hidden rules of daily co-existence.

Extract from my own diary, 25 June 2009

It is remarkable to observe how much car mobility has in time created a public sphere in which Palestinians negotiate their space and boundaries as well as their identity.[33] Each Palestinian views it as a political message where the complex social and political realities can be distilled in a moment of time.[34]

2.24 Hitchhiking 'illegally' in the Jordan Valley.

Here on the slopes of hills,
facing the dusk and the
cannon of time,
close to the gardens of
broken shadows,
we do what prisoners do,
and what the jobless do,
we cultivate hope.

[Mahmoud Darwish]

Samer's 'soft tactics' to survive the hardships of living in a blurry boundary between Palestine and Israel also accumulate to become a lifestyle. As he proudly notes:

> There is a round I do every night picking up workers from a factory. And there is a shortcut I take in Givat Shaul, [neighbourhood in western Jerusalem] It is a one-way street going the wrong way. It is only 15 metres, but it saves me ten minutes. I have two passengers in the car. A police car signals for me to stop. I think to myself: 'I can't afford a 1000 shekel fine and a 10 penalty points on my license'. As the police officers approach I tell my passengers in Arabic: 'Hold tight, I need to play a little here, everything will be OK'. They are regular clients from East Jerusalem, workers whom I take home. So I meet the police halfway and say softly: 'Guys, I saw your patrol and came right to you. You've got to help me. These two passengers got in, and I have a funny feeling about them. Please check them out. So the police checked their IDs. They came back to me and said: 'it's OK, they've checked out fine'. I say: 'Are you sure? It's your responsibility!' They thank me for my vigilance, shake my hand, and wish everyone were as alert as I am – a model citizen. And so off we went. I wasn't afraid that they'd rough up my passengers; they were policemen in blue uniforms, not border patrol thugs. I said to myself: 'The fine would be 1,000 shekels. If the passengers get beaten, I'll have to give them half that sum, say 250 each'.[35]

Playing with Israel's imposed borderlines has thus created even further lines on the map. By putting together these micro-scale events, Palestine is reshaping its dead spaces and urban voids in which people wait, remember and resist. The intensification of the borderlines does not leave any other alternative but to occupy the margins, which in turn creates a new spatial quality and intensity to the 'dark points' on the map. As Cupers and Markus write:

> These margins get their meaning through opposition rather than coherence. While they remain unnoticed to the majority, they become platforms for their temporary hosts and for unofficial activities.[36]

Nonetheless, occupying these margins was never a formal strategy or tactic of ordinary commuters or

2.25   Night hunters waiting for the right moment to cross to the other side of the wall.

cuts in our landscape are dividing but they are also j

2.26   The West Bank in fragments.

the Palestinian Authority, and thus the need to rethink the map today given these facts has become urgent. The unconsciously emerging networks, the invisible and silent forms of resistance to overcome and adapt, are now transforming boundaries into ritual spaces in which Palestinians can reconstruct their social relationships on a daily basis. It is in fact re-drawing a 'virtual' map that can overcome oppression and the labyrinthine boundaries being enforced by Israeli forces on Palestinians.

TOWARDS AN INVISIBLE COUNTER-PLAN

If we return to the question of what might be the role of a Palestinian architect within these fragmented spaces, the key issue is whether it is their job to criticize and renounce the entire idea of occupation?

Or is it to accept the conditions and unequal maps already created by the Oslo Agreement, adapting their thinking to limitations of the current situation, and proposing an alternative that envisages changes? What can the act of architectural resistance be in such circumstances? And does it have the same meaning as it might have had 20 or even 60 years ago?

In my search among the various lines, documents and maps to find the possibility of spaces without chains, it appears that neither the peace agreements, or the current planning strategies envisaged by the Palestinian Authority, have managed to overcome Israeli occupation nearly so much as the actions of Palestinian daily life has done. There have of course always been historical alternatives to accepting the unequal forces of power. However, given that Foucault has written that 'Power as such does not exist, what exists is a power relation', then the counter-map lies in looking for such relationship. There is no doubt that mass organization gave every Palestinian a sense of empowerment during the *First Intifada*. Ze'ev Schiff and Ehud Ya'ari have referred to its profound effect in their book on that subject:

> This was a sharp psychological turnabout for a public that had discovered what it could do – and how to exploit the enemy's weaknesses.[37]

Another *Intifada* may not be the best answer today; far more important are the social relationships and collective processes that manage to empower every individual during an *Intifada*. In terms of current events, it is evident that the collective acts, which have become a permanent reality, are suggesting new modes of urban resistance born out of social choreography. Therefore, what is needed now is a strategy to put the Palestinian community back into the front line so that they can take over the act of resistance, and draw their own maps. If silence, invisibility and subversion are in fact the key tools, then it is time for the Palestinian architect to nourish them with responsive design interventions. Israeli occupation mightn't require the concepts of architecture in the way these have hitherto been imagined: instead, it suggests an architect-figure who is able to distill the essence of the community's patterns of capturing spaces, and thereby let them become the core for incremental design solutions. Simply put, to facilitate the kinds of conditions that will create more of these 'subtle' networks. The foundations are already there in Palestine and overtaking at the margins. All that is required is for us to re-draw the map so that it corresponds with the new matrix of everyday life.

As long as one doesn't ever forget what 'normal' is, as long as one does not forget while enjoying the walk through the blossoming trees full of almonds and pomegranates, that the top of the hill is full of illegal Israeli settlements – housing occupiers who are the very reason behind the contorted journey in the first place – then invisibility will eventually reach a point at which there is no power to obstruct it. If this will to go on with daily life is viewed by some as giving up, or as hiding away from reality, then I instead regard it as reality itself. It offers the space of possibility to create a sense of energy and to accumulate power all across the West Bank – indeed, across Palestine as a whole. Before looking at the implications of this approach in terms of new design proposals, it is worth first looking in more detail at the issue of historical centres and how these too can become a creative tool for creating spatial possibilities in Palestine.

2.27   Stripping the map of its boundaries.
Searching for possibilities through the voids.

2.28   Occupying the margins. Underneath the
skin of the troubled land.

NOTES

1 Part of this chapter has been presented as a paper for the conference on 'Occupation: Negotiations with Constructed Space', University of Brighton, 2–4 July 2009.

2 Karkar, S. 'The *First Intifada*, 20 years later', *The Electronic Intifada*, 10 December 2007. Available at: http://electronicintifada.net/content/first-intifada-20-years-later/7251 [accessed 26 February 2009].

3 Hammami, R. (2004) 'On the Importance of Thugs: The Moral Economy of a Checkpoint', *MERIP Middle East Report*, Vol. 34, pp. 26–34.

4 Further to President Obama's speech on Thursday 19 May 2011, which called for two-state solution and an independent Palestinian state created on the borders of 1967, Prime Minister Netanyahu stated that this does not make any sense as it ignores the 'solid facts on the ground'. Netanyahu added that he expects the USA to allow them to keep all major Israeli settlements in the West Bank. He also stated that: 'the viability of a Palestinian state cannot come at the expense of Israel's existence'.

See Mualem, M. 'After Obama speech, Netanyahu rejects withdrawal to 'indefensible' 1967 borders', *Haarez*, 19 May 2011. Available at: http://www.haaretz.com/news/diplomacy-defense/after-obama-speech-netanyahu-rejects-withdrawal-to-indefensible-1967-borders-1.362869 [accessed 24 May 2011].

5 Dovey, K. (2008) *Framing Places: Mediating Power in Built Form*. London: Routledge.

6 According to Hammami, initially, only 'licensed' Ford vans were working along designated routes between cities and villages, but later in early 2001 the unemployed realized the potential profit from the van business. If one can't buy a second-hand Ford van for 15,000 shekels or so, they can do with unlicensed ones; some buy these for 2,000 others 3,000 shekels.

7 Hammami, op. cit.

8 Checkpoints usually create three areas; two ends with an entrance and exist, separated by a 'no-drive' zone in-between. This is where cars are not allowed, but commuters are able to walk across.

9 Hammami, op. cit.

10 For further details on this issue, see Hammami's work on the Surda Checkpoint.

11 See also Anon. 'Checkpoints', *Palestine Monitor*, 17 March 2010. Available at: http://www.palestinemonitor.org/spip/spip.php?article8 [accessed 21 April 2011].

12 Hammami, op. cit.

13 Bayat, A. (1997) 'Un-civil Society: The Politics of the "Informal people"', *Third World Quarterly*, Vol.18(1), pp. 53–72. Available at: http://abahlali.org/files/Iran.pdf [accessed 26 May 2011].

14 Bayat's theory on the 'quiet encroachment of the ordinary' reflects on these habits in both Cairo and Tehran. Bayat, op. cit. See also Bayat, A. (1997). *Street Politics: Poor People's Movements in Iran*. New York: Columbia University Press.

15 Ibid.

16 The lack of job opportunities on the eastern side of the wall forces Palestinian workers to cross to the Israeli side to look for work, accepting almost anything, even with minimum wages. This rate is estimated by B'tselem (Israeli Information Centre for Human Rights in the Occupied Territories) to be as low as $9 a day. With the no-building permits policy, Palestinians are stripped from any right to work in Israel; hence thousands of Palestinian workers risk their lives tying to sneak through the border controls. See B'tselem, 'Workers from the Occupied Territories', *B'tselem*. Available at: http://webcache.googleusercontent.com/search?q=cache:zwHWCgbQWAgJ:www.btselem.org/english/Workers/+low+wages+of+palestinian+workers+in+ISrael+btselem&cd=1&hl=en&ct=clnk&gl=uk&client=safari&source=www.google.co.uk [accessed 21 May 2011].

17 De Certeau, M. (1984) 'General Introduction', *The Practice of Everyday Life*. Berkeley: University of California Press, p. xix.

18 Quoted from Barclay, A. 'Resisting Spaciocide: Notes on the Spatial Struggle in Israel–Palestine', MA thesis, Cardiff University, 2010. Available at: http://www.scribd.com/doc/51342175/Resisting-Spaciocide-in-Palestine-by-A-Barclay [accessed 2 April 2011]. See also Kossak, F. (2010) *Agency: Working with Uncertain Architectures*. London: Routledge.

19 After the Separation Wall was erected, one of the key tools for penetration was the sewage tunnels. The purposely-installed concrete pipes, which are supposed to transfer Palestinian water resources towards the Israeli side, have also been collecting sewage along the way. Back in 2004, one of the famous gateways to enter Jerusalem was the famous 'women's route' – as some villagers of Beit Hanina used to call it – as it was easier to cross without having to jump over the wall. All what was needed then is a plastic bag to cover the sinking feet before the 100-meter long journey starts. Whenever Israeli bulldozers blocked these routes, they got revitalized again by what the locals refer to as 'tunnel operators'.

20 Amiry, S. (2010) *Nothing to Lose but Your Life*. Doha: Bloomsbury Qatar Foundation.

21 Barnes, quoted in Dovey, op. cit., p. 101.

22 After 12 years of not having seen Gaza, I managed to get through in September 2010, and finally met up with my family there. My little cousin is now running the family small flower business: 'We are not allowed any flowers through Israel since 1997. People are fed up with carnations [the only flowers growing locally in Gaza] so I have to use the tunnels. I pay $80 each time I want to smuggle a small box of flowers from the Egyptian side otherwise, my business will die. With the help of my friend, we have designed new flower boxes that can handle

the heat and the difficult journey underground. Even though this has reduced the risk slightly, we still have few occasions where the flowers never arrive to Gaza. This means an extra $50 in the hands of Omar on the Gaza side, and a similar one to Ayman on the Rafah side. This is only to guarantee the arrival of the big deliveries whenever a rich family decides to have a proper wedding' (26 August 2010).

23 *Al-Quds Newspaper*, 'Tunnel between Egypt and Gaza for VIPs only', 27 December 2008.

See also Issacharoff, A. and Haaretz Correspondent. '"VIP Tunnel" Smuggling Wealthy Gazans into Egypt', *Haaretz*, 25 December 2008. Available at: http://www.haaretz.com/print-edition/news/vip-tunnel-smuggling-wealthy-gazans-into-egypt-1.260177 [accessed 2 June 2011].

24 Cupers, K., Meissen, M. and James, W. (2002) *Spaces of Uncertainty*. Wuppertal: Muller und Busmann, p. 122.

25 As a mean to criticise normalising the Separation Wall, a columnist at *Al-Quds* newspaper called Maher Al Alami wrote an ironic letter to those who advertise themselves on the wall. He questioned the daily life and reminded Palestinians that the wall is only there to divide. The article was written at a time when the possibility for preliminary elections was looming: 'Dear candidates who are busy advertising yourselves on the Separation Wall, did you ever think of the contradiction this is bringing? Did anyone of you include the wall as part of his or her agenda in the election programme? You are turning the wall into an advert board rooting the division in our hearts . . .'. [Arabic text].

26 This culture of checkpoints and non-places has become a prolonged theme in Palestinian work of creative art, including cinema, dance, music and fashion design. See for example the movie, Rana's *Wedding*, for the views of the director Hani abu Asad who picks up on this subject. See also 'Chic point: fashion for Israeli checkpoints for Sharif Waked'. Available at http://universes-in-universe.org/eng/nafas/articles/2005/waked (accessed 21.5.11).

27 Amiry, op. cit., pp. 115–18.

28 BBC, 'Dye-job Donkeys Wow Gaza Children', *BBC News*, 9 October 2009. Available at: http://news.bbc.co.uk/1/hi/8297812.stm (accessed 17.5.10).

29 Ibid.

30 'Flying checkpoint' is a term used to represent random hasty checkpoints set up by Israeli forces between Palestinian roads, which are usually done at unpredictable times and locations.

31 Beersheba is the Israeli name for the Palestinian village of Beer Sabe' located in the southern desert of Nakab. It was occupied in 1948 and consequently all its original residents were forced to exile; mainly fled on foot towards Gaza. Today it is a large city referred to as 'the capital of Negev', and is occupied by many immigrant Jews from Ethiopia.

32 The information website cited below pinpoints few guidelines for those who plan to hitchhike in Israel: 'It's common to get rides from Arab Israelis and from religious Jews. So it's wise to avoid talking politics unless you really know your ways and who you're talking to . . . Some Orthodox Jews prefer to speak only Yiddish, so it may be helpful to learn a few basic phrases in this language . . . it's significantly harder to hitchhike at junctions close to Arab villages. Somehow cars coming out of the village are less likely to pick up hitchhikers. This could be because their wife is sitting next to them or someone of the closely-knit network of the village is driving behind them. In such cases it makes a lot of sense to try to find out of the previous or next junction has different traffic (e.g. predominantly Jewish or further away from Arab villages) and to move on or back there . . . *Note*: Israel shares borders with these countries; however, due to hostile relations between the states, it is *illegal* and probably impossible to cross over to Syria or Lebanon; Getting into Palestinian territory in the West Bank is quite straight forward, usually flashing your passport in the checkpoint is enough. Getting to Gaza should be problematic. Egypt and Jordan should be fine'. See http://hitchwiki.org/en/index.php?title=Israel [accessed 18 May 2011].

33 For right-wing Israelis, the stickers are located everywhere on the high roads to remind them of their duty to exclude and expand the land of Israel: 'Together in the tank together at the bank'; 'Hebron, for our forefathers and for us'; 'The land is also ours'; 'Hebron, our Patriarchs' city for generations to come', and many others.

34 According to Yaccov Garb, a lecturer at the Hebrew University, Palestinian drivers would also go to the extreme by tying the orange ribbons on their antennas. This was mainly during the disengagement from Gaza period in 2005. Then, there was a strong campaign by right-wing Zionists against disengagement. They distributed orange ribbons to be tied everywhere as a form of rejecting the plan. According to Garb, even though the stickers might bring some sort of satisfaction to the drivers with their hidden meaning, some drivers saw it as 'going too far'.

Garb, Y. (2006) 'The Softer Side of Collision', in Rieniets, T. and Misselwitz, P. (eds), *City of Collision: Jerusalem and the Principles of Conflict Urbanism*. Basel: Publishers for Architecture, pp. 286–93.

35 Garb, op. cit., p. 293.

36 Cupers and Meissen, op. cit.

37 Schiff, Z. and Ya'ari, E. (1990) *The Intifada*. Jerusalem: Schocken, p. 102.

BRINGING LIFE BACK TO THE HISTORIC CENTRE OF BIRZEIT[1]

PREFACE

This chapter forms a key part of my journey in search for spaces of possibility and enact spatial change within the current Palestinian/Israeli conflict. Throughout the process I have been looking for different tools to explore and understand the conflict and its power relations emerging with different readings and site experimentations. This section however, adds a new dimension with its practice-based nature that involves a 'live' project, which aims to assist the process of analysis and healing. Working in collaboration with Riwaq – a leading NGO for architectural conservation in Palestine – on regenerating the historic centre of Birzeit (an important university town, just north of Ramallah) is thus one of the key investigative tools I have used to explore the spatial potentials of historic centres in re-constructing Palestinian space and identity. This experience involves a 'live' project that has in a way expanded my role towards critical architecture practice; one, which I believe, is urgently needed to engage with the kinds of social and political realities found in their most devastating state in places such as Palestine.

Being critical in architecture is often stereotyped as being 'negative' and sometimes it can even be dismissed as merely a 'luxury' for developed western countries, as Fraser[2] provocatively suggests. However, critical architecture practice needs to become an urgent and a vital part for the redevelopment of Palestine – a country without many basic resources and still living under a state of occupation. Where, then, can a critical form of practice be developed? Regrettably it is their traditional cultural heritage that is now viewed by some Palestinians as a 'luxury' that Palestine apparently can't afford to think about or deal with at this moment of political duress.[3] As a result, it remains one of these buried potentials left on the margin to decline and fade away despite its obvious value. Only a few organizations like Riwaq are arguing that the protection of cultural heritage can become another tool to make a difference for Palestinians in their struggle against occupation and in their assertion of the right for self-determination. Indeed, it is what Riwaq describes as 'being *political by being a-political*' that brings a unique dimension to their work. Even within the current political crisis they are managing to make powerful political statements through heritage conservation as a tactic against the deliberate destruction of Palestinian identity and memory. It represents another mode of what I call 'soft urban resistance' that can engage within the Palestinian cultural landscape and mend what has been fractured.

The regeneration of the historic centre in Birzeit – which later won the 2013 Agha Khan Award of Architecture – is thus an experimental project to explore what could be done with limited resources, to cultivate possibilities for change within Palestinian historic fabrics. Relating the work in Birzeit to other urban centres in Palestine is also another way to create different matrixes and networks that operate when needed to overcome Israeli strategies of occupation.

In the context of rapid change in Palestine today, the examination of day-to-day practices and their relationship with place is becoming more crucial and urgent; being included and excluded from the map under political and economic pressure works to shift the dis/ordinary practices into a state of norm. As much as this folds danger underneath it, it also reveals more possibilities and potentials. Not only are these ordinary practices 'creatively' taking place

3.1 Traditional rural fabric in the West Bank.

at the Israeli checkpoints, or along the borderlines of the West Bank, or the alternative routes Palestinians are creating to avoid siege, they are also being reflected in rural areas which are forming new attitudes towards space. Palestinian historic centres offer some of the best of these 'hidden' spots, which are being pushed further back due to the shifting social and political boundaries. It is a gold mine loaded with potential and waiting to be revealed and directed towards reconnecting the fragmented communities.

My contribution to the urban strategy for Birzeit and the wider Riwaq concept of reconstructing 50 villages – which I will explain in this chapter – is a

follow-on from what I was doing between 2002–2005 when I used to work with Riwaq. However, my argument today is that for the process to be enhanced, given that the role the Palestinian community has been playing recently in shaping the built environment mans that the local cultural context with its social networks and everyday habits needs to be seen as the key source for rebuilding sustainable communities and spaces. It is also an attempt to explore and re-define the concept of 'heritage' on the urban scale, breaking away from any conventional or static beliefs associated with heritage, or conservation of historic buildings. Heritage architecture in this context is no longer seen as a passive act to prevent change, rooted in romantic values, as is so common in countries like Britain; rather, it can be a dynamic form of resistance and change that not only engages with built urban space, but also leads to greater self-sufficiency in the use of resources to create sustainable communities. As will be explained later in this chapter, the concept and definition of heritage is going through a process of rapid change opening up possibilities towards new readings of urban spaces, buildings as well as individuals. These possibilities also embrace the contemporary activities, meanings and practices that one can draw from the past to shape the future.

I will first introduce briefly the challenges being faced by Palestine in terms of cultural heritage. It will shed light on Riwaq and the '50 Villages' initiative, which aims to protect and regenerate 50 historic centres in Palestinian rural areas. The chapter will then refer specifically to the regeneration process that has taken place in Birzeit since this is the testing ground and starting point to engage practically with the realities today in the West Bank.

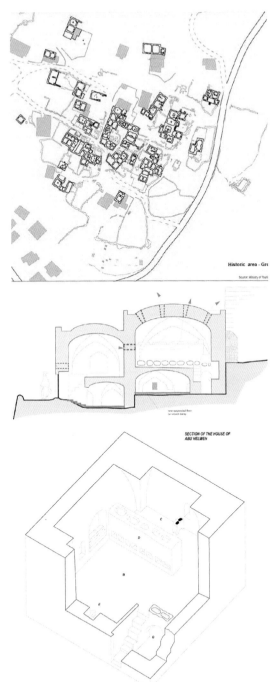

Historic area - Gr

SECTION OF THE HOUSE OF
ABU HELWEN

3.2   Typical traditional built fabric with
its many courtyards.

3.3   Traditional Palestinian village house
with its multiple levels.

WHY HISTORIC CENTRES?

In retrospect, the changes that took place in the Palestinian landscape were relatively minor up until 1948, when, following the initial formation of the initial Israeli state, hundreds of villages were completely destroyed and indeed erased from the map for the purpose of Israeli occupation. Later on, after the 1967 War, further dramatic urban change came about in Palestine with even more destruction, land zoning and confiscation. However, it is also right to point out that another key change that has affected Palestinian villages as a result of Israeli occupation has been the form of 'westernized capitalism' – as described by Jubeh[4]– that has been imposed on its population. It is the destruction of traditional economic structures which has mostly affected people's perspectives, beliefs, taste, needs, and most importantly, their lifestyles and day-to-day practices. The relationship with the land changed gradually when farming was no longer seen as a source of income and ex-agricultural workers started to search for possibilities in the urban centres and big cities or even seek work in Israel as waged labourers.

With this capitalist transformation, as a result of higher incomes earned in the Israeli market and the money flow coming back from emigration,[5] the new buildings erected in the West Bank started to take on a different shape, as has been mentioned in earlier chapters, and the social and economic value of land changed dramatically. Rapidly built concrete-and-block work structures began to replace traditional stone buildings,[6] in time, the encroachment of residential buildings took over agricultural land, and when horizontal expansion on the map became impossible, the alternative in the West Bank has

So the question today is what kind of change is required for Palestine? And what could the limit of 'normal' become, before it again becomes abnormal?

> ... five-to-ten story height buildings became 'normal' in the Palestinian countryside. By the same token, it became 'normal' to see the old towns or parts bulldozed for one reason or another. It became 'normal' to see the continuous encroachment on agricultural land ... it became 'normal' to build on the river beds and rainwater courses, just as it became 'normal' to violently extract rocks in order to sell them to Israeli contractors for the construction of quays at the ports or breakwaters on the beaches of Tel Aviv, Netanya and Askalan, so that bathers could enjoy a calm sea. It has become utterly 'normal' to extract stones from historic buildings and sell them for the nucleus of heritage collection in Israel or even for reuse in the construction of Israeli villas[7] ... the worst thing for us is that we can even find these stones in the construction of new buildings in Jewish settlements built on land that was once part of the same village'.[8]

been high-rise buildings that are now destroying, alienating and taking over the fabric of the cultural landscape.

Today, therefore, most of the Palestinian historical fabric has been lost, and what is left is mostly abandoned; rural areas now suffer the most given their peripheral location.

The separate identity of rural architecture is vanishing so fast that it is almost impossible to see now where the city starts and the village ends. The weakness of executive power held by Palestinian local authorities, plus the lack of a proper legal framework and related land ownership, master plans, national agendas and planning policies, are all leading to destruction. At the same time however, they also present a potential ground for change.

3.4   Mazare Alnobani village. Courtesy of Riwaq Photo Archive.

3.5   Beit Wazan village. Photograph by Mia Grondahl. Courtesy of Riwaq Photo Archive.

This impassioned quote shows why the architectural focus should now be directed towards towns and villages in these contested rural areas, and is precisely the reason why Riwaq is now heading towards a more 'aggressive' approach to protect and regenerate these rural areas.

RIWAQ

Riwaq is a non-profit organization based in Ramallah that was set up with the aim to protect and develop architectural heritage all over Palestine.

It was founded in 1991 by Suad Amiry, a well-known architect, as well as the author of several remarkable books. Today, Riwaq consists of 20 competent architects, as well as archeologists, artists and anthropologists, in addition to a permanent workforce and the involvement of a large number of students from Birzeit University and Al-Najah University who take part in research projects and actual physical conservation work.

It is worth stressing the importance of Riwaq as a network. Before the birth of the Palestinian National Authority (PNA), the spirit of what can be called the 'network society' created a unique social order in which politics, identity and daily life operated as one 'net' within occupied Palestine. This was very much related to the national movement which offered a big role to the local community during the *First Intifada*, as has been noted in earlier chapters. In that era of the late 1980s and early 1990s, key individuals and local leaders in Palestine stepped in to put forward alternatives during the difficult economic and political periods of occupation when institutions like schools or health care centres were closed. This resulted in a network of locally formed initiatives that were later transformed into the infrastructural framework of NGOs in Palestine. Suad Amiry was one of these central figures in Palestine who started working with the local community to protect and reconstruct Palestinian cultural identity, in her case through Riwaq.

It is no exaggeration to say that Riwaq today is the only institution that has taken the initiative to protect historic fabrics all over the West Bank and specifically in rural areas,[9] with its intention to extend the concept of conversation far beyond its conventional 'passive' act of prevention of change. In fact, the work has always been about change and a dynamic form of resistance that not only approaches building but also looks into revitalizing the human life within them. After the formation of the PA in the post-Oslo period, Riwaq's development was strengthened substantially as the range of their operations were widened; they have since been working with local communities while also building partnerships with local government. Their clear aim is to establish a powerful and dedicated group of believers in each town and village to take this challenge on their shoulders. Of course, having Suad Amiry and Nazmi Jubeh – Riwaq's former co-director and one of the influential politicians in Palestine – has added another value and dimension to their contribution.

In working in collaboration with the bodies of local government, Riwaq has been trying to draw attention to the need to make conservation and redevelopment a national responsibility for Palestinians, calling for wide participation from a number of other institutions. In 2003, Riwaq raised the issue of how to structure policies to protect heritage, and so began work on legislating for adequate regulations to protect the Palestinian cultural heritage more systematically.[10] This has since led to the *Palestinian Law for Cultural and Natural Heritage Protection, Management and Enhancement* under the leadership

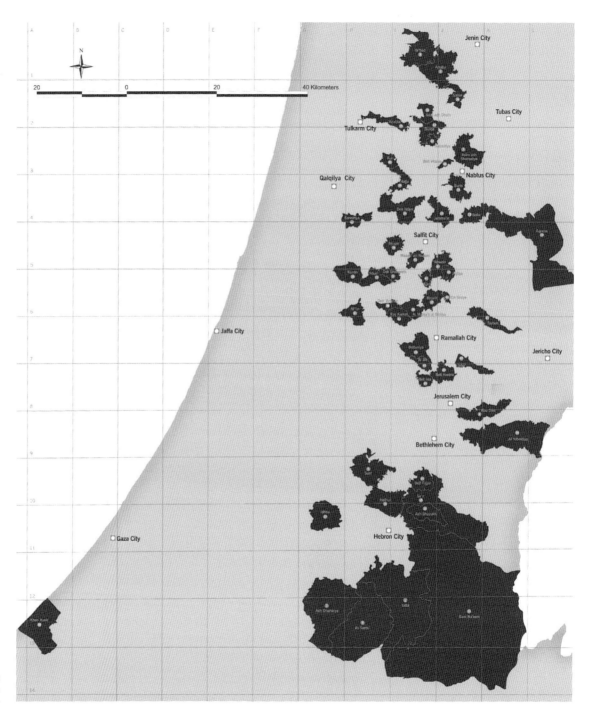

3.6   Palestinian historic centres on the
      list to be renovated by Riwaq.
      Courtesy of Riwaq Photo Archive.

of the Law Institute at Birzeit University, and with the support of the World Bank.[11] Even though this law has not yet been fully ratified by the PNA, the Palestinian Higher Planning Council in March 2006 has approved the general guidelines and by-laws for the protection of historic areas as well as single historic buildings. These ordinances, developed by Riwaq through their work to date on protection plans, are now considered to be part of the current planning by-law and are intended to be applied to all historic buildings in Palestine.

Riwaq's National Register of historic buildings is another remarkable achievement, being the only registry of its kind in Palestine compiled since 1880 – i.e. the registry compiled by the British occupiers – for the most endangered components of cultural and natural heritage in the West Bank and Gaza Strip, including Jerusalem. The practical interpretation of this registry has led to many projects and initiatives; Riwaq has shown its commitment to the new cultural heritage legislation by starting work on the national inventory to accompany the law. This releases a real financial and technical burden off the PA.

The tentative list for World Cultural and Natural Heritage sites in Palestine is another important achievement derived from the NR.[12]

In undertaking this task, the main focus was to nominate key sites that would cover a relatively good percentage of the Palestinian architectural heritage to be recognized, protected and managed with the support of UNESCO. As a result, and further to the training of the World Heritage team, Riwaq chose two themes to include on the list; the 'Throne Villages'[13] which applies to 24 rural historic centres (including rural areas inside the 1948 border), and the cultural landscape as a whole with its olive tree terraces and watchtowers, which constitutes more than 60 percent of the landscape of the West Bank. This experience offers therefore another form of expanding the economic potential of cultural heritage and exploring its impact on the political map. Not only are these sites nominated for their outstanding universal value,[14] but the broader aim is also to look at how heritage can be utilized as a mean to achieve political gains. It is thus seen as a political statement to assert that Palestinian cultural heritage, memory and identity still exist and should be identified and protected on the global map, despite the chronic political problems.

The above achievements have expanded Riwaq's role and position nationally and internationally far more than any other conventional NGO in Palestine, and indeed far beyond any conventional conservation or heritage institution elsewhere. The National Register and its outcomes demonstrate an intellectual modernity born from heritage conservation – a characteristic, which has made Riwaq one of the 'most distinctive and cutting-edge institutions' in Palestine, as described by Leyla Shahid, the representative of the Palestinian Authority to the European Commission in Brussels. Later on, and when the possibilities of its activities in the field became more limited due to the Israeli blockade, especially after 2001–2002, Riwaq has had to think of alternatives to keep its beliefs of conservation protection alive. This has encouraged it to explore new ideas, in which art and architecture could merge, triggering the beginning of the '50 Villages' concept.

Yatta, Arraba, Addahriya, Abu Dies, Surif, Aş Samu', Asira Alshamaliya, Ya'bad, Deir Ghassane, Attabta, Bani Na'eem, Burqa, Beita, Halhul, Sa'ir, Silat aldaher, Idhna, Rahtis, Aqraba, Alshuyukh, Nilin, Aboud, Birzeit, Burin, Deiristya, Beit Iksa, Beitunya, Jamma'in, Hajja, Beit Hanina, Al'Ubeidiya, Taybeh, Sabastya, Ebwein, Sanur, Beit Fajjar, Burqin, Deir Ammar, Al Mazra'a Al Qibliya, Mazari' Nubani, Jilul, Sanniriya, Al Jib, Beit Wazan, Jiliiliya, Ein Sinya, Jaba', Kur, Ras Karkr, and Khan Yunis.

50 VILLAGES, 50 DREAMS

Ever since its establishment in the early-1990s, Riwaq has had a clear aim to sustain the historic buildings and urban centres in Palestine, in spite of often terrible odds. Their role has gone through different phases, beginning with the protection of single historical buildings, then the wholesale recording and documentation of the built heritage, followed more recently by a series of projects for the 'preventive conservation' of entire historical fabrics in West Bank towns and villages. However, the sheer urgency for critical architectural thinking and action prompted by the political and social conditions, especially in rural areas of Palestine, implied a self-reflective process with new experimental approaches to design and planning, aiming to embrace all the social, cultural and economic assets of the historic centres. The different ideas have begun to be put into historic centres in the past few years, but needed a strategy to frame them. This has since been formalized by Riwaq's programme to regenerate the fabrics most at risk. Realizing that it would be extremely difficult to regenerate Palestine's entire built heritage – which according to Riwaq's register comes to about 50,320 historic buildings in 422 sites all over the West Bank and the Gaza Strip – instead, a list of key 50 villages was identified by Riwaq as a national priority. Regenerating those villages will lead to the protection of almost 50 percent of the historic buildings still existing in Palestine.[15]

Thus the '50 Villages' initiative is loaded with potential to generate new patterns of life within the wider urban context of the West Bank, specifically by seeing historic fabrics as rural and suburban 'bridges' that can overcome the isolation enforced upon inhabitants by Israeli occupation. It is also a

3.7   The 50 Palestinian villages in the West Bank and Gaza Strip.

3.8 The historic centre of Birzeit.
Courtesy of Riwaq Photo Archive.

way to explore 'ideologically' the concept of cultural heritage and its potentials to link with other urban centres. This new approach can be seen as a prolific source of ideas, especially with the absence of legal framework, since it could lead to formulating and realizing what was only before an impossible dream.

The '50 Villages' concept is currently nourishing with new urban priorities in mind. It has started with Birzeit as a case study, and very recently Hajja, Deir Ghassane, Beit Iksa, Taybeh, Ebwein, leading on to proposals that are yet to come for Yatta, Arraba, Addahriya, Abu Dies, Surif, As Samu', Asira Alshamaliya, Ya'bad, 'Anabta, Bani Na'eem, Burqa, Beita, Halhoul, Sa'ir, Silat aldaher, Idhna, Rantis, Aqraba, Alshuyukh, Ni'lin, Aboud, Burin, Deir Istya, Beituniya, Jama'een, Hajja, Beit Hanina, Al'Ubeidiya, Sabastya, Sanur, Beit Fajjar, Burqin, Deir Ammar, Al Mazra'a Al Qibliya, Mazare Al Nobani, Ajjul, Sanniriya, Al Jib, Beit Wazan, Jilijliya, Ein Sinya, Jaba', Kur, Ras Karkr, and hopefully, Khan Yunis in the Gaza Strip.

BIRZEIT REGENERATION STRATEGY

The historic center of Birzeit – as noted, a well-known university town just to the north of Ramallah – is the one out of the fifty selected significant sites chosen as a pilot project for the regeneration process. Work on Birzeit historic centre started in 2007 in partnership with the local municipality[16] and in collaboration with Birzeit University (BZU) and later the Rozana[17] Association. The intention has been to set out a model that can formulate a better understanding of

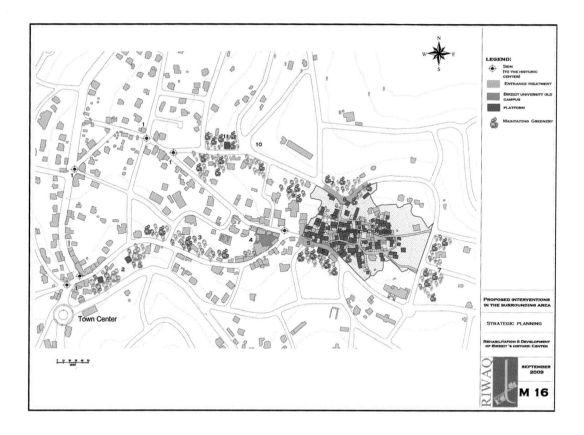

3.9 Map showing the historic centre and the extended part of Birzeit. Courtesy of Riwaq Photo Archive.

rehabilitation, protection and urban regeneration. Its main aim has been to bring life back to the mostly deserted historic centre by encouraging those who are currently living there to stay, and create conditions for new comers to move to and contribute to the place.

The project for Birzeit has aimed consciously to create a conceptual shift from the documentation and conservation of single historic rural buildings to a more extensive strategy of regeneration based on creating better habitation and renewed commercial activity for the historical centre, linking also to the wider regional context of surrounding towns and villages. It is embedded within a conscious approach to overcome current problems by setting out a social,

economical and physical framework for regenerating Birzeit historic fabric and the communities which live there. Unlike previous cases which could have dealt with conservation of buildings without relating it to the bigger context, the direction in Birzeit has been more towards creating a sustainable community that is armed with social and environmental awareness, and which can commit itself to the site regardless of the volatile conditions imposed by Israeli occupation. It is a strategy for Riwaq led by Farhat Muhawi that I have been working with for years. I later re-joined the team as a consultant along with Nasser Golzari from NG Architects in London. Many others were also involved to develop the strategy and conceptual ideas on Birzeit as part of Farhat and Riwaq's initiative to widen the network. Below are some of the ideas and thoughts that emerged as part of the experience while working with the team, which I thought are worth sharing. While some were discussed and implemented, others were left aside yet, became influential in setting up the basis for the projects that followed later, especially for Hajja and later the village of Beit Iksa which has won the 2013 commendation Holcim Award for Sustainable Construction for the MENA region.

Changes in thinking about Palestine's built environment are currently taking place on two levels: firstly, the legislative level at which general guidelines and by-laws have been prepared for adoption under the umbrella of the Palestinian Ministry of Local Government; and secondly, the level below at which we are focusing on the strengthening of local communities as a visible manifestation for reusing historical centres. Working on these two levels is crucial to achieve a sustainable and responsive strategy that can rebuild fractured communities as well as places. Hence in the Birzeit suggested designs there is an emphasis both at the scale of the street, with its patterns of daily customs and habits, gradually reaching up to address issues that operate at the regional/national level. Our approach has been to negotiate the 1:1 of bodily scale in terms of project details, and feed these into our thinking at the scale of 1:10000 to relate to the wider context.

The regeneration strategy for Birzeit therefore started by us putting some critical questions onto the table for discussion. How could one create a balance between protection, development, comfortable habitation and aesthetic values? What is there to protect in the historic centre and, above all, how

3.10   The courtyard of the People's Museum. Photograph by Majdi Hadid.

can we regenerate it? Should one promote a relocation of business investments? Should we perhaps try to enhance cultural tourism? Do we really need iconic buildings or distinctive architectural features to regenerate the historic centre of Birzeit? Extensive debates, and indeed disagreements, took place with local participants about the best approach. To aid with the design front, an interdisciplinary team of consultants consisting of leading architects, planners, anthropologists, environmentalists, theorists and economists from Palestine and abroad was set up – which we have named the 'Think Net'.[18] The richness of their input helped to link all of these initiatives together into a new design matrix that was eventually ready for testing and making on site.

3.11 Private courtyard.
Courtesy of Riwaq Photo Archive.

BIRZEIT BETWEEN PROTECTION AND DEVELOPMENT

Choosing Birzeit[19] as the test case was very much based on its nature as a pivotal location in the West Bank, and its relationship with the surrounding cities and villages, which makes it a good representation of the condition in rural areas.

The name Birzeit is translated in English as 'the well of oil', referring to the olive oil wells used by the local inhabitants and which exist till today. Birzeit, like many Palestinian rural villages surrounded with olive tree terraces, was primarily an agrarian society relying mainly on olive picking as its main source of livelihood. And as in most villages located in the central highlands of West Bank today, Birzeit's historic centre represents the typical traditional Palestinian rural architecture with its clusters of one and two-storey residential houses and domes blending naturally with the landscape. Despite the cultural and aesthetic richness of many of these buildings, the historic centre has fallen into a state of disrepair with some concrete-and-brick additions and insufficient infrastructure for the few families living there.

Even though Birzeit is a relatively small town with a population of only about 4,529 people,[20] and its small historic centre has just 174 historic buildings, it has its share of the present-day migration patterns caused by the Israeli strategic occupation in the West Bank. Today, Birzeit hosts students from all over the West Bank and the Gaza Strip, as well as daily commuters and working classes from the villages and towns to the north who seek job opportunities in Ramallah. The majority of the original local residents of Birzeit who managed to migrate to Ramallah, or even the USA, have facilitated the birth of a new social structure now occupying the vacant gaps of the town.

The effect of this new strong edge-development around Birzeit, and the competition with larger urban centres like the nearby city of Ramallah, as well as the prevalence of Israeli checkpoints, has resulted in the marginalization of its old historic centre and shifting of the focus of development even more towards its edges. Being located – as are most other West Bank rural areas – mainly on 'Area B' land, combined with the complex issue of ownership within the historic fabric,[21] this has caused more decline and pushed the historic centre even more towards the margin of Palestinian priorities. This has made the shift between dream and reality, theory and practice, a very intricate balance in Birzeit.

3.12 Existing concrete addition in Taybeh village. Courtesy of Riwaq Photo Archive.

The outcome on the ground has been complete chaos created by the deliberate destruction of the town's historic buildings and the rampant unorganized extensions around what has been left. This urged Riwaq to rethink its ideas about the 'balance' and 'compromise' between aesthetic, cultural and social values, so as to make sure they don't push out what are left of the local inhabitants of the old historic centre.

The dialectic process between dream and realization in Birzeit has offered and sometimes enforced different readings to the map, not least in the conversation about accepting 'spontaneity' and constant change if these can contribute to sustaining the site. Various concrete extensions have been negotiated from being seen as a dull concrete boxes that damage the environment and need to be demolished, to potential sources of livelihood that can bring in new values to the space – whether this is as an informal meeting place for coffee or

a tree house, a mechanic's garage, a bike repair shop, or even just a corner for gossiping. Given such uncertainties, the empowerment of local citizens in Birzeit became a main issue. But empowering who and for what reason? To be related to the community and those who actually use the site, we felt that any architectural interventions needed to respond to and celebrate the daily habits and rituals of the locals who contribute the most to the identity of the historic centre of Birzeit. It's a tough challenge to push for change and continuity at the same time.

MAKING THE ORDINARY SPECIAL

The design proposal put forward by the team, introduced a new angle. Messy leftover spaces that were once disregarded are suddenly seen as key generators of social dynamics which need to be celebrated and encouraged. Many of these leftover spaces have thus now been identified and located on the map of Birzeit. While they might not possess great meaning on their own, we conceive of them as essential ingredients to the context in the way they create urban and social bridges between the old historic centre and the surrounding context.[22] To help to uncover new ways of reading the place, the technique of social mapping was used to record a spectrum of 'invisible' moments, using these to plot social activities and emotional responses onto the site. Given that social mapping is a relatively new investigatory method in Palestine, the experiment in Birzeit hasn't always proved easy; our main challenge has been to get others to appreciate specific activities or observations as signs of dynamics in the site, not as minor aspects with no meaning. The effort has been to read the activities of inhabitants as a significant if largely unseen social network, and to emphasize their

role. As has been noted by Maurice Mitchell during similar work in Kosovo:

> none of the activities mapped have meaning on their own, it is the matrix of these activities, the networks that make them alive the key tool. It is the collectiveness of these activities that gives the town its meaning[23]

The act of plotting invisible activities onto the map of historic Birzeit led to the identification of dynamic spots to assist the design. The bike-repair shop, for example, which was created by Ameer and his brother Amjad, is one of the dull concrete boxes which can suddenly be seen as a crucial 'organic' element. Their building is no longer an ugly room to be removed; after all, it is their dream, their hiding place, and a key spot that brings local children together. But perhaps, if it were to be carefully reproduced and relocated, then it might encourage even more children to come back and use the historic centre. The route taken through the site by girls on their way to school, the bakery rooftops, the clusters of gossipy neighbours, and many other moments are all potential networks that might be spread further across the historic centre.

The focus in the above approach is thus to celebrate the ordinary ensuring that it is seen and made special, as Hamdi[24] refers. This also brings an entirely new dimension to the reading and alteration of urban space. 'Slowing down' the design process to observe these day-to-day habits, incidents and narratives – plotting and relating them back to a program of activities to create a more sustainable historical centre – became crucial. What is remarkable is that these moments, often little fragments which are almost too small to be noticed, possess a unique state of invisibility, but yet if pulled together within a program they can contribute immensely to the regeneration of a place. The approach has therefore been much less about confrontational design interventions, and more about celebrating 'normality' and bringing it gently to the surface.

DESIGN INTERVENTIONS

The work in Birzeit has consisted of a thoroughgoing process of research and data collection covering a wide range of social, cultural, architectural, economic, legal and planning issues. Amplified by the process of social mapping, was then overlaid onto the map to suggest a programme for regeneration.

3.13 Existing concrete additions in Birzeit historic centre. Courtesy of Riwaq Photo Archive.

3.14   Hosh Kokab is one of the key meeting
spaces for women.

3.15   The bike-repair space created by the
children of the village.

The actual design work was carried out in parallel with a series of collective events and projects organized with the local residents of old Birzeit as means to create dialogue, build confidence, and uncover even more about the potential of the site.[25] This is also another reason why such interventions by Riwaq have always taken place in historic centres while people are still living there, which is to make sure that it is not socially disruptive. On the contrary, their work tries to understand local needs and provide additional services for inhabitants to improve their living conditions and link them more with the site.

The multiple layers used to form the general strategy for Birzeit were initially viewed at the large scale of 1:10000 to try to connect the historic centre with the complex urban context around. Two main linking routes were proposed as a result; these two routes are thus seen as the backbone stretching across the historic centre and connecting it with the rest of the town and the surrounding villages. The two routes were chosen for their geographical and historical importance, based on the findings of our social mapping, which had indicated certain 'given lines' on the map. One is named provisionally as the 'Trade Route', given that it contains the main trading and commercial activities in the historic centre, while the other is the 'Caravanserai Route' (it includes the oldest building inside the historic centre, a disused caravanserai dating back to the fifteenth century).[26]

These two routes already between them contain a number of key activities which currently generate daily life in Birzeit's historic centre, such as the bakery shop, internet café, mechanic's shop, hairdresser, mosque, Christian church, Rozana

Community Association, as well as other residential and public spaces. We have then proposed further social programmes at an urban scale through specific activities and design interventions to take place along these two routes. These new interventions are located in what we refer to as 'urban pockets', again identified by mapping the little fragments of activity. The focus in the design is hence primarily on the regeneration of public spaces and associated buildings in old Birzeit, not least as a convenient way to avoid the otherwise highly complicated issues of private ownership if one tries to make changes to ordinary buildings.

3.16   The tree house by the locals is now one of the main 'living rooms' in the neighbourhood.

3.17   Riding along the 'Trade Route' in Birzeit.

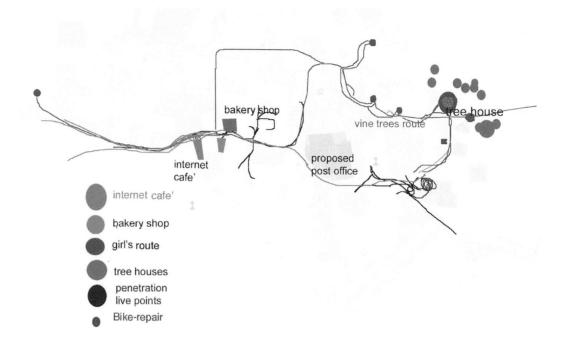

internet cafe'

bakery shop

girl's route

tree houses

penetration
live points

Bike-repair

3.18   Mapping some key moments, locations in the historic centre.

To kick off the regeneration process through a pattern of 'small changes', Riwaq has already repaved and identified/renamed all of the main routes, urban pockets and key buildings within the historic centre. They have done this by drawing on existing narratives collected on site to associate places with their history, thereby attaching the new changes with local meaning. This initiative attracted widespread attention from the local population, who were closely involved in collecting narratives and choosing the names for their neighbourhoods. 'Hosh Kokab', or the lemon tree courtyard – as some now call it – is for example specifically associated with a previous owner of that house. Its name comes from a lady, called Kokab, who became famous for a passionate love story that caused a major conflict between two local families around 50 years ago.

Shifting between the larger urban scale and the small intimate scale of 1:1, the physical interventions along the 'Trade Route' began with tiling the street to provide easier access and better public infrastructure on one hand, and also to start identifying the key areas and attract some activities there. The policy of 'carve your name on your tile' was an idea proposed by students at Birzeit University to help locals associate themselves with the project. Given that Birzeit is famous for its quarried stone, the proposal offers locals to contribute by placing their own stone tiles in front of their houses.

The impact of the street tiling has left a huge imprint on Birzeit's historic centre; ever since the tiling work began on the two new routes, the sense of urban space has gradually become more formalized, and the old centre is already hosting more visitors. Locals find it more convenient, clean and safe to

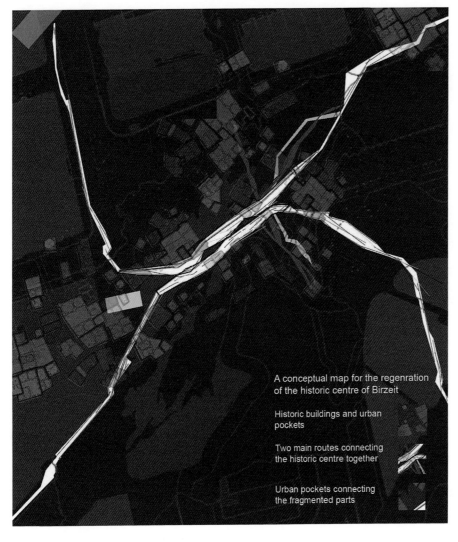

A conceptual map for the regenration of the historic centre of Birzeit

Historic buildings and urban pockets

Two main routes connecting the historic centre together

Urban pockets connecting the fragmented parts

ideas about how to use the public space have been emerging.

As a way to change the stereotyped image of historic buildings in Palestine as that of a 'dirty place' or as a 'place for the poor', Riwaq worked on renovating historic buildings to provide a physical example of how they could be used and renovated. The aim has been to show how the conservation of these historic buildings could actually be cheaper than destroying them to erect new concrete structures.

Conservation of historic buildings has always been a major challenge in Riwaq's work, as previous experience was not comprehensive enough to resolve key issues to do with new services and environmental qualities that could encourage people to live and use the space. The result in many of its previous conservation projects was beautifully renovated buildings, yet many remained empty either due to the lack of environmental comfort or modern-day amenities.

On the other hand, and to be fair to Riwaq, their experience of conservation was also a reflection of the different political, social and economic layers that Palestine has gone through. This collage has left its impact on design decisions, levels of interventions and priorities for conservation – from just conserving single historic buildings, to preventive conservation of the exterior skin of the fabric, and now the regeneration and development of the whole historic centres. 'Job creation through conservation' is an example of a key phase for conservation projects in terms of creating job opportunities to alleviate unemployment in economically disadvantaged areas, while conserving buildings to be used for public services. Despite the success of the policy in

3.19 Conceptual approach towards regenerating the historic centre of Birzeit with the two main routes acting as the spines of activities and events to take place.

3.20 Proposed regeneration plan for Birzeit's historic centre.

use the space during the day and night – especially children and women, who are consciously or unconsciously creating their own new social centres and meeting points.

The initiative has also attracted a few institutions and investors who started appreciating the hidden potentials of the site. In this way, more demands and

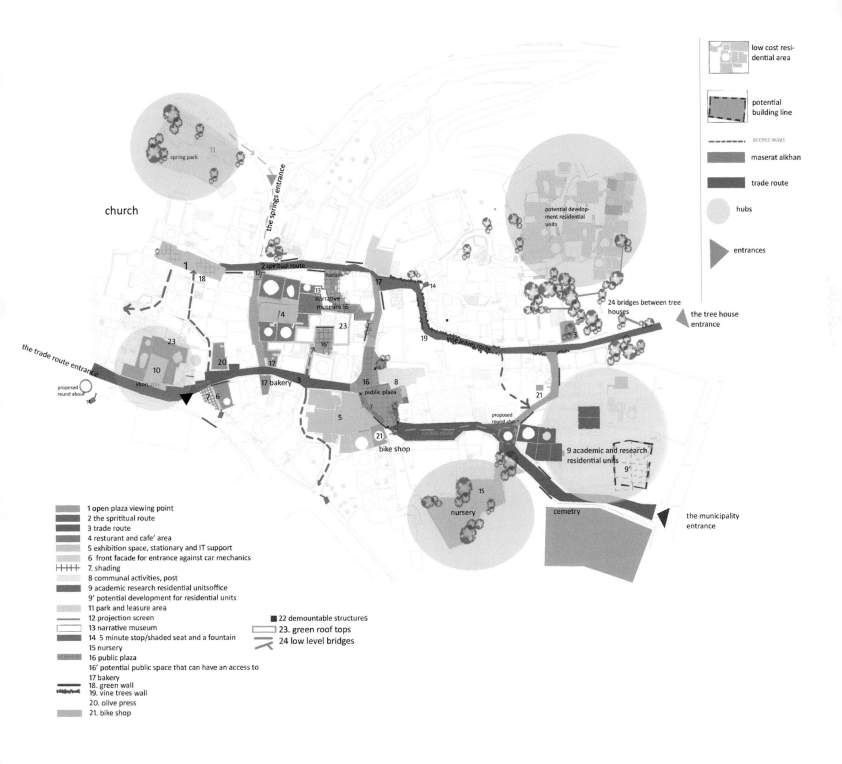

church

the springs entrance

spring park
11

1
18

2 spiritual route
12
fontain
13
narrative
museum 16
4
23
17
16'

23
10
short stay
20
17
7 6

the trade route entrance

proposed
round about
14

17 bakery 3

5

7
21

bike shop

potential develop-
ment residential
units

17
14

24 bridges between tree
houses

the tree house
entrance

19 vine leaves route

3

16
public plaza
8
7

21

proposed
round about

cyclists route

9 academic and research
residential units
9'

the municipality
entrance

nursery
15

cemetry

Legend (left column):

1 open plaza viewing point
2 the spiritual route
3 trade route
4 resturant and cafe' area
5 exhibition space, stationary and IT support
6 front facade for entrance against car mechanics
7. shading
8 communal activities, post
9 academic research residential unitsoffice
9' potential development for residential units
11 park and leasure area
12 projection screen
13 narrative museum
14 5 minute stop/shaded seat and a fountain
15 nursery
16 public plaza
16' potential public space that can have an access to
17 bakery
18. green wall
19. vine trees wall
20. olive press
21. bike shop

22 demountable structures
23. green roof tops
24 low level bridges

Legend (right column):

low cost resi-
dential area

potential
building line

access ways

maserat alkhan

trade route

hubs

entrances

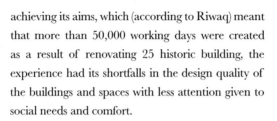

achieving its aims, which (according to Riwaq) meant that more than 50,000 working days were created as a result of renovating 25 historic building, the experience had its shortfalls in the design quality of the buildings and spaces with less attention given to social needs and comfort.

Dealing with the concept of conservation has always been an accumulative process of research and practical experimentation, and Riwaq is constantly revising its work and exploring the different practices and schools of conservation around the world to uncover what conservation could mean in a context like Palestine. The approach is now gradually developing from just that of to 'conserve to protect' into a different school of conservation that focuses best on the role of the community, human activities and the relativity of values as referred to by Jokilehto.[27] UNESCO's recommendations regarding the 'Safeguarding and Contemporary Role of Historic Areas' also set up a clear guidance for Riwaq's recent approach:

> Every historic area and its surrounding should be considered in their totality as a coherent whole whose balance and specific nature depend on the fusion of the parts of which it is composed and which includes human activities as much as the buildings. All valid elements including human activities, however modest, thus have a significance in relation to the whole which must not be disregarded.[28]

And it continued:

> That historic areas are part of the daily environment of human beings everywhere, that they represent the living presence of the past which formed them, that they provide the variety in life's background needed to match the diversity of society, and that by so doing they gain in value and acquire an additional human dimension.[29]

Throughout this process, it has also been crucial for the team to ensure that the identity and memory of the sites are kept alive, as it is not only through the destruction of heritage that memories and identities are erased – as Bevan[30] points out – but also through careless rebuilding of architecture which is then lost. Therefore, within Birzeit we have attempted to suggest interventions which do not deny or erase the frequently messy, so as not to end up 'faking the past'.

3.21 Work in progress, tiling and repairing the 'Trade Route' in Birzeit's historic centre.

3.22 Work in progress, tiling and repairing the 'Trade Route' in Birzeit's historic centre.

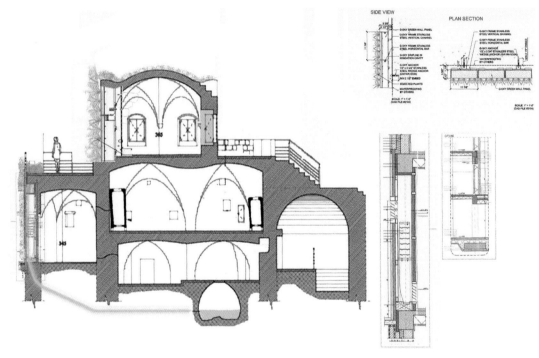

3.23 Local builder fixing traditional mud-bins known in Arabic as *Khawabi* used to store crops. Courtesy of Riwaq Photo Archive.

3.24 Traditional mud-bin in Ein Sinya. Photograph by Giorgio Palmera. Courtesy of Riwaq Photo Archive.

3.25 Proposed design intervention for the attic incorporating some passive environmental measures.

This entails a closer attention to conservation and design decisions, as can also be seen in the relatively more tolerant attitude to modern interventions in older buildings in recent years.[31]

In this sense, the renovation of a building named Rabi Attic (*Eliyyet Rabi*) in Birzeit's historic centre, which according to local residents was previously the traditional guesthouse in the town, provides a starting point to test the new conservation approach. A project was implemented to convert this three-storey building cluster, with its serene courtyard, into the Municipal Services Centre for Birzeit. It is based on a mixed-use programme initiated by the municipality to support small-business initiatives and keep the

3.26   Children with their own food stand in a cultural festival organized in collaboration with different institutions.

building active throughout the different seasons. The new Municipal Services Centre has been partially converted into a café. It is already becoming another key meeting point, in the area especially with the public space created in front. Whether the building is open or closed, local children can still find their way into it by climbing over the rooftops. They have managed to claim the place and use it in the best way possible.

The work in historic Birzeit also aimed to reconfigure a typical dwelling as a prototype model where people can physically experience what can be done by simple modifications and extensions to existing buildings to improve the environmental qualities. Responsive, yet largely invisible, alternative environmental technologies and design interventions were proposed to one of the old houses to demonstrate how to save energy and enhance thermal comfort. Additionally, we were looking – with help and support from the 'Think Net' team – at ways to raise consciousness about architectural design which engages with day-to-day cultural practices and responds to climatic factors. Above all, this is intended as a political reaction to current Israeli policies which are draining the Palestinian landscape of water resources and such like. Our intention is to find alternative 'invisible' ways for inhabitants to become less dependent on having to buy water and electricity at inflated prices from Israel; they can only achieve this by being more self-sufficient in such matters.

BUILDING NETWORKS

The urban strategy for Birzeit has created a network of local citizens and institutions, which have now started to see a feasible example on the ground. It has paved the way for new ideas and initiatives on different scales; the People's Museum is one of the interesting outcomes whereby a group of local artists worked together to renovate a courtyard as their place of residency. Since then, different interactive art projects have taken place with local inhabitants, which left a positive impact. As noted, the Rozana Association is another new initiative by local residents and property owners. It emerged in 2008 from a group of stakeholders to create an institution to promote Birzeit's cultural heritage and attract projects in.

With the support of Riwaq, Rozana has since become a key partner in the regeneration process with a number of activities and projects to be negotiated and developed. This might sound promising, as it is raising awareness about the potentials of the declining historic fabric. But in fact it also rings an alarm bell for Birzeit not to repeat the Barcelona experience of regeneration, or at least not the one where privatization ends up inserting new 'alien' symbols that then push locals out.

Indeed, the vision and approach of some stakeholders and private investors is more towards creating a museum-like village for the 'original' families of Birzeit to live in, and which does not have

any perceived 'foreigner' in it. They refer mainly to the northern part of the historic fabric which hosts many 'informal' residents who chose to live there with minimum services because they are so poor. But while this group should be accommodated, it is wrong not also to look to provide accommodation for students at Birzeit University. The fact that Birzeit is a student town means that some students tend to live in the old historic centre because of the lower rents which is seen by some as a negative point rather than a generator for urban life.

To overcome this conflict of interest, and create a linkage with the Rozana Association and other different partners, the design team has encouraged 'cultural tourism' as a concept to connect with surrounding historic centres, and specifically Riwaq's '50 Villages' initiative. This is not about creating a localized seasonal touristic place; rather it is a collective process to celebrate the area, its festivals and culture, and relate these back to the narratives and history of Birzeit. This is a collective project involving the surrounding villages through the two thematic routes that extend to connect all over the West Bank.

Some proposed routes would for instance link Birzeit with the agricultural terraces of Jifna, famous for its seasonal plum-picking festival, or with Taybeh with its local beer industry.[32] This project is being further developing to include what Riwaq has been calling 'the nineteenth- and twentieth-century architecture and spaces in between'. It is a three-year project in partnership between several Mediterranean countries, namely France, Italy, Morocco, Palestine and Tunisia. The aim is to investigate and promote the more modern heritage in rural Palestine by setting up tourist trails which will highlight the nineteenth- and twentieth-century architectural heritage of the region.[33]

THE 3RD RIWAQ BIENNALE, FROM VENICE TO PALESTINE

Physical interventions are only one component of the regeneration process. Riwaq's 3rd Biennale was another activity carried out alongside to promote and publicise the concept of '50 Villages' internationally.

Its starting point was the 53rd Venice Biennale in June-September 2009, where, the artist Khalil Rabah (who made a radical shakeup to the concept of Biennale through his playful artwork 'Biennale within a Biennale') put together an exhibition along with six other artists from Palestine under the banner of 'Palestine c/o Venice Pavilion'.[34]

The subject of Khalil's work also celebrated the '50 Villages' project, with Riwaq's entire team – myself included – being transferred to Venice to become part of the living artwork and to lead a series of lectures, discussions and presentations.[35]

> Khalil Rabah's presentation at the Biennale is an account of the restoration work undertaken in 50 Palestinian villages by the Palestinian architectural NGO, Riwaq. His aim is clear: 'Riwaq has created an opportunity not only to investigate the trappings of our visual and cultural codes, but also to look at ways to reconnect isolated and walled Palestine to the international art world'.[36]

Later on, the 3rd Riwaq Biennale in Ramallah from 12–16 October 2009 drew in a large international audience. Artists, social theorists, planners, architects, environmentalists and many others joined in a series of journeys to the 50 selected villages, as well as other disparate locations, as a way to reflect upon the fractured territory of Palestine and uncover its potentials. These journeys were conceived as one of a series of networking activities between the villages in Riwaq's overall programme, offering them opportunities to create dialogue and new visions.

WHAT IS NEXT?

The design process continued for Birzeit with more events, tests and projects to take place. Many key issues were discussed and negotiated. For instance, accepting vertical extensions within the historic centre was welcomed by the Riwaq team, despite the limited land and financial resources. However, for me the concept is subject to consideration if organized within a suitable program; the issue is not only about aesthetics, but also about building a sustainable community. I'm not suggesting here that aesthetics can be ruled out, or even compromised, rather I'm suggesting new avenues that can add a new and maybe different meaning to the term 'aesthetics' formed by social relations. This in return can imply accepting and recognizing the role and touch of everyone in that society, a town needs to develop and expand without creating 'conflict'. I believe therefore that we should consider seeing historic centres as collages that reflect the different layers while we as initiators should organize and sustain them – even if this means deconstructing and accepting the meaning of a concrete room added to a rooftop.

The clichéd idea of bringing in a 'star architect' like Zaha Hadid to leave an iconic form in the town – as was proposed by some of the team members – is never going to revitalize Birzeit, certainly not in the way that will create a sustainable community. If architecture is not going to provide a stage for the

3.27 Trail route across the watch towers
passing through the villages of Silwad and
Taybeh. The route marks the key traditional dry
stone towers used in agricultural fields and olive
terraces. Courtesy of Riwaq Photo Archive.

locals to perform on, then it won't get far before collapsing. As Mitchell puts it:

> we do not want to run in danger with the aesthetics, to live with a beautiful person who has little to say.[37]

However, within this clash of paradigms, I accept that I might also be wrong given that the current competition for 'capital flow' in the region is proving to have more than two edges. I can understand the psychological motivation behind bringing big-name architects in; it places the weight internationally before locally, and politically before physically. This could – and will for sure – direct the attention towards the other side of the Separation Wall, just as Santiago Calatrava's bridge in Jerusalem did. Still, we need to be very careful about the impact it will leave in the long run on space and communities, as this is no longer about a 'sexy' form.

Al Reehan[38] and Rawabi offer examples where big-name architectural offices were brought in to take part in designing a whole new city to the north of Ramallah under the name of 'economic recovery'[39] – a curious strategy when more than 70 percent of Palestinian historic centres lie abandoned. Regardless of the reason behind whom it targets, or how it is being

advertised, the layout of these new developments does not differ at all from any Israeli settlement, which is now occupying the hilltops of Palestine. If anything, it reflects a confused identity falling apart under the umbrella of modernity. I myself would not call it 'economic recovery', or 'economic peace'[40]; I think the best term to describe it should be that given by David Harvey,[41] as it is just another example of competition for 'capital accumulation' through which the logic of power is moving culture and identity on its own terms. Ultimately the grasping at big-name architects is a dead-end.

This point then raises an urgent question: why, in the midst of such massive investments, is cultural heritage still not being seen as a means for development despite its obvious potential? Is this related to a lack of awareness and suitable planning strategies? Or is there a conflict of interest between politicians, investors and the community needs?

Of course there are many common obstacles to heritage investment shared by many countries around the world, and which have to do – according to the World Bank research – with public policies and complications related to land value, land ownership, market prices, and the lack of heritage management programs, etc.[42] Palestine, however, encounters

3.28   The Israeli settlement of Modi'in.

3.29   Rawabi as marketed in its promotional brochure. Courtesy of Lana Joudeh.

3.30 Israeli settlements constructed between the traditional Palestinian built fabric in the West Bank. Photograph by Majdi Hadid.

other barriers created by Israeli occupation which dominate all policies in the Occupied Territories and push investment and consumption towards specific areas, mainly in the city of Ramallah. However, the major gaps are also caused from within the Palestinian system itself; the protection of cultural heritage as a technical and managerial discipline does not exist within the PA agenda, as previously mentioned. Initiatives by the PA have so far been limited to a few feasibility studies and proposals for establishing 'museums' to house vestiges of the past. There has been no wider view of heritage development that looks into the social need of the community until very recently, now that Riwaq has started promoting the concept of regeneration as developed in the Birzeit project.

Added to this, the impact of the 'post-Oslo' period. It has created a fertile ground with incentives for capital investment in all sectors of the Palestinian economy from both local and foreign corporations registered to do business in Palestine. Construction since then has become one of the biggest sectors of Palestinian economy.

The impact of Palestinian's private investment and spending has been disappointing. It has widened economic inequality, creating an upper-middle class of Palestinians who are now trying to sustain their power. Their investments, especially in Ramallah, did not establish a solid basis for long-term economic growth within a pre-planned national agenda; instead, they have been mainly concentrated in buildings that can further sustain

their social ambitions through restaurants, cafés and luxurious dwellings.

Today, these economic forces are themselves shaping the Palestinian landscape. Land and empty building plots are the main source of investment given their scarcity, which in turn raises land prices up very high.[43] Quoting Jakob Jakobsen during his visit to Ramallah:[44]

> The fear today is the control of special lobby of investors who are now taking over all vacant land in Palestine for further development and investment. They are in control of what kind of investment that is going to happen. The same people are the people, who are allowing Arab investments to come. They have enough money to buy cultural heritage sites and totally destroy them in order to build high-rise buildings. Nobody can stop them.[45]

Municipalities and other local organisations have limited control in practice over these investors, and even if some investors wish to promote cultural heritage as a viable source of development, they would need a network of governmental and non-governmental institutions that work together on a national agenda to direct their investments with the

3.31 Turmos Ayya village being turned into mansions of stone and red roofs similar to the surrounding Israeli settlements.

necessary technical and managerial expertise. It is something Palestine still lacks due to the economic resources and the different priorities for its national agenda. If anything, the current condition is unfortunately helping to fuel social and political differences; it represents a neo-colonial strategy from within that serves as – argued by scholars like Jakobsen – to fragment the Palestinian community through acts of controlled consumption.

This is the reason why the major challenge in the regeneration of Palestine's historic centres, and Birzeit's in particular, is to work on different levels to establish the necessary networks that can abolish social and economic inequality, and create the ground for self-sustained institutions that are no longer economically dependent on Israel. It is a strategy that is not dominated by the same tiny web of wealthy companies and private investors, who in many cases also happen to be the political leaders of Palestine as well.

If the aim is to make a difference through heritage, then the concept of conservation can't be dissociated from the political and social agenda. It needs to involve a change that goes far beyond any conventional perception of just 'dealing with the historic and artistic work of the past'[46] or of 'keeping buildings as close to its original condition as possible for as long as possible'. Indeed, conservation in this sense is more towards an adaptable and modern definition; one that tackles the 'change of values in contemporary society'.[47]

The danger I see facing Palestine today is that both regimes – the Israeli occupier and the wealthy sector of the Palestinians occupied – are 'dismantling' slowly the social values and memories embodied within society. This is the main reason why conservation and the protection of the Palestinian cultural heritage have to aim far beyond an image or a character of place. It is now about regaining missing social values by giving each member of the community an active role once more. The investor, the politician, the farmer, the businessman, the housewife and the student need to all come together to bringing life back to 50,000 historic building and 420 historic sites all over the West Bank and the Gaza Strip.

The issue is also about reconstructing the memory and identity that is being distorted. Dolores Hayden,[48] in The Power of Place writes:

> Place memory encapsulates the human ability to connect with both the built and natural environments that are entwined in the cultural landscape.

Buildings are not important just because they are buildings. Memories are attached to places because of the social and political meanings that people link to their physical form and aesthetic beauty. Thus, the process of creating a new future at the current ruins of destroyed local distinctiveness has to be put into place, and urgently.

'50 VILLAGES' AND BEYOND

At a time when Palestine is facing setbacks in the political and economic spheres, the '50 Villages' project hopes to make a qualitative addition to the structure of Palestinian networks. Just as I am looking for spaces of possibility, we equally need to think and look for the possible networks that can create or sustain these spaces without any conflict of interest. Working with a local NGO like Riwaq has thus for me paved the way for endless possibilities of spatial resistance that could be achieved.

NGOs are clearly now playing a key role in shaping the Palestinian community, since they are essential to a multitude of basic requirements in the West Bank and Gaza territories, as well as Jerusalem. Their contribution can't be undermined.[49] Thus the need to work with them is vital. The challenge is to ensure that they carry out policies that empower the local community and sustain the civic values of its society. It is something that Riwaq as well as many other local NGOs have successfully and consciously managed to achieve. I believe that this local networks of NGOs has managed to shift the nature of the Palestinian/Israeli game from ping-pong to chess, referring to an ironic description by a prominent left-wing Israeli journalist called Amira Hass: 'Palestinians play ping-pong while Israelis play chess'. This time around however, the Palestinians are the ones playing the more complex game.

In an article published on the Jewish Political Studies website by Steinberg,[50] he reflects Israel's dominant view about the role of NGOs in Palestine:

> This community has exploited the 'halo effect' of human rights rhetoric to promote highly particularistic goals. In most cases small groups of individuals, with substantial funds obtained from non-profit foundations and governments (particularly European), use the NGO frameworks to gain influence and pursue private political agendas, without being accountable to any system of checks and balances.[51]

This Israeli opposition and counter strategy should not be viewed as an obstacle that is going to impede future ability of NGOs in Palestine. Indeed it is a proof that NGOs are managing to be influential and thus are essential to be sustained and empowered as a key ingredient against attempts to destroy the identity and civic values embodied within Palestinian society.

There is no right way – or indeed just one way – to design, and thus there always needs to be an element of 'critical' practice incorporated into design. Concepts and ideas are born, while others are questioned, tested and sometimes excluded. It is the process of making space and society that has shifted our work on the Birzeit development plan to a new level. Dialogue, collectiveness and teamwork, listening to the locals, reading their daily habits and arguing about the level of compromise, is giving a different meaning to the project. After all Birzeit is just one of 50 historic centres on the agenda. Neither Riwaq nor I will be able to protect all of these centres and realize the bigger dream on our own. That is why we are trying to build networks and communities that can take over and stand up on the front line by themselves. Above all it is about the 'strategic' link being made to connect rural areas with urban spaces. This is the shift where I think one is able to contribute the most, bringing what was happening outside the historic centres into the equation.

For me, the accomplishment will be when heritage protection will no longer stop where historic centres are. Heritage as a concept in Palestine is now wide open to discussion, interpretation and debate, and this will lead to endless scenarios for the concept of the '50 Villages' project.

In Palestine, even the definition of built heritage is still blurry.[52] Different attempts have taken place over the past two decades to rediscover the meaning of it over the past two decades; this has been not only limited to historic buildings but also to its cultural landscape, music, handicrafts and food. Such efforts, as Bshara suggests:

Demonstrate both the willingness to re-write history, incorporate new findings and the fact that the concept of heritage is changing rapidly.[53]

These new readings of urban spaces, buildings and even individuals who embody important historical values, despite their relative newness, opens up a huge web of possibilities when reading the Palestinian landscape. Refugee camps set up since the 1948 relocations are just one of the examples, since they represent a stark demonstration of what heritage might be seen as: not for its physical value as such, but for its historical importance. Indeed, the uniqueness of such phenomena extends the very meaning of refuge into that of an involuntary permanent residency, as born out of emergency.[54]

In a different sense, Yasser Arafat's old residence – now his memorial in Ramallah – is another example of contemporary architecture built on top of ruins, yet its value stems from the historic and political meaning behind the figure that once lived there. Examples such as these demonstrate what one might start to be included as an integral part of the cultural landscape, and which could possibly turn these structures into a state of 'normality'. Likewise, the Israeli Army checkpoints, the hidden routes used by Palestinians, impromptu markets at the side of roads, depleted stone quarries, and many others – if not yet regarded as a key part of Palestinian culture – could well in future be added to the litany of built heritage. In other words, everyday life will witness a change; what people have been fighting against on the basis of destruction of urban character could in turn be our next target to protect, simply because something represents a specific social, historical or political memory. Bearing this idea in

3.32 Amari Refugee Camp, Ramallah, 2005.
Photograph by Majdi Hadid.

mind, the possibilities for extending Riwaq's network of 50 villages becomes endless.

And as much as this is painful to admit, we can imagine the day when we will be discussing whether to include an Israeli checkpoint or an Israeli settlement – or even more dangerously, a rapacious housing development like Rawabi[55] – on the list of Palestine heritage. Once one enters into the cultural aspects of heritage protection, it is almost bound to lead to the most unexpected of end results. Here we need to keep in mind Edward Said's call for the re-affirmation of 'the power of culture over the culture of power'. If we can do this, then we believe that built heritage in Palestine will be on the right track.

Just as I tried in this chapter to nurture possibilities for change through design from within the historical fabric – which I believe is crucial process while building the Palestinian state – my next chapters will take the existing conditions even further trying to offer new design interventions that can interweave these networks with new potential ones born from the map. I will show how the collective power of informal networks, with their 'soft' tactics of resistance, can also collide with the moments of weakness that Israel is concealing, which in effect paves the way for another subversive map. These subversive design proposals cannot be grand or iconic: instead they should aim for invisibility, and seek to build upon everyday habits of life.

If all of these attempts can be put together, I believe we will eventually reach the necessary alternative strategies for change.

105

NOTES

1 Part of this chapter has been published as a joint paper. See Golzari, N. and Sharif, Y. (2011) 'Reclaiming Space and Identity: Heritage-led Regeneration in Palestine', *The Journal of Architecture*, Vol.16 (1), pp. 121–44.

2 Fraser, M. (2007) 'Introduction: The Cultural Context of Critical Architecture', in Rendell, J., Hill, J., Fraser, M. and Dorrian, M. (eds), *Critical Architecture*. London: Routledge, pp. 249–51.

3 Historical fabrics form less than 1 percent of the total Palestinian built-up areas in the West Bank and Gaza Strip. They are widely seen as one of the key representations of Palestinian national and cultural identity. Yet, they lie abandoned and in a state of decline and deterioration. This has been caused both by the Israeli bulldozers which strategically mean to erase forms of Palestinian identity, and also by Palestinians who tend to replace this kind of older cultural identity with high-rise buildings that can accommodate the increasing population within the limited area available.

4 Jubeh, N. (2009) 'Fifty Villages and More: The Protection of Rural Palestine', in *Geography 101* (catalogue published for the 3rd Riwaq Biennale). Ramallah: Riwaq, Vol. 1.

5 After oil prices went up after the 1973–4 'oil crisis', many Palestinians migrated to work in the Persian Gulf and many others went to the United States.

6 The Oslo Peace Agreement and the consequent birth of the Palestinian Authority (PA) in 1993 has also opened the doors wide in Ramallah and other West Bank towns for investors, who since then have contributed in almost 60 percent of the buildings we see today.

7 Stone has become a political tool under Israeli occupation to create a sense of false identity and 'roots' to the land: a subject and a cultural currency to be fought over. This is one of the issues that I will be addressing in the coming chapters.

8 Jubeh, op. cit.

9 Riwaq's conservation work has covered more than 90 buildings, plus the preparation of rehabilitation and protection plans for almost 20 historic centres all over the West Bank, including Jerusalem – in addition to research and documentation of all historic Palestine including Jaffa and Acre.

10 The protection of cultural heritage in Palestine is under a technically weak umbrella, namely the Ministry of Tourism and Antiquity. Archeological sites dating back to 1700 BC are the only protected elements of heritage within the current legislation, leaving the majority of most recent historic buildings and historic sites without any legal protection.

11 The uniqueness of this experience is that for the first time carefully chosen and competent academics, practitioners and intellectuals from different spheres – nationally and internationally – are coming together to understand and come up with a meaning of heritage, conservation and protection that best fits Palestine and its condition. Different laws from six selected countries were thoroughly studied and put into a matrix to assist the drafting of the new Palestinian law: English, French, Spanish, Tunisian, Egyptian and Jordanian law, of which Palestine is still under its jurisdiction. The main achievement of the new legislation is that it covered not only archeological sites but also included architecture and all the important natural heritage sites all over the Palestinian territories.

12 In 2002, the World Heritage Committee took a decision in Budapest to provide technical assistance in favour of the protection of the Palestinian cultural and natural heritage[12]. As a result, a one-year program implemented by UNESCO happened in close consultation with the Ministry of Tourism and Antiquities to formulate and train a specialized Palestinian team for World Heritage nominations. Riwaq's team was put in charge of preparing the inventory for the architectural nominations, while other cultural institution covered archeological sites and natural heritage.

13 As mentioned in earlier chapter, during the eighteenth and nineteenth century, the central highlands of Palestine were divided into 24 administrative domains (sheikdoms), ruled by sheikhs who belonged to rich or noble origins. The villages in which the sheikhs and their clans resided were called 'throne villages'. Throne Villages are remarkable for their architectural style; they are distinctive in the scale and spatial organization, which introduced semi-urban architecture within rural areas.

14 See criteria for selecting sites on the World Heritage List. Available at: http://whc.unesco.org/en/nominations

15 See Riwaq's National Register for historic buildings. Available at: http://www.riwaq.org/register/register.html [accessed 10 June 2011].

16 It is worth mentioning that the Birzeit municipality is the owner of the project while Riwaq is responsible for the execution and overall management of the regeneration project in partnership with other local organization and BZU. It is important to also mention that two architectural student workshops were held during 2007 between Riwaq, BZU and both La Cambre University in Brussels and the Technical University of Dortmund in Germany.

17 Rozana is a stakeholder groups from the locals of Birzeit who gathered under the umbrella of this organisation to promote cultural events and initiate projects that can further enhance the town.

18 Along with Nasser Golzari from NG Architects, we initiated the UK team. This included Richard MacCormac, Murray Fraser, Fergus Nicol, Peter Barber and Michael Edwards. Others members were also involved from USA, Belgium, and of course Palestine.

19 Having an understanding municipality, as well as Birzeit University and a conscious local community, which appreciates the quality of the historic centre, are other key factor for choosing Birzeit. Also, Riwaq has done a few conservation projects in and around Birzeit, and this has also helped to facilitate communication and set up the basis for the upcoming work.

20 The population of Birzeit is estimated according to the census carried out in 2007 by the Palestinian Central Bureau of Statistics.

21 The issue of ownership became complicated ever since the British Mandate when the systematic survey and mapping of Palestine first took place (between 1920–48). The British maps delineated only land parcels within the historic fabric, leaving the far more problematic issue of ownership unresolved.

22 For example, the famous tree house at the eastern entrance of the village which, throughout the years, has hosted the activities of the local children in the morning and their parents in the evenings. There is also the informal public meeting space at the edge of the main road, the rooftop terrace of the bakery shop which was transformed into a living room, the neighbour with his 'iconic' chair in the street, and many other informal spaces which changed the meaning and spatial value of Birzeit's historic centre tremendously.

23 Mitchell, M. (2003) *Rebuilding Community in Kosovo*. Powys: Centre for Alternative Technology Publications.

24 Hamdi, N. (2004) *Small Change: The Art of Practice and the Limits of Planning in Cities*. London: Earthscan, p. xix.

25 This included preventive conservation for 50 historic buildings and public spaces in different parts of the historic centre, and conservation work to one of the buildings to be used as the Municipal Service Centre. Additionally, Riwaq and the local municipality have managed to raise funds to provide new infrastructure and paving for the main public spaces and routes inside Birzeit's historic centre.

26 The 'Caravanserai Route' has national value given that it was once part of the famous caravanserai trade routes linking Palestine with the rest of the *Mediterranean* region. It is the only building protected by the current antiquity law as it dates back to the fifteenth century.

27 Jokilehto, J. (1999) *A History of Architectural Conservation*. Oxford: Butterworth-Heinemann, p. 290.

28 Ibid.

29 Anon, 'Recommendation Concerning the Safeguarding and Contemporary Role of Historic Areas', *UNESCO*, 26 November 1976. Available at: http://portal.unesco.org/en/ev.php-URL_ID=13133&URL_DO=DO_TOPIC&URL_SECTION=201.html [accessed 13 January 2010].

30 Bevan, R. (2006) *The Destruction of Memory: Architecture at War*. London: Reaktion Books.

31 This viewpoint spans from Ruskin's views about restoration right up to modern conservation philosophies which form the basis for a critical process for the definition of what is to be conserved and how.

32 Taybeh already attracts a good number of visitors who come to its historic churches as well as the Beer festival. Riwaq has already started on a number of conservation projects and activities in Taybeh village, again to set up the basis for historical awareness and urban regeneration.

33 Another phase as part of the regeneration process in Birzeit was the design of the main four entrances to the historic centre and some selected 'urban pockets' along the routes. This was done through a design competition set up with students of architecture at Central Saint Martin's in London and at Birzeit University, in collaboration with UNESCO.

34 The name reflects Palestine's historic condition of always being 'looked after' by someone else: i.e. the Ottoman Empire, the British Mandate, Jordan, Egypt and now Israel.

35 During the Biennale I myself presented different ideas as to what the concept for regenerating 50 villages could be and how Birzeit could be approached.

36 Anon. (2009) 'Reflect and Resist', *The Guardian*, Saturday 13 June 2009. Available at: http://www.guardian.co.uk/artanddesign/2009/jun/13/art-theatre [accessed 27 October 2009].

37 Mitchell, op. cit., p. 19.

38 Anon. *Al Reehan*. See: http://www.alreehan.ps [accessed 1 November 2009].

39 McCarthy, R. (2009) 'Rawabi, the new Palestinian city that could rise on the West Bank', *The Guardian*, 8 September 2009. Available at: http://www.guardian.co.uk/world/2009/sep/08/new-palestinian-city-west-bank [accessed 28 October 2009].

40 As part of Israeli support for Rawabi, Ashkenazi, the director for the economic research division of Israel's Office of Regional Cooperation under Minister Silvan Shalom says: 'Israel views with great importance assisting economic projects in the Palestinian Authority. We believe economic peace will improve our relations and help bring us to a place of dialogue and the real basis for the future'.

41 Schouten, P. (2008) 'David Harvey on the Geography of Capitalism: Understanding cities as polities and shifting imperialisms', *Theory Talks*, 9 October 2008. Available at: http://www.theory-talks.org/2008/10/theory-talk-20-david-harvey.html [accessed 20 October 2009].

42 Stefano, P. (1996) 'Economic Analysis of Investments in Cultural Heritage: Insights from Environmental Economics'. Available at: http://www.elaw.org/system/files/Economic.Analysis.Investments.Cultural.Heritage.pdf [accessed 10 January 2010].

43 Further to a conversation with one of the big entrepreneurs in Ramallah – who prefers to remain anonymous – I was told that when Rawabi project was first promoted, land prices in that area went up tremendously. Bashar Masri, the manager of the project, sold a huge amount of the land plots, for the complex. The reason was to get more profit even if it meant reducing the amount of public spaces around, and these sales provided the main income for the second big project in the area.

44 Jakobsen, J. (2008) 'Ramallahisation', *The Ramallah Lecture*, 14 July 2008. Available at: http://theramallahlecture.blogspot.com/2008/07/ramallahisation.html [accessed 2 January 2010].

45 Ibid.

46 Jokilehto, op. cit., p. 290.

47 Jokilehto, op. cit., p. 295.

48 Hayden, D. (1995) *The Power of Place: Urban Landscapes as Public History*. Cambridge, MA: MIT Press.

49 Of course some NGOs – specially international NGOs – have their danger of acting in international interests, since most of them are internationally funded, and some funders might gear their efforts towards their state's cultural and political agendas while 'serving the Palestinian community'. Yet, while bearing these dangers in mind, the networks of NGOs could form a key vehicle in developing Palestine – especially, in the field of planning, heritage, environment, healthcare, education and human rights.

50 Steinberg, G. (2004) 'Abusing the Legacy of the Holocaust: The Role of NGOs in Exploiting Human Rights to Demonize Israel', *Jewish Political Studies Review*, Vol. 16 (fall), pp. 3–4. Available at: http://209.85.229.132/search?q=cache:YU4xd36PZtAJ:www.jcpa.org/phas/phas-steinberg-f04.htm+role+of+ngos+in+palestine+political+agendas&cd=2&hl=en&ct=clnk&client=safari [accessed 20 January 2010].

51 Ibid.

52 Apart from the aforementioned draft legislation for the protection of cultural heritage in Palestine, which however has not been endorsed yet by the Palestinian legislative authorities, it will work to protect any item of cultural heritage by recording it in the National Registry. The draft law refers to cultural heritage as historic buildings or historic sites which are at least 50 years old. This date was used as a reference point to include all what has existed up to 1948. The process is accumulative and later amendments will also be introduced to cover a lot of more recent architecture.

53 Bshara, K. (2009) 'Preserving the contemporary: Palestine refugee camps – from destiny to destinations', in *Geography 101* (catalogue published for the 3rd Riwaq Biennale). Ramallah: Riwaq, Vol. 1, p. 39.

54 Ibid.

55 Rawabi offers an example of where big-name architecture offices have been brought in to take part in designing a whole new district to the north of Ramallah under the name of 'economic recovery' – a curious strategy when it is estimated that more than 70% of Palestinian historic centres lie abandoned. Regardless of the reason behind the project, or how it is being advertised, the layout of this new development does not differ at all from any of the imposed Israeli settlements now occupying the hilltops of Palestine. If anything, it reflects a confused identity falling apart under the umbrella of modernity. We think the best term to describe it is that given by David Harvey, in that it is just another example of competition for 'capital accumulation' through which the economic logic of power is trying to move culture and identity on its own terms.

See Schouten, P. 'Theory Talks #20: David Harvey on the Geography of Capitalism: Understanding cities as polities and shifting imperialisms', *Theory Talks*, 9 October 2008. http://www.theory-talks.org/2008/10/theory-talk-20-david-harvey.html (accessed 20.10.09).

Plate 1   Traditional rural fabric
            in the West Bank.

Birds redefining the West
Bank's aerial map

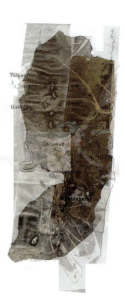

Plate 2   Re-reading the West Bank
through its margins.

Off the road

Plate 3   Artifacts of resistance emerging
at the margins.

A conceptual map for the regenration
of the historic centre of Birzeit

Historic buildings and urban
pockets

Two main routes connecting
the historic centre together

Urban pockets connecting
the fragmented parts

Plate 4   Conceptual approach towards
regenerating the historic centre of Birzeit with
the two main routes acting as the spines of
activities and events to take place.

Plate 5   Re-reading Birzeit stone quarry.

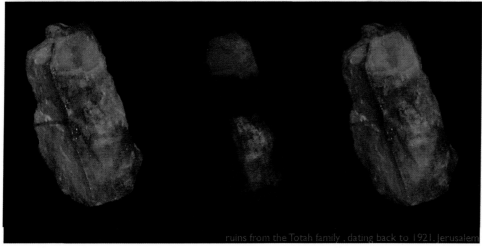

ruins from the Totah family , dating back to 1921. Jerusalem

Further to archaeological excavations, scientists has recently found new traces of land registry documents trapped in amber. The amber also include traces of hair and other DNA contents. After investigation it appears that the family registry document is matching the DNA forensics. Both belong to members of the Totah Family. Contents reveal that the Totah family owned the land back in 1920. In 2003 a new house was built by the family, but was later demolished in 2004 by Israeli army to expand the 'Big Jerusalem' plan known as E1, which aims to expand Jewish neighbourhoods and erase slowly the Palestinian ones.

Given the fact that these settlements were then considered illegal according to Geneva Convention and international law, the Totah family is now intending to reclaim their stolen land back, now that the Palestinian state has been finally founded.

Plate 6   An imagined scenario in 2028 showing excavated pieces of stone. The trapped DNA elements reveal the right of a displaced family to reclaim their land. This scenario is inspired from a real story of land confiscation and house demolition that took place in 2004 for the Totah family.

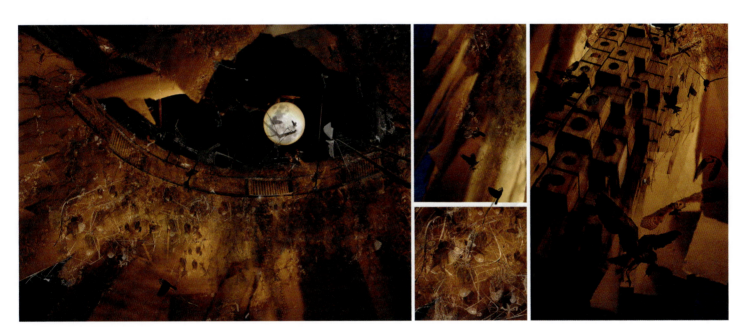

Plate 7   Making the 'Bird Machines'.

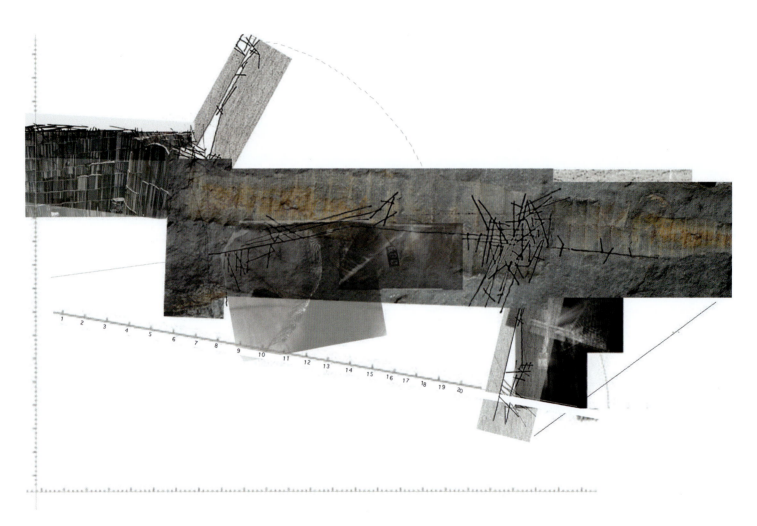

Plate 8   Bringing back the dismantled layers.

UNDER THE
SURFACE

To collect together the pieces of the land and draw a coherent mental map of Palestine remains difficult. It is not only the complexity of borderlines and the different fragments on the surface caused by the power of Israeli occupation, but also the invisible traces of occupation and the corresponding resistance forces in the voids. Thus, this chapter will instead put emphasis on the need to step underneath the exhausted surface of land in Palestine, so as to explore different layers below the surface of the 'conventional' map. I will be looking for an invisible contradictory landscape where it is difficult to identify who owns what, or even who is occupying what. In doing so, I will be cutting through the surface to reach another dimension with its invisible layers and codes.

The current map of Israel is built on a fight over identity, domination and ownership of the landscape. This 'structured chaos' makes it even more confusing to understand where the limits of the map might start or end. But despite the complexities of these lines, legal and territorial realities above the surface in terms of colonization of the land has been relatively straightforward, with a process of suppression and land grab which is brutal, elastic and thick – as described by Weizman.[1]

What is far more dangerous is what happens underneath, away from the physical borderlines, especially when Palestinians are being used and exploited. This is when the land starts eating itself and deteriorating from inside. By going below the surface, one enters another level of war, which is the war of stone, sewage and water; it's an ongoing crisis which has changed the Palestinian landscape from a homogeneous continuous space into a complex matrix full of gaps, dead and leftover spaces, which could any minute literally collapse.

Hence, I will use this chapter to highlight the invisible forms of Israeli occupation below the surface, some of which other scholars have addressed before. My emphasis will be on stone as a central tool used to erase history and create a new identity; something that has not been yet dealt with and exposed enough by architects, planners and urban critics. Stone in Israel today is a material loaded with political and historical codes which work on different time scales, as Weizman[2] suggests. The short-term interest is reflected by the instant design interventions while the long-term strategy seems to be to eat away slowly and quietly the Palestinian landscape and cultural identity in order to allow for the creation of the Israeli dream.

In the text, I will try to uncover how the strategy of occupation emerging from power operates below the surface of land, and how again this collides with the tactics of resistance of the weak. Within such a context there is always also a degree of Palestinian power and Israeli weakness, a place of resilience and defiance, which is nurtured by the everyday forms of Palestinian opposition. Social and economic innovation is born from need below the ground, just as much as is the case above the ground; indeed it is actually developing faster and easier below the surface due to its invisible nature. These elements of decay are producing another thin layer of urban possibility below the surface, are in which sewage pipes, tunnels and even stone quarries are working together as bridges to create an otherwise impossible space.

THE WAR OF STONE
SETTING

Historic Palestine is characterized by extreme topographical variations, ranging from the lowest

4.1 A journey across the mountains of the West Bank its stone layers. Courtesy of Riwaq Photo Archive.

point on earth, 413 metres below sea level, on the shores of the Dead Sea, up to 1,000 metres in the central highlands, usually known today as the West Bank. The West Bank represents a mosaic of steep rocky hilltops, composed of deep horizontal layers of limestone, and intersected by a network of small and fertile valleys with a light brown loamy skin of soil which has been reshaped over time to form the olive trees, crops and vegetable terraces. Across the West Bank, all one can see is hills followed by hills until they slope gently towards the coastal plain of the Mediterranean on the western edge, or the Jordan Valley on the eastern edge with its sharp slopes that meet the Jordan River.

Although this central highland is a relatively small area, it actually forms the region's backbone due to its unique topography. The face of the land with its beautiful brown soil and green olive

terraces, mushrooming between the predominantly limestone rocks in rich colours ranging from white, yellow, pink and honey – gives the land its significance. The stone below, which now provides most of the reconstruction material given that it is relatively easy to cut, also adds to the unique character of the landscape. It has become a key ingredient – as well as a curse, as I will be explaining later in the chapter – to the typical biblical image imagined by the west.

Hence, what is really shaping the land of historic Palestine is how the surface wraps underneath, and what can penetrate through to reach the substrata. The mountains forming the West Bank consist mainly of sedimentary rocks formed from compressed and solidified layers of limestone. These layers with their porous nature hold ground water coming from the *wadis* and create the various

4.2 The West Bank's typical topography with its rich layers of limestone and thin skin of brown earth. Courtesy of Riwaq Photo Archive.

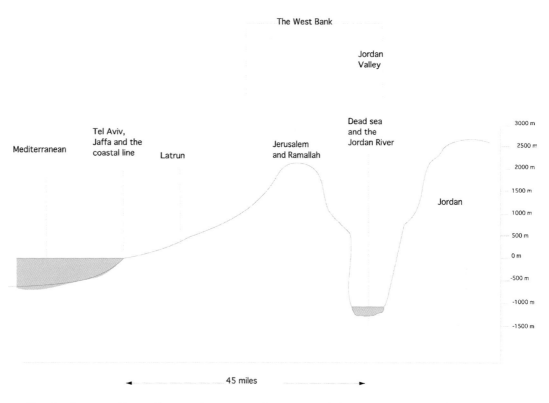

The West Bank

Jordan
Valley

Dead sea
and the
Jordan River

Tel Aviv,
Jaffa and the
coastal line

Mediterranean

Latrun

Jerusalem
and Ramallah

Jordan

3000 m

2500 m

2000 m

1500 m

1000 m

500 m

0 m

-500 m

-1000 m

-1500 m

◄——————— 45 miles ———————►

aquifers in the area. Depending on the nature of the rocks, in terms of texture and composition, these aquifers take on different shapes and depths. In the case of historic Palestine, wells and water springs are the main source of water supply in the region; they have identified by their location the main habitable areas, and thus the cities and villages, that we know today.

So what has been enforced on the surface and what has penetrated through to the sub surface of the land has also changed the natural geological formation of the region. The solid boundaries, walls and settlements above are strategically located to isolate the Palestinians and grab the natural resources of the land beneath. This fight over the land and its resources has thus not only been a fight for water

or stone; it has also been a fight for the 'materiality of the land' to engrave traces of Israeli history and root Zionist identity in the depths of a land that they otherwise found 'unfamiliar'.[3] It is a direct policy of confiscating Palestinian history to 'inject' a new Israeli one.

GOING BACK IN HISTORY

Who would have thought that the sub-strata with its complex layers would have been a subject so fought over today? In the case of Israel, it seems like working on the surface runs parallel to working from below ever since the Zionist state was established. David Ben Gurion – the first Israeli prime minister – once summed this up clearly when talking about the Jewish right to take over the Palestinian land. As he claimed,

4.3   Topography of Palestine, a cross section.

'it is based on digging the soil with our hands'.[4] Some believe that he was referring then to the two main practices seen as essential for establishing the Zionist state of Israel: agriculture and archeology. Today, we can't exclude the materiality of stone as one of the key ingredients in forming the Israeli state and Jewish identity. As one rabbi, in an interview with the *New York Times* in 2007, said proudly:

Today, every synagogue in the world has Jerusalem stone in it.[5]

During the Oslo Peace Process, which aimed to reach some sort of agreement about land ownership, the surface of the West Bank and the Gaza Strip was discussed back and forth. However, the Palestinians seem to have forgotten to discuss what lies underneath, or maybe they thought it is less problematic, or important. As a result, Israelis were given sub terrain control over all Palestine/Israel. Regardless of whether this was a result of Palestinian weakness, the imbalance of power, or a subject that was overlooked, the price the Palestinians are now paying is so high.

Consequently, a massive infrastructural system has been used by Israel to strip Palestine of its resources and to fragment it from below. Water has been one of the key tools, as referred to later in this chapter. However, what is most alarming is the literal 'peeling' away of stone from the West Bank to 'insert'

4.4   Traditional structures used by farmers to store their agricultural products. The towers are mainly built from natural stone pieces collected in the fields. Photograph by Majdi Hadid.

4.5   Inside a cave in the central highlands. Courtesy of Riwaq Photo Archive.

4.6 Stone terraces characterising the West Bank's landscape. These Terraces are mainly built in agricultural fields out of the excess of natural stone to protect the earth from being eroded by rainwater. Photograph by John Tordeh. Courtesy of Riwaq Photo Archive.

4.7 Deir Ghassaneh village to the west of Ramallah. Courtesy of Riwaq Photo Archive.

it strategically in Israeli areas. This issue is still mostly overlooked, and will lead to dangerous consequences if left to expand further. Only recently, when the cuts into the land became too big to ignore, and the scars erupted in a collision between water and sewage, has the issue of stone quarrying come to light.

The aggressive approach that Israel is taking towards acquiring stone is thus leaving a strong impression on the Palestinian economy and cultural landscape, mixing social values with the exploitation of natural resources and human rights. The idea of stone becoming a new form of cultural currency that is squabbled over is a critical twist in the Palestinian/Israeli conflict and especially in its architectural terms. On one hand one sees Palestinian land being eaten away, traditional stone buildings being erased

4.8   Ibwein village. Courtesy of Riwaq
Photo Archive.

and replaced with new buildings, and on the other hands, Jerusalem and illegal Israeli settlements all over the West Bank being intensified by the use of stone cladding. It is as if the Zionists want to build themselves forever into that land, enforcing history – compressed through layers of sand and stone – to justify their right to occupy the land.

This of course brings up the tricky question of what is Palestinian architecture in the first place? Suad Amiry, reminds us that it is definitely less problematic to talk about 'architecture in Palestine' than it is to talk about 'Palestinian architecture'. The former refers to all the influences that the region has had during different time periods, whether one is talking about Mandate Palestine, Ottoman, Mamluk, current day, etc. Influences have been mainly concentrated in cities, and more specifically in areas like Jerusalem or Acre.[6] According to Amiry, one feels more at ease in rural villages to talk about Palestinian vernacular architecture, as it seems to have prevailed there for centuries – maintaining its architectural features even if political and economic changes have transformed the social and spatial characteristics gradually with the shift from an agrarian society to the wage-labour community noted in earlier chapters.

The essentially picturesque setting of the typical Palestinian village exists until today, with its stone house located on top of the hills overlooking the valleys of olive trees and rocky landscape. This is a captivating image that the Zionist state has become strongly attached to. Indeed, conflict soon emerged when the Israeli state was initiated, and the search for architectural identity became a dilemma in terms of appropriating the identity of the 'occupied' to the new identity of the 'occupier'. Alona Nitzan-Shiftan, in her article on 'Israeli Place in East Jerusalem', refers to Israeli architects taking over Palestinian aesthetic after the 1967 war: 'the colonizer appropriates the culture of the colonized in order to define an authentic national culture of their own'.[7]

This Israeli adoption of the Palestinian traditional architecture – characterised by its unique stone structure – to localise 'the new Israeli state' and associate it with its roots, was in fact first facilitated during the British Mandate, even before the initiation of the Israeli state. On 1918, a by-law enacted by the first military governor of Jerusalem, Ronald Storr, mandated different kinds of limestone as the only material to be allowed for exterior walls in the city. The rule remains in effect until today, with its building specifications[8] being lifted only for a short time in the 1930s after a stonecutters' strike. The strike paved the way for few modernist buildings to emerge, especially briefly in the 1950s with the rush to build subsidized housing for the new Jewish immigrants. Storr's rule may be the most important single act of city planning ever in Jerusalem.[9] Later on, and as part of the attempt by Israeli architects to search for their own identity, they introduced clusters and broken masses that engaged more with stone cladding, also incorporating elements of traditional Palestinian village-like forms,[10] as can be seen in the new Jewish suburbs in Jerusalem such as Yemin Moshe, Ladbroke Development, David's Village, etc.

Today the typical design specification is not only limited to stone cladding or to areas of Jerusalem;

4.9 Beit Wazan village. Courtesy of Riwaq Photo Archive.

in order to achieve a recognizable Israeli identity, the visual codes of Israeli identity have also become about the geometry of buildings, shape of roofs, window openings, courtyards, wells, massing, street illumination, housing typologies, alleyways, fences, quarries, phone networks, water, sewage and even designated green areas – to assure that the so-called 'perfect kingdom' is somehow 'rooted' to the land. Again, as Nitzan-Shiftan has revealed, this has created an internal paradox within Israeli architects who were unable to stay away from the Palestinian rural architecture, if not through form, then definitely through the use of the particular materiality of West Bank stone.

GOOD AESTHETIC TASTE MAY BE SEEN AS BAD POLITICAL JUDGMENT

The dilemma of shaping a 'national idiom' is still the main focal point within Israeli architecture. Even for architects who call self-consciously for Israel to divorce itself from the past,[11] stone remains a key ingredient for most of the new designs. Very recently, Frank Ghery contributed to Israeli architecture with his proposal for the 'Museum of Tolerance' in Jerusalem. The museum is designed as a combination between titanium cladding and a massive wall clad with stone to emphasize on the Israeli relation to the context. Maybe he was attempting to forge a 'national idiom' that combines the Middle Eastern with western character. The site is located – of all places – over a Muslim holy site. Since then, Ghery has had to step down from the plan to build the project after the protest of architects, human right activists and local citizens against the 'intolerant' approach of erasing Palestinian people and their memories from their own place.[12]

However, it is not only in Jerusalem, or even in Israel, that the quest for identity and the endless appetite for stone and specifically for what is called 'Jerusalem stone' – which is mainly the limestone from villages and cities around Jerusalem, Bethlehem, Hebron and Ramallah – has been used. All around the world, it seems to be a tactic to reflect and emphasize Jewish identity.

For example, Leyla Dawson in an article on Jewish identity in contemporary architecture noted:

> The various 'Jerusalem stones' are employed worldwide in Jewish buildings as a symbol of Jewish identity. It has been used this way in many Jewish Community Centers, including the one in San Jose, Costa Rica, in Hillel buildings such as the Columbia/Barnard Hillel building, in Jewish memorials including the Holocaust Memorial on Miami Beach, in many Jewish schools including the Charles E. Smith Jewish Day School in Rockville, Maryland and in numerous synagogues, including the 1901 Ades Synagogue in Aleppo, Syria and the new Jewish Chapel at the United States Naval Academy, in Annapolis, Maryland.[13]

This obsession with stone and other materials is also manifested in practical attempts to 'steal' existing architectural elements from deserted Palestinian historic centres to reuse it in Israeli areas. Having worked with Riwaq on the conservation and protection of historic buildings, I came across so many cases in the West Bank, where houses had been half-stripped of their tiles, ironwork and of course stone. Unfortunately, this phenomenon is becoming even more alarming today as some desperate Palestinian families in need become their own worst enemies, and find in this business a new source of income, albeit selling their history.

PALESTINIANS RECLAIMING THEIR LOST IDENTITY

For Palestinians, the use of stone has developed far more slowly, and has not been as a reminder of identity, since they never had the dilemma of proofing their roots or relation to the land. Rather, it has always been for them an image of wealth and resilience. Stone through history has thus been the main construction material used for traditional buildings in Palestinian cities and villages. It was used with simple carvings and decorations for the main facades to document ownership, or to 'protect' the house with engraves from the Quran (or Bible). However, some buildings took this to the extreme,

4.10   Shahwan House in Beit Jala.
Photographs by Mia Grondahl.
Courtesy of Riwaq Photo Archive.

4.11   A new stone-built mansion in Ramallah.
Photograph by Mia Grondahl. Courtesy of
Riwaq Photo Archive.

like the famous Shahwan family mansion in the town of Beit Jala, with its extraordinary carved facades.

This was a reflection of the western effect on Palestinian architecture, after to the migration of rich families to the west Palestinians brought back with them new styles to celebrate in stone. The story of the Shahwan house is best remembered because of the famous drunk stone sculptor who preferred to get a bottle of *arak* for every carved piece he makes. This passion for *arak* resulted in unique architecture with exaggerated carving of animals, people, and plants decorating every corner of the house, and which every Palestinian has talked about ever since.

To quote Diala Khasawneh, in her book on Memoirs Engraved in Stone: Palestinian urban mansions:

Sitting in the salon, we were told the story of Yacoub Rabba'a. Born in Beit Jala, he was the artist responsible for all the sculptures and the stone detail in the house. He may have also worked on the other houses in Beit Jala, Qaser Jasir in Beithlehem, and the Shahwan house in Jerusalem. Here the story of the house as it was narrated to me:

Rabba'a (drunk and totally broke): What would you like me to sculpt for you now?

Yaccoub: Nothing thank you. Do you realize we have over 2600 pieces of your work already?

Rabba'a scratching his head and trying to focus: Come on, another piece for your bedroom, huh?

Yacoub: No.

Rabba'a: (burp) Come on . . . a nice little statue.

Yacoub: Go carve me a monkey if you wish, just get off my back . . .

Up till today it is still fashionable and prestigious for Palestinian families to build with stone. This has gone so far to the degree that a city like Ramallah has been literally flattened to decorate its mansions and

4.12 Shaping and cutting new stone pieces to replace missing ones in Palestinian historic centres. Courtesy of Riwaq Photo Archive.

high-rise facades with stone cladding. The richer one becomes, the wider the marble columns, the better the stone carvings, textures and colour varieties on the exterior of the house as a manifestation of class difference and social status. This phenomenon is widespread in Turmos Ayya, Kufor Malek, Taybeh and many other villages, where many locals migrated to America and then came back with a probably confused identity and enough money to reflect their wealth and power into eternity.

THE WHITE GOLD: STRIPPING THE WEST BANK'S STONE

Roaming around the West Bank, one is struck by the amount of damage being caused to the environment and the cultural landscape of the region, especially near to the big cities of Ramallah, Bethlehem, Hebron, Nablus and Tulkarem. In this case I'm not referring to the physical boundaries of concrete walls and checkpoints, or to the construction of high-rise

building in historic centres, or to the illegal Israeli settlements occupying the top of the hills. What I'm talking about are the sudden cuts one sees in the landscape of olive terraces whereby whole mountains and hills are being completely flattened to create formal and informal clusters of stone quarries. The Bani n'eem area near to Hebron, Aseera near to Nablus, Birzeit, Kalandia, Jaba' and Rafat near to Ramallah, and Beit Fajjar in Bethlehem region, are all suffering extensive topographic change as well as environmental consequences.

Historically, the number of stone quarries in the West Bank was relatively well balanced to the needs of the area over the years, with just a few known Palestinian family-run enterprises. This started to change from 1991, when Israel began using the West Bank to quarry stone to meet its building and financial needs in and outside Israel.

Beit Fajjar, as noted a village close to Bethlehem, has earned a reputation for the best stone in the West Bank. It is estimated that out of the 650 stone-cutting enterprises set up in the West Bank by 2000, producing a rich range of pink, sand, golden and off-white stone, Beit Fajjar by itself has 138 stone production outlets.[14] Business was run for hundreds of years in the village, and the old workers tell stories of their grandfathers transporting stone from the quarries around Bethlehem and Hebron to Beit Fajjar on camel back. Unfortunately, the stonecutters which produced the major quantities to serve Israeli areas in the last decade are facing a crisis. Today, the entrance of the village is a mound of white stones leftovers. The economy of the village, which has been home to so many stone workers throughout the years, is now deteriorating. Prices of stone are completely unregulated, sometimes forcing

sellers to offer their goods below cost just to close a deal.

This is because the stone business today has been taken over by the Israeli quarries who themselves are confiscating lands and initiating new outlets inside the West Bank area.[15] In a report published by the *Palestine-Israel Journal*, it is estimated that Israel has confiscated an area of at least 18,700 dunums in the West Bank to construct seven quarries in various locations.

> The largest is the Wadi Al-Teen quarry in the Tulkarem district, on an area of 9,685 dunums. Wadi Al-Teen represents an important natural grazing area, which supports many livestock farmers in neighboring Palestinian villages. It also serves as the main catchment area for runoff rainwater.[16]

These new Israeli-run quarries represent a systematic pirating of Palestinians' natural resources and the destruction of their environment.[17] It is also a clear contravention of human rights regulations and the 1907 International Hague Convention rule, which states clearly that any occupier is not allowed to exploit any of the natural resources of the occupied country, and that any gain obtained from their exploitation must be kept in a designated fund for the local population.[18] Add to this the economic exploitation, which Israel is enforcing on Palestine, depriving Palestinians from importing, exporting, or even benefiting from their own resources. Agriculture, water, electricity, even dumpsites, are all controlled by Israelis and sold back to Palestinians at double the price. Stone is now becoming the worst case:

> It is estimated that 12 million tons; a fifth of the gravels used for building in Israel each year, comes from the West Bank.[19]

This whole situation with quarries and stone cutting has been kept in the dark until very recently, indeed until March 2009, when an Israeli human rights organization, Yesh Din, took the Israeli military, Israeli civil administration and a number of Israeli mining companies to court for breaking international laws.[20] The human rights group alleges they are illegally stripping Palestinian West Bank quarries of raw construction material for the benefit of Israeli.

4.13 Stone quarry on the edge of Ramallah and Jerusalem expanding towards the Israeli settlement of Kohav Yakov.

Yesh Din also accused ten Israeli mining companies located in the West Bank area of:

> illegal practice of brutal economic exploitation of a conquered territory to serve the exclusive economic needs of the occupying power that bluntly and directly violates basic principles of customary international law . . . Israel is transferring natural resources from the West Bank for Israeli benefit, and this is absolutely prohibited not only under international law but according to Israeli Supreme Court rulings . . . this is an illegal transfer of land in the most literal of senses.[21]

However, the danger doesn't even stop there; it becomes the mystery of what follows next. According to the report by Yesh Din, there has also been an Israeli government study in 2008, which predicted that a serious shortage of raw building materials will occur within a decade in the West Bank, due to the rate of extraction, since three quarters of what is quarried in the West Bank goes directly to Israel. The remainder is bought by Palestinians on the open market at a higher price.[22]

This form of exploitation of resources might be different to other countries, nevertheless the essence is the same, and especially once a full market economy arrives in a country like Palestine/Israel. If one skims through the region's political map today, the formula is quite clear – indeed it compliments what is going on in Iraq and the Middle East since the American invasion.[23] The war on Iraq was always about oil; a clear exploitation of the country's 'black gold'. Within the common justified slogans of 'democracy, axis of evil and terrorism', only 'them' in the west can turn a blind eye towards human rights and do what they want to root themselves deeper in the land.

It is really a surprise that the outcome of the Iraq war lead to oil pipes plans running directly to Israel through Jordan? It is also no surprise to know that USA has played a smart game by appointing a new Iraqi government to find a way around the Hague Convention rules. According to a report by Kryss Tal,[24] the USA began talks in May 2003 with the USA-backed Iraq National Congress to build an oil pipeline between Iraq and Israel. James Atkins (a former US ambassador to Saudi Arabia) declared

> There would be a fee for transit rights through Jordan, just as there would be fees for those using what would be the Haifa terminal. After all this is the new world order now. This is what things look like particularly if we wipe out Syria. It just goes to show that this is all about oil, for the United States and its allies.[25]

According to Tal's report, the plan was originally put forward by Henry Kissinger back in 1975 and was revived later by another American conservative, Donald Rumsfeld. The favoured company to build the pipeline is Bechtel, one of the supporters and contributors to the Republican Party and of course of ex-President George W. Bush.

On 19 September 2003, the US administrator for Iraq, Paul Bremer, enacted a new law called 'Order 39'. This allowed the privatisation of 200 state industries including electricity, telecommunications and engineering. This law also enabled foreign companies to take full ownership of banks, mines and factories, with taxes reduced from 45 percent to 15 percent. Companies or individuals are now allowed to lease land in Iraq for 40 years. Again, all these changes were in violation of Iraq's

4.14 Lunch break for Palestinian workers in an Israeli quarry in the Jordan Valley. There are no services or forms of shading available in a hot climate that can reach up to 38 degrees in summer.

constitution as well as the Hague Convention, as an occupying country must respect 'the laws in force in the country' and 'shall be regarded only as an administrator'. But in reality the changes mean that profits from Iraq's resources will go the USA companies. Just a few weeks ago, in August 2010, president Barack Obama declared that American troops would get out of Iraq, leaving only few thousands behind, to look after the companies. Is the Iraqi occupation really over, or has the mission simply changed face?

Given these neo-imperialist American tactics in the region, what will happen to the Palestinian landscape? Are the Palestinians going to poison the well they are drinking from? In ten years' time will they find an alienated land completely flattened by the hands of the Palestinian workforce? Some of the richer Palestinians might do, especially those in power who are already benefitting from the so-called 'economic Peace',[26] but certainly not the Palestinian quarry workers who are being ruthlessly exploited.

Recently, 42 Palestinian workers broke through the climate of fear to report their exploitation by Israeli companies quarrying in the West Bank. One of the quarries that is located near to the illegal Israeli settlement of Ma'ale Adumim employs Palestinians from both East Jerusalem and the West Bank. Given the West Bank ID holders have no residency status in Israel they only receive minimum wages in cash, with no records of their employment. They also have no health insurance or safety measures, and are subject to sudden redundancy any minute. The Jerusalem-based residents are not in any better condition apart from the fact that they receive vague pay slips yet, they also have no rights and only with minimum facilities.

In a report by *Challenge* magazine, one of these labourers, M.V., who has been working in the quarry for more than a decade, described the conditions to the Workers Advice Center (WAC):

> There is no town nearby. There are big tractors and trucks, there are machines for the dirt and gravel, and there's the asphalt plant. All this takes place in the desert heat. There is always dust in the air, a great deal of noise and filth. After 24 years the quarry still lacks restroom facilities for us. There is no room to eat in. We only have cold water because we pooled money and bought a fridge.[27]

According to the reporter, the quarry management was shown the report but there has not been much change to the condition of the workers apart from a letter received stating that they will start building a dining room and toilets. The employers however, have still not take any steps to protect workers from the stone dust, which can cause asthma and cancer, even though government regulations state that workers must be provided with protection and regular inspections carried out to determine the amount of dust in the air.[28]

This situation typifies what more than 20,000 Palestinian workers have been going through over the last decade. Not only they don't have any legal status or rights to protect them while working; now with the ongoing quarry closures, lack of permits to work inside Israel, and the Separation Wall going up, they also have to risk their lives to sneak through from one place to the other. The lack of job opportunities on the Palestinian side forces them to accept almost anything in the Israeli side, meaning minimum wages as low as $9 a day.[29]

The issue of stone quarrying has become even more charged today, as not only is the Israeli government bringing in firms from Israel to work in West Bank, they are also obstructing Palestinians from working their own quarries by denying them permits to cut stone or even to export. Most Palestinian quarry owners are now facing difficulties and mobility restrictions themselves, which is causing massive losses for their businesses and forcing the small businesses to close down. According to the Palestinian Marble and Stone Industry records for 2005:

> Before the intensified closure policy in 2000, stone used to be the key backbone of Palestinian economy. Palestine used to contribute 4% of the world's total stone production making it the 12th largest stone producer in the world, double the production of Germany and almost half the production of Turkey.[30]

KALANDIA QUARRY: 'TORA BORA' ROUTE

Heat, wind, dust, garbage. Cars stuck in line, jammed bumper to bumper – probably a two-hour wait. I squeeze through the few inches between an articulated lorry and the next car. On the other side is a porter shifting two television sets tied to his cart weaving in between the oncoming traffic . . . Up through the first set of blocks, the wind blows up white dust from the quarry; the peddlers clutch their sun umbrellas. I pick up my pace, as it's rush hour. Through the second row of blocks and I can see the crowd up ahead, spilling out from under the zinc roof and concrete pens of the crossing. I reach them and ask an old man, how long he's been waiting: 'From the time I was born' . . .[31]

My first encounter with this quarry culture was not really related to stone in particular, but in fact came about due to my journeys around the West Bank when Palestine was all about checkpoints and roadblocks. At that time, Palestinians were banned from entering Jerusalem from Ramallah and vice versa, so the only way out was through Kalandia quarry, or what we call in Arabic *kassarat*. As mentioned in earlier chapters, the owners of the quarry allowed Palestinians to cross through, since it was the only invisible route able to bridge us to the other side of our small world in the West Bank. The artificial topography caused by the stone quarrying has also contributed towards people's creativity. The so-called 'Tora Bora' route that crossed Kalandia was named after the quarry's dramatic landscape, which by time has created a similar image to what one sees in hilly Afghanistan. The image was not the only issue associated with the route; there was also the experience of walking through the 'unpredictable' routes that which commuters had to use in the no-drive zone until they reach the shared taxis to be picked up to the different parts of the West Bank. The dusty walk in summer or the muddy walk in winter, took about 15 minutes up a steep hill and a large pile of rubble to overcome, as well as possible Israeli snipers to avoid.

PALESTINIANS CARVING THEIR OWN LAND

The appetite for stone and cultural identity underneath the land has thus very much influenced the re-organization of the surface by both Palestinian and Israelis. Palestinians have started looking at their landscape as a viable source of economic income, even if it is for a small-scale quarrying business. Ghaleb – a farmer that I met, and an owner of a land near Tulkarem – has initiated his own small manual quarry as a way to get around the blockade. Ever since he became unable to reach his farm behind the wall, he made use of his wife's bare rocky land, a new potential for business emerging from cutting and selling stone.

> When my wife inherited this piece of land, we were so disappointed as it has no potential for agriculture. Today, after 15 years, we bless every millimetre of it; we are not only inheriting the surface, we can go as deep down as we want, and so our new business has no limits anymore.[32]

Roaming around the West Bank today, one can observe all of these sudden tiny cuts in the land due to small quarries.

Unfortunately, stone is becoming Palestinian's own worst enemy. What is particularly dangerous is the contribution of Palestinian capitalism to destroying the land under the slogan of 'soaring demand of Palestinian economy'. Palestinian containers are also carrying thousands of square metres of stone all over the world with no process of control or records of what goes where. The land is literally being sold off beneath them.

The stone business – for those who can afford the shipping costs through Israeli ports – has even quietly managed to expand to reach the UK, America and

4.15   Kalandia stone quarry.

4.16   A small quarry business opposite the
village of Jibya, 2008.

4.17   Jaba' stone quarry.

Europe. Mohammad, a Palestinian entrepreneur and one of the quarry owners in Palestine, is now moving tones of stone containers to Sunderland. His market targets anyone interested in buying some of the stone of the 'Holy Land', regardless of their politics or background, just as long as his business runs smoothly.[33]

PRACTICING ARCHAEOLOGY

Israel has clearly lost any innocence when it comes to archaeology. Practicing archeology has become just another form of Israeli desperation to legitimize their existence and prove its sovereignty, borders and political existence in the land. This practice – currently going on in parallel with stone cutting – is overshadowed by obvious political motives which aim to ideologically re-read and re-write history to support the cause of the Zionist state. The policy is very much based on exposing facts that can be seen to deepen the roots of the state ancestral land, while also ignoring or erasing anything that might not be in line with the Israeli state's aims.

Thus one finds Israeli historians playing with archaeology as a new form of cultural representation, emphasizing certain periods and exploiting or erasing others. The Bronze and Iron Age sites, the Second

4.18 Stone pieces displayed at the entrance of Hebron for sale.

4.19 Israeli-run quarry on the edges of Ramallah.

4.20 Quarry located in the Jordan Valley.

4.21 Jama'een village near to Nablus is known internationally for its local stone. The village has 70 stone quarries scattered over its land, causing a major environmental problem for the 20,000 residents.

Temple ruins and Crusader archaeology are well maintained and presented as national sites to Jewish people, as they are seen as links to the ancestral past. However, any upper layer that might be to do with Palestinian, Muslim or Ottoman patrimony is dismissed, either to be erased, or to be built over.[34] Taking the Haram Al Sharif – the famous religious site in East Jerusalem – as an example, the official Israeli history has always ignored any Muslim layers affiliated to the site. Consequently, countless excavations have caused important sites as well as artifacts to be destroyed and removed in the West Bank and the Gaza Strip. Jerusalem – both east and west – is currently going through an intensive

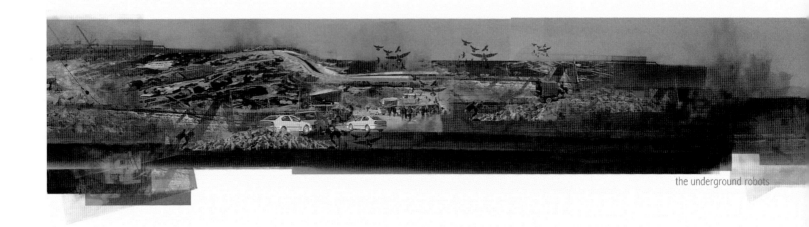

the underground robots

4.22 The Underground Robots.

process of cultural cleansing under the name of reconstruction or heritage protection, as has been well recorded in the press.

On many occasions what is believed to exist under the surface erupts above the surface through new projects for settlements or physical boundaries that unwrap what is hiding underneath. Tal Rumeida in Hebron is one such manifestation; it is built over what is believed to be the 'City of David'. Ironically the excavated zones in most cases happen to be located in Palestinian built-up areas. This automatically ends any possibility for Palestinians to expand or even live there, while giving all possibilities for Israelis to occupy the land under the slogan of 'archeological excavations'. Archeological sites are thus just another way of claiming the surface of the land.

The above point is best expressed by Robert Bevan, author of *The Destruction of Memory: Architecture at War*, who wrote about cultural cleansing in modern history. This very much represents the political forces at work in the case of Israel, even though Bevan was not referring to that context specifically:

> The first step in liquidating a people is to erase its memory. Destroy its books, its culture, and its history. Then you have somebody write new books, manufacture a new culture, invent a new history. Before long the nation will begin to forget what it is and what it was.

Abu El Haj,[35] in her 2001 book *Facts on the Ground: Archaeological Practice and Territorial Self-Fashioning in Israeli Society*, caused a radical shake up when she

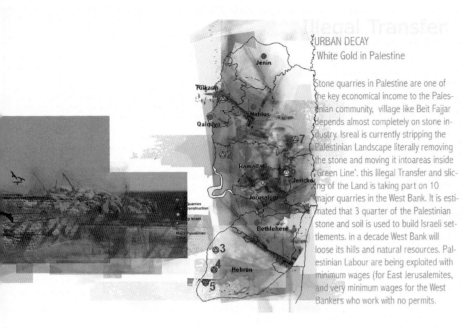

Illegal Transfer

URBAN DECAY
White Gold in Palestine

Stone quarries in Palestine are one of the key economical income to the Pales-inian community, village like Beit Fajjar depends almost completely on stone in-dustry. Isreal is currently stripping the Palestinian Landscape literally removing the stone and moving it intoareas inside 'Green Line'. this Illegal Transfer and slic-ng of the Land is taking part on 10 major quarries in the West Bank. It is esti-mated that 3 quarter of the Palestinian stone and soil is used to build Israeli set-tlements. in a decade West Bank will loose its hills and natural resources. Pal-estinian Labour are being exploited with minimum wages (for East Jerusalemites, and very minimum wages for the West Bankers who work with no permits.

shed new light on the subject of politically motivated archaeology, and how material remains have been furnished with tendentious national and ethnic meanings in the case of the Zionist state. She zoomed in Israeli strategies of using 'scientific' methods as means to exploit and erase history. Abu El Haj showed how bulldozers in Israeli excavations were used to get deep down to the earlier strata to assure their national significance as quickly as possible in areas like Jerzeem and Al-Haram such that they became the ultimate sign of bad science.[36]

Prior to his death, Edward Said reflected on the work of Abu El Haj in his book on *Freud and the Non-European* (2003):

What she provides first of all is a history of systematic colonial archaeological exploration in Palestine, dating back to British work in the mid-nineteenth century. She then continues the story in the period before Israel is established, connecting the actual practice of archaeology with a nascent national ideology – an ideology with plans for the repossession of the land through renaming and resettling, much of it given archeological justification as a schematic extraction of Jewish identity despite the existence of Arab names and traces of other civilizations. This effort, she argues convincingly, epistemologically prepares the way for a fully fledged post-1948 sense of Israeli-Jewish identity based on assembling discrete archaeological particulars – scattered remnants of masonry, tablets, bones, tombs . . .[37]

Meron Benvenisti has also commented:

Israeli historians, geographers and archaeologists did not have a difficult job in sanitizing the landscape and ridding it of the identity of its former inhabitants because the British authorities had be quested to them a valuable legacy: the definition of 'antiquity' as 'any construction or any product of human activity before the year 1700 AD' . . . it reflects the view prevalent in Britain during the twenties, according to which an object was considered an antiquity only if it had been produced before the death of Queen Anne in 1714.

Meanwhile, new thinking had evolved in Britain regarding the question of when the 'past' ends. The conclusion reached was 'that the past continues right up to the present', and thus all human activity that found expression in the creation of physical objects was entitled to respectful treatment.[38]

This political use of archaeology leaves no choice but to rethink all of these underground narratives compressed by sand and stone. The underground seems to be suffocated; just as the surface is now exhausted with physical boundaries, underground cuts are disturbing the sequence of logic. What is below is no longer older than what is above; archaeology in Palestine/Israel is becoming again a state of superimposition of history and identity, a state of conflict between past, present and future. Critics of the Israeli policies have referred to archaeology in Israel as being pressed into the service of the present, while the excavated stone is being pressed to serve the longer-term interests of the future.[39]

With this rearrangement of the underground layers built up of stone, soil, and archaeological traces, one wonders what Israeli archeology will be doing in ten years' time? Will we ever live to see the British antiquity law 'enforced' today, recognizing what is left to rot below? If not, then maybe it is time for the Palestinians to rethink their sub-terrain through new invisible layers, injected and superimposed, over and between the past and the present to reclaim their lost identity. After all, archaeology is not a reflection of the past and the way people lived based on the things they left behind. In the case of Palestine, it is also a reflection of the chaotic rebirth, or indeed reinvention of the present.

The danger arises when archaeology is called upon to resolve such issues. But what if one looks through the cuts and can no longer recognize the features of the land? The scars will always remain, and it is then an ethical decision to decide how to heal the landscape without distorting facts. It is all about confrontation with one's own identity.

TROUBLED WATER

The inequality in access to water between Israelis and Palestinians is striking. Palestinian consumption in the OPT is about 70 litres a day per person – well below the 100 litres per capita daily recommended by the World Health Organization (WHO) – whereas Israeli daily per capita consumption, at about 300 litres, is about four times as much. In some rural communities Palestinians survive on far less than even the average 70 litres, in some cases barely 20 litres per day, the minimum amount recommended by the WHO for emergency situations response (Report by Amnesty International).[40]

SETTING[41]

As previously mentioned, the location of the West Bank in the central highlands of Palestine, with its unique topography of slopes, mountains and valleys has determined throughout history the location of the main Palestinian cities and villages around water extraction points. Even though the main sources available for water in Palestine/Israel are the Jordan River, and the groundwater aquifer centralized in the West Bank and the coastal areas, about 80 percent of the region's water supply is actually located under the surface of the West Bank. The water cycle in the region is caused by the evaporation of water off the surface of the Mediterranean Sea, which is condensed in the form of clouds driven by the eastern winds towards the central highlands. The clouds then break against the mountain peaks, with heavy rain picked up by the valleys. The rainfall runs back again through the western slopes in streams through the coastal planes into the sea again. Some rainfall infiltrates through the soil and the porous limestone rock to refill the ground aquifers, recharging the impenetrable sedimentary layers.

The natural outlets of the water sources are the springs, which have recently also determined the location of the Israeli illegal settlements and military zones. The path of the Apartheid Wall has captured within its boundaries over 60 water

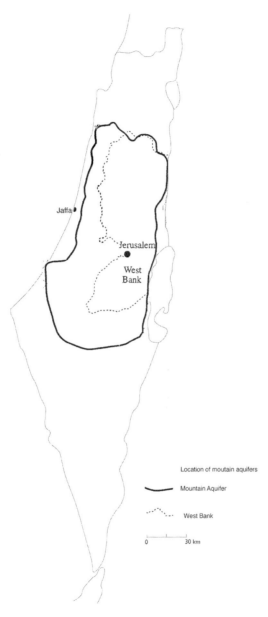

4.23   Location of mountain aquifers.

Location of mountain aquifers

——— Mountain Aquifer

······· West Bank

0   30 km

springs, and thereby assured the penetration of the rest of the water resources through its drainage system of pipes, tunnels and gullies to benefit the Israeli side.[42]

LEFTOVERS FROM 'OSLO 2'

Israel has enforced full control over Palestinian water ever since its military occupation, depriving Palestinians from benefitting from their own natural resources. This was manifested by restrictions on drilling any new wells, or even taking water from existing wells – if not closing them or destroying them completely. In a report published by B'tselem (The Israeli Information Center for Human Rights in the Occupied Territories), Palestinians were allowed to dig only 13 wells between 1967 and 1996. This is far less than the number of wells which dried up during the same period due to Israel's refusal to deepen or rehabilitate existing wells.[43] The lands close by the Jordan River were also declared as closed military zones, meaning that farmers were deprived from irrigating their agricultural lands. Moreover, some water springs were also considered to be natural reserves with limited use that required a complex system of permissions and fees.[44] Today, the 450,000 or so Israeli settlers, who live in the West Bank, use as much or more water than the Palestinian population of some 2.3 million.[45]

Unfortunately, the interim agreement that Israel and the Palestinian Authority signed in September 1995, known as 'Oslo 2', gave Israel total control over the Palestinian natural resources, and most importantly, water. The Oslo Accord process has thus singularly failed again to provide equal water shares for Palestinians and Israelis. Moreover, it prevented the Gaza Strip from benefiting from water resources in the West Bank, which means a complete dependence on limited aquifers below the average needs of the Gazans – leaving it perennially short of water.[46]

According to B'tselem, even though the accord initiated a joint water committee (JWC) by Palestinians and Israelis – which sounds very convincing at first glance – Israel was still able to veto any Palestinian request to drill wells or obtain additional waters. However, Jewish settlements have been given full access to pumping wells, which do not require any permission from the JWC. Consequently, this means that Israeli settlers now utilize six times more water than Palestinians in the West Bank.[47]

Regardless of who owns the surface of the land, Israeli politicians believe that Israel future depends on its water resources.[48] Although these aquifers are the only source of water for the residents of the West Bank, Israel uses over 83 percent to benefit Israeli cities and settlements, while the Palestinians in the West Bank use the remaining 17 percent.[49] The result means that hundreds of thousands of Palestinians in the West Bank and almost all in Gaza Strip receive only a limited amount of water, irregularly.

In practical terms – taking my own family as an example – this literally means that water is constantly cut off, and thus all the daily activities of any Palestinian family has to be calculated carefully to ensure that washing can take place one day a week for each neighbourhood (Tuesday is the day allocated for our area, while house cleaning and gardening are only on Fridays). The rest of the lucky times where we get water we have to fill it into emergency tanks for the 'dry' days, while watching the Israeli settlers washing their cars, irrigating their gardens and filling up their swimming pools. Some villages, which often suffer total cuts, have to find alternative water

sources, so they end up buying expensive water from tankers.

In an ironic comment by one of the Palestinian residents living opposite an Israeli settlement, he declared:

> the water in Ariel Settlement is never cut off. We feel lucky because we look out onto beautiful settlement houses with green yards, while Israeli settlers view the gloomy scene of our poor, parched community.[50]

Israeli policies of occupation and control in this aspect are again related to the depth of the land. While Israeli water pumps are allowed to go as deep down as they can, Palestinians are restricted to shallow layers nearer the surface. This offers a state of *déjà vu*, from the Irish/British colonial conflict that led to the 'Potato Famine'; it was not that there was no food available; it was just that the Irish were deprived of it. Equally in the case of Palestine/Israel, it is not that there is no water, it is just that Palestinians are deprived of it.

Using the topography of the land as routes to divide and control, has worked in most cases for the benefit of the Israelis. Yet, it has also allowed the 'anonymous daily heroes' to use it as a tactic to penetrate through the tunnels and pipes (as the case around the separation wall). However, the danger is when the liquids are flowing at their maximum, with sewage joining water, as will be explained later.

It is clear that the struggle between Palestine and Israel has never been about culture, or religion; it has always been about the land and its every little detail, with water playing a central role. However, what the Palestinians are calling for today is no longer just a right; it is an urgent crisis and a need to survive. Human intervention in the natural water cycle has exceeded such limits that Palestinians can no longer capture water in its liquid state; the moment it touches the surface of the land it disappears in the darkness of the underground tunnels, to be controlled by Israeli companies. Maybe the only way out is to let it evaporate; only then it is able to fly in the eastern winds back to the central highlands crossing all boundaries. Hopefully it can be captured equally one day, or at least maybe one could capture as much as possible on the rainfall's invisible journey of disappearance into the underground layers.

SEWAGE

In my visit to Palestine in July 2010, I visited a village called Hajja in the north of the West Bank, near to the city of Qalqilyah. The journey was memorable as I accompanied one of the Ford van drivers whose common nickname is 'Superman', given he is known for driving through difficult sites while avoiding the intricacy of roadblocks and checkpoints. Ashraf started his career as a Ford van driver in 2000 after becoming unemployed as a construction worker in Israel, joining the network of the informal drivers who are bridging Palestine together. His journey route was one of the extreme beauty traveling through a landscape of olive groves, pomegranates and figs. The journey started by crossing Birzeit, Atara, the natural park of Umm Safa, passing by Nabi Saleh, which became known on the map since the construction of an iron gate by Israel to block all villages of the north from entering Ramallah. From Nabi Saleh we descended down the no-drive zone through the valleys towards Wadi Qana. We passed by Deir al Sudan, Arura, Mazare Al Nobani,

Bruqeen, and Qarawat Bani Zeid to face afterwards the industrial zone and the complex road network of Ariel settlement, before crossing to Hajja on the other side of the military area.[51]

DESCENDING BELOW SURFACE

The journey down these valleys and groves was so uplifting as one could feel that the landscape of Palestine with its *wadis*, springs, cliffs and ancient ruins is not vanishing completely – apart from the Israeli settlements' sprawl on top of the hills. We did not mind the two-hour labyrinthine drive across the fields. The play of light and shadows on the terraced landscape showed they are relatively unspoiled, yet the journey conceals stories to be explored and witnessed below the surface of the land. The names of the Palestinian villages on the road signs were crossed out with black paint to be replaced with Hebrew names by the illegal settlers. The deeper we went down the valley, the more tragic such stories become.

Bruqeen, Kufr al-Dik and Qarawat Bani Zeid, were once known for their natural treasures of water springs stretching along the olive groves. As in the rest of Palestine, every *wadi*, spring, hillock and cliff has a name. Some are Arabic, others are Canaanite or Aramaic, and these names are usually an indication to how the land was inhabited, with key characters associated with the formation of the land.[52] Today, their beauty has become a curse, just like the rest of the 'blessed biblical land' that everyone seems to be after; the main seven wells and springs are no longer living wells. They have become deserted due to the force of military rule, if not destroyed by Israeli settlers who make sure they 'visit' from time to time. As is the case in so many villages, Palestinian land is currently becoming a dumping ground for illegal Israeli settlements, causing severe damage to ground water resources and the general environment in the West Bank. Sewage pipes and networks are being used again to penetrate through the impossible boundaries, as a strategic tool infiltrate, dislocate and occupy Palestinian land.

The location of the Ariel settlement on top of the hills, combined with the topography of the *wadi*, guarantee that of all the sewage and untreated waste water must pass down the valley towards the Bruqeen, Kufr al-Dik and Salfeet area, contaminating the springs and other sources of fresh water used by Palestinians. In addition to the purposely-redirected sewage dumping caused by settlers, other kinds of toxic hazardous waste – which they find much cheaper to dump at Palestinian side than processing inside Israel – are currently causing great threat to human lives and the natural environment. In fact, what is left from the landscape that is not yet vanishing is being eaten out from below; the land is going through a process of slow death.

In a conversation with a farmer from Bruqeen about his situation he remarked:

> I'd rather join the workers sneaking to Israel, as my crops are all infected because of sewage and the lack of clean water. We can't dig wells, so we have the surface only, and our surface is Ariel sewage in which we daily inhale, drink, and eat . . .

The head of the village council of Hajja, has also expressed his frustration about these sewage, water and electricity problems. Being close to settlement areas, the villagers are blackmailed daily by the Israeli authorities; any water or electricity services to be activated for their village is conditional on allowing new networks of infrastructure serving the Israeli settlements to pass through their lands, otherwise they will be cut off from water and electricity. Not only locals, but also NGOs suffer when trying to provide services to Palestinian areas. According to *Eco Peace* and *Friends of the Earth Middle East*, Israel's approval for internationally funded sewage and water projects is made conditional on extending these services to the illegal Israeli settlements. Of course, this is rejected by both Palestinians and donors, which leads either to the delay or cancelation of projects.[53]

> it is hard to monitor the numerous dumping sites used by Israel because the dumping is done both overtly and covertly, sometimes during the night. The locations used vary, and the Israelis cover up the sites afterwards.[54]

In places like Shuqba, Salfit, Broqeen, Kufr al-Dik – as well as areas in the Gaza Strip – Palestinian built-up areas are drowning with sewage mixed with water in their pumping stations, threatening their water supply and agricultural lands. 300 pirate-dumping sites are where truckloads of sewage were dumped by Israeli settlers into the valleys in the absence of any infrastructure, even though it is a legal duty of the occupying force to manage sewage. Israeli companies have also used sites in West Bank to dump Israeli sewage from Tel Aviv area, especially in the large disused quarries near to Nablus.[55]

To quote Fareed Taamallah:

> According to the Applied Research Institute of Jerusalem, 80 factories from Ariel's Burkan industrial zone discharge 0.81 million cubic meters of wastewater per year into nearby valleys. All this wastewater and the sewage have formed a river through the agricultural lands of the villages of Kufr al-Dik and

4.24   Raw sewage from the
Israeli settlement of Ariel polluting Bruqeen
village and the natural springs in the area
around Wadi Qana.

Bruqin. These poisonous streams have led to the death and ruin of trees and crops located in their immediate vicinity.[56]

However, the Separation Wall, just as it cannot block water from penetrating underground towards Israel, it also can't block the sewage from reaching the western side. Palestinian sewage – which is not managed by the Palestinian Authority due to the lack of financial resources – becomes mixed with the settlements' sewage; following the contours towards the Israeli side. The fortified wall, which was made to separate, is currently working as a bridge that carries the sewage through purposely-installed water pipes, trapping all the solid waste and raw material around the wall.[57] Only because of these circumstances, Israel has decided to release some of the money allocated for the Palestinian Authority to install sewage system, especially in areas around Jerusalem to avoid diseases, which are not familiar with the concept of boundaries, ethnicity, or even the 1967 division line.

THE MUDDY ROUTE

The two villages of Beit Hanina are separated by the Separation Wall, which annexed one side to Israel and the other to the West Bank.[58] Not only Ramallah and the northern cities and villages are separated from Jerusalem by the wall, but locals are also separated from their families. Marian, an old university friend who lives in Beit Hanina and works in Ramallah, found herself one day living on the other side of the wall from her parents just opposite. Her only way through to them since 2004 has been the sewage pipes:

> I moved opposite my parents so they can baby-sit my kids. After the wall was erected, we were in a state of shock; not only couldn't I see my parents, but I'm now considered to live in the West Bank side and my Jerusalem identity card will be lost. Ever since the wall came, I use a ladder to get my children to my mum every morning, and in the evenings, I take them through the sewage tunnel back home.

These anonymous daily commuters from Ramallah to Jerusalem, are thus still penetrating through the Separation Wall; they have found in pipes and sewage runs another method of bridging which is far more easier to use for women and children than jumping or squeezing through narrow gaps. All it takes is a plastic bag to wrap around oneself:

> Ordinary women and men, wearing plastic bags on their feet, pulling their pants up to knee level, clutch their children to their chests and roam along a 110-metre dark tunnel of sewage to cross from the Israeli-occupied West Bank to East Jerusalem.[59]

Such tunnels are still operating, even though every now and then they are blocked. The phenomenon has multiplied all along the separation wall wherever a sewage or water pipe is connected. In Beit Hanina, it is estimated that 150 people cross these every day, even when the Israeli blocked off the passage with rocks; what is referred to as 'tunnel operators' ensure that commuters squeeze through the gaps.

Indeed, the land in the West Bank, which has been pulled apart with sharp contours on the map, is thus being 'stitched' together by sewage and dirt, which has deconstructed and redefined the meaning of boundaries as well as of bridging. Hopefully, with the Israeli phobia from sewage the wall will be torn apart rather than solidified, given that it is proving

4.25 Commuters crossing the
sewage pipes from Ramallah to Jerusalem.

to be so porous regardless of its visible height above the ground.

TIME FOR A CULTURAL WAR

In the course of living in Palestine and working on my research, I have come to realize just how much history is traded, faked and distorted. The surface and the sub-surface are now left with physical and virtual gaps resulting from fear and denial; if left to expand, the land will eventually collapse. Palestinians have been watching their land changing contours, shadows and colours to match the views, dreams and aspirations of those Israelis who have occupied it. Indeed, long ago the western imagination made it one of the most visited lands for pilgrims, travellers as well as occupiers over the centuries. The description of the land in books, images and maps was never familiar to the Palestinians who actually inhabited it, rather it was the imagination of those who wrote and reinvented it. As Shehadeh in his book on *Palestinian*

137

Walks reveals, the very people who cultivate the green olive orchards and render the landscape biblical are themselves excluded from the panorama:

> the long tradition of Western travelers and colonizers who simply would not see the land's Palestinian population. When they spared a glance it was to regard the Palestinians with prejudice and derision, as a distraction from the land of their imagination.[60]

Today, this tradition is taken further by the Israeli occupation through more peeling, erasing and inserting. Maps are still being distorted on the surface while history is being reinvented from the deep layers underneath. The story beneath the folded skin of the land cannot thus be told or imagined without reflecting what is going on the surface – not only in terms of settlements, borders or military occupation, or the land grab, but also in mind of how much the anonymous daily heroes of Palestine face this with the persistence to go on. What the underground struggle is obstructing is really the right to live in dignity, stripping all human rights from the Palestinian people, that the struggle is now reflecting itself in everyday practices. However, the danger only really occurs when inequality is normalized in people's minds.

Unlike the politics of verticality of the Israeli occupation described by Weizman,[61] the Palestinian counter-verticality is not a strategic one; it is a tactical form accumulated from the need to survive. What is needed today is thus to transfer the underground conditions into a strategy to resist. It is time for Palestinians to fill in the gaps, inject them with new overlapping layers that stitch and connect. After all, the potentials in Palestine seem to be lying just where the scar is created, in its gaps and leftover spaces. Hence, the elements of decay below the surface are themselves producing spaces of possibility with stone, sewage, and water working together as boundaries and bridges to otherwise seemingly impossible space

I'll end this section with Abu Youssef's story. He has been working in Israel for over 28 years as a construction worker, and lately has had to become part of the invisible illegal workers who sneak to Israel to look for job opportunities. In a conversation with Suad Amiry, when she asked him about his feelings about constructing Israeli settlements, he insisted that he has reached a stage far beyond being questioned or lectured as to whether this is right or wrong, in that he has no other choice. Nevertheless, he lives in a paradoxical situation:

> Listen, when I am in a bad mood, and I am sitting on that construction site, I say: 'Al 'arsaat! This occupation will never end. They keep taking more land and building more settlements. We will never have a peace with these 'arsaat'. These bastards! So in a day like that, when I am in a bad mood, I decide: 'Okay, I'm gonna put less portion of cement in the concrete mixture'. But sometimes, when I'm in a good mood, I think: 'All occupations in this world have ended, and Palestine cannot be any different. And these settlements will become Arab's, and most probably will become for the refugees and poor people like me'. And that day I say: 'Y'allah ya walad! Put in more cement!'[62]

Meanwhile, what is urgently needed in Palestine today is a continuous questioning of the situation in order to find out how Palestinians can reclaim their vanishing cultural identity in a few years' time. What will be left over on the surface and underground

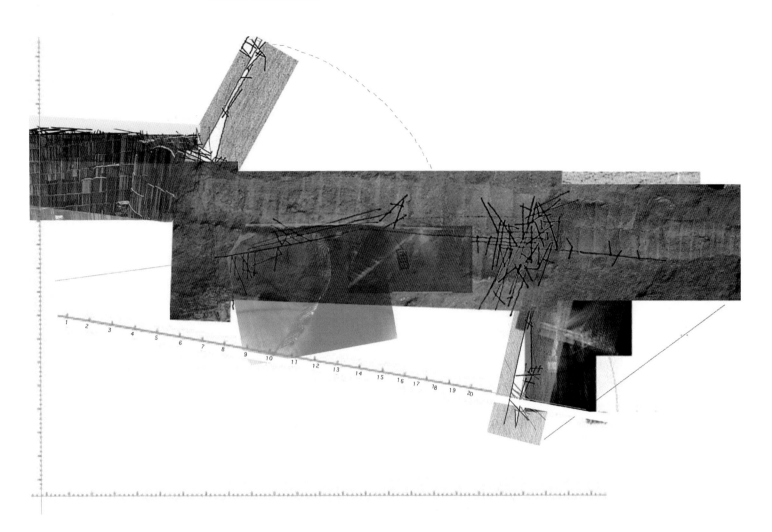

4.26 Bringing back the dismantled layers.

when illegal Israeli settlements are 'decorated' with stones, windows and tiles 'borrowed' from traditional Palestinian villages? How will Palestine bring back the dismantled layers over the years? Should they fight for the land, or the materiality of the land? What Palestine should call for now is Antonio Gramsci's 'war of position', where the dominant voice of the masses rule over the hegemonic discourse of the maps. It is time for a 'cultural war' that will raise consciousness within the masses of civil society, and ensure that the normality of the Israeli occupation will indeed come to an end in time.[63]

MOMENTS OF POSSIBILITY
IMPLANTING DNA

With the topography of the West Bank being in crisis, re-designing the existing quarries of the West Bank can be employed as a tool to respond to the dramatic loss of the land. They have the

139

potential of hosting the clandestine people who do not fit – neither in the Israeli map, nor in the Palestinian context – yet, have found shelter there. The proposal I will explain here is built over the footprint of the existing Birzeit quarry. One of the key stone quarries in Palestine which has a relatively big number of workers from all over the West Bank. The design is seen as one of the emerging space, where decay becomes a process for place making, and a point where the 'invisible traces' can make imprints somewhere else.

Through a multi-faceted process which already taking place inside the quarry, and while the stone is being sliced to be moved and sold to Israel, I envisage that amber is injected in between the sedimentary layers of the removed limestone to record secret narratives; a form of 'implanting' memory into the sub-strata.

Before inserting the fragments of amber, it is to be heated, pressed and then mixed with hair, nails, skin cells, teeth fragments, data and other microforms of Palestinian identity. These secret capsules will be taken away and built into Israeli homes for the meantime.

The proposal offers a new way of collective fossilization of history, by compressing narratives to avoid their loss with the constant changes enforced by Israeli occupation. Fossils are of course the preserved traces of animals, plants, and other organisms from the remote past. The totality of fossils, both discovered and undiscovered, and their placement rock formations and sedimentary layers is known as the fossil record.

Amber or 'tree resin' is readily available from the pine trees in Palestine. These were never indigenous species to the region; rather, they were strategically brought in during the British Mandate by the Jewish National Fund and lately used by Israel on top of the hills to surround its settlements. By making scars on the trees, Amber will be produced; this is another way of marking a statement against the enforced acclamation of the land in 1930s when over 1.7 million trees were planted on confiscated Palestinian lands, and later strategically multiplied as instruments of concealment to hide the ruins of the Palestinian villages which were 'ethnically cleansed' after the Jewish state was created. This 'covering up' process has also been a way to assure that the exiled would have nothing to come back to anymore.[64]

Throughout the process of 'implanting memory', amber will be gradually heated in an oil-bath, to become soft and flexible. Amber fragments are thus united by smearing the surfaces with oil, heating them, and then pressing them together while hot to create 'amberoid' or 'pressed amber'. The pieces are carefully heated with exclusion of air and then compressed into a uniform mass under intense hydraulic pressure. The process of heating the amber and mixing it with oil (which in this case will be the common olive oil) will also produce aromatic scents, which will be a constant reminder of the roots yet to be revisited.

It might eventually require DNA forensics to reveal the micro-objects implanted in-between the stone pieces, but for Palestinians, these dull fragments of amber will preserve the roots of their land, awakening it once more. Over time, the content of the amber can be revealed; scanning

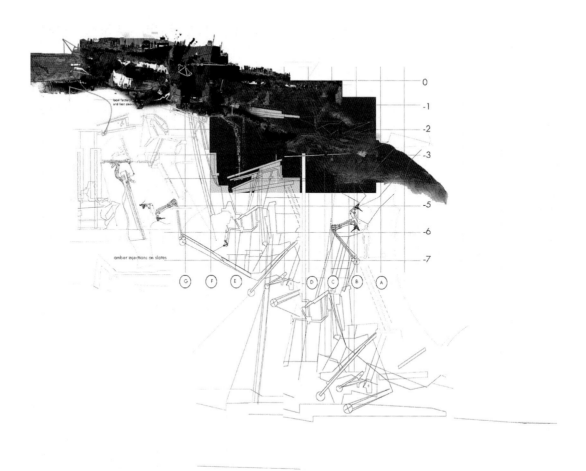

4.27   Injecting the land with memory.

stone will offer a new kind of insight into the past to coming generations of Palestinians who claim back their lost territory.

THE SPONGE BAGS

While the hidden networks create voids and decay under the surface, in the West Bank, people using them are faced with water and sewage colliding with one another. The useful rainwater needs to be captured before it disappears to the deeper invisible layers run by the occupier. Clusters of sponge bags are thus placed to suck in the water before it dissipates through the porous rocks. These sponges expand and later contract when water is squeezed and filtered for reuse in watering the dried out agricultural lands. Collectively these sponges create what I term 'water pockets' as silent nodes of Palestinian resistance.

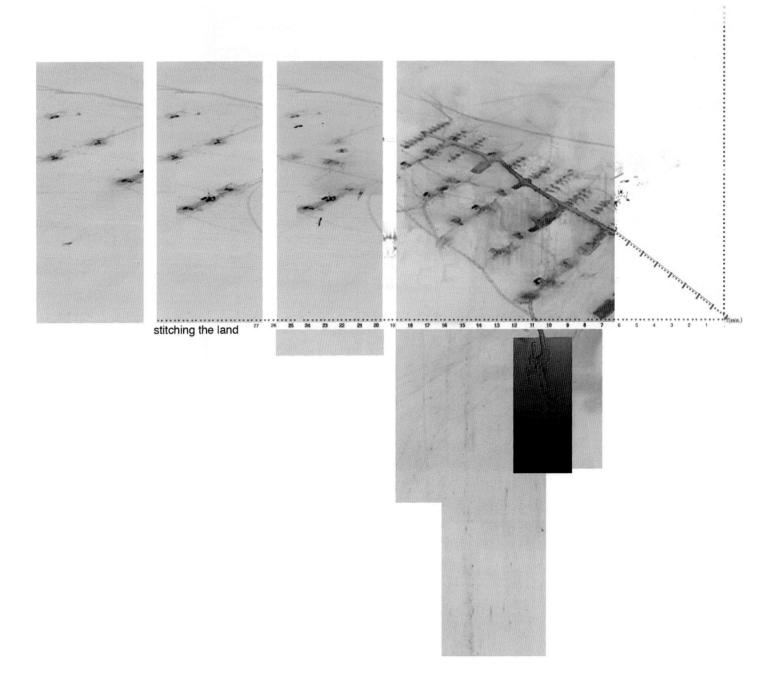

stitching the land

4.28 Stitching the land.

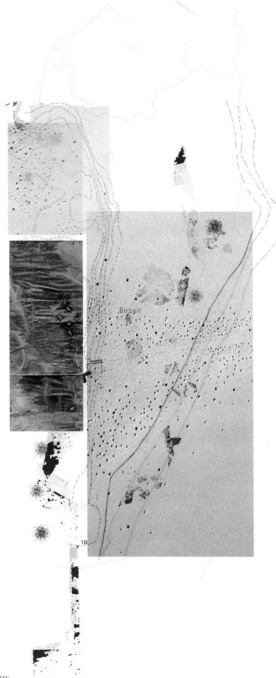

4.29   Re-reading Birzeit stone quarry.

These 'water pockets' are made and tailored by women from the excess of leftover fabrics they use. Over the past 20 years or so, Palestinian women have found in tailoring and fabric business a new form of income generator. A home-run business that is currently serving so many families against the unemployment and imprisonment enforced on their family members. The role of women making, fixing and replacing these 'water pockets' is a response to the urgency and need for clean water which has been throughout history their responsibility, as they usually collect water from the springs. Until today this role of collecting the water and waiting by the springs is associated with poetic narratives and love stories that all the folk songs refer to. However, the role of Palestinian women in shaping the cultural and political history of Palestine was never limited to this. Palestinian women – especially those waiting by the springs to collect water – have been part of the Palestinian resistance movement; they have taken key roles in facilitating different conditions for the men to fight while observing the fields and being the secret messengers between those outside prison and others inside.[65] Therefore, I see in this subversive task a continuation to their role.

FILTERING GREY WATER

Sand filters for wastewater provide a good natural solution for rural sewage treatment. In the case where sewage might get mixed with the water supply – as the case of most Palestinian villages – it is more advisable to treat sewage separately and return it to the earth. In return, water can be extracted from the ground on a low-cost basis

4.30   Section through the Birzeit quarry.
        A moment of injecting and stitching.

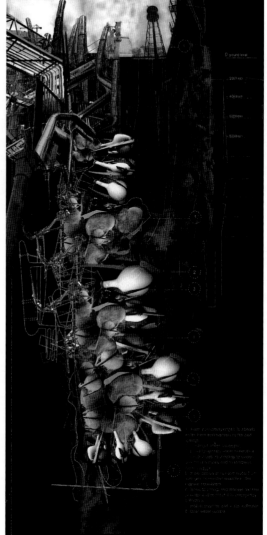

(full filtration is a very costly process that cannot be afforded within Palestinian rural context). This proposal is thus intended for the instant use of filtered water for agricultural purposes in villages that currently struggle to get a decent daily amount of water. However, when waste-water is to be stored for long term purposes, special tanks can be used with shallow soakaways, since these are easy to install and much more affordable than any high-tech treatment products.

This process of treatment in the quarries involves collecting the grey water from the saturated 'water pockets' by automatically squeezing the sponges. Water is then released and directed towards sand channels. There, it passes through different grades of filtration before it gets re-collected again and directed towards the agricultural fields.

AIR FILTRATION

As a way to reduce the environmental impact of quarrying, 'green belts' are also proposed at the edges of the quarry to capture the dust and filter the air from the harmful particles. This is

4.31 A section through the quarry showing the proposed sponge bags used to capture water before it disappears to the deeper invisible layers run by the occupier.

air get mixed in a relatively slower paste to that of the heated quarry air. This in effect reduces the emission of pollutant chemicals and particles, which are temperature dependent.

The quarry is also composed of stone slicing and stone cutting stations to replace those located at the entrance of the village. Each of these stations has an archiving point where the locals can bring in their 'DNA elements' to be later injected within stone layers. Birzeit residents have already started this archiving collection in 2008 and are currently being collected by the People's Museum.

The proposed elements within the quarry are all available and easy to run and maintain by the local residents who either live in Birzeit or the commuters who pass by everyday on their way to and from Ramallah. All can take part, either in connecting their fields to the water channels, replacing the 'water sponges', manufacturing them, or even in injecting stone with their own roots. All is done meanwhile more underground tunnels are created to expand and connect Birzeit tunnels[66] with the rest of the quarries in the West Bank.

The whole quarry proposal is seen as an alternative/subversive way against Israeli strategies to limit building for Palestinian communities and ban it in Areas B and C land. It is a new form of empowering and multiplying the community underground, especially that its becoming more likely to approve permissions for installing stone quarries in Areas B, if it means stone can be transferred to the Israeli side.

mainly concentrated around stone crushing stations within the quarry to extract sand and gravel. The 'green belts' also help reduce the air temperature around the quarries and thus reduce the atmospheric mixing such that cooler

4.32   A section/collage illustrating how waste water will be collected and filtered.

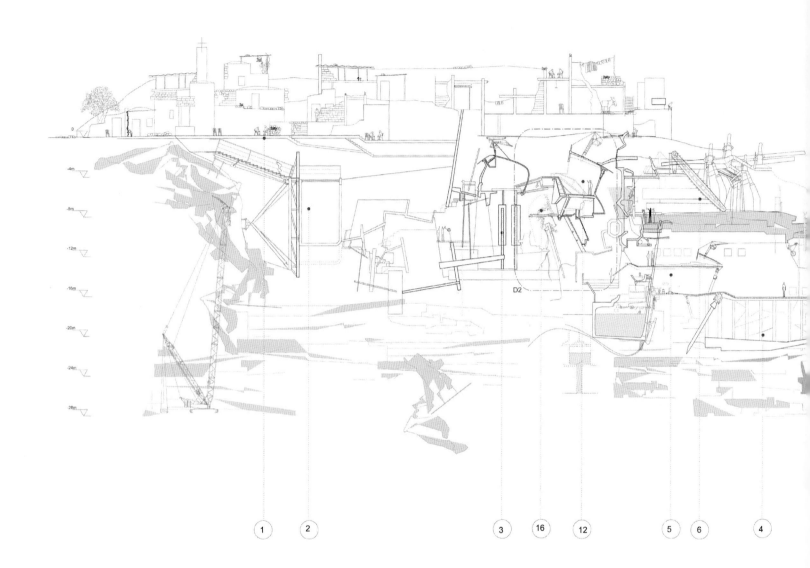

-4m

-8m

-12m

-16m

-20m

-24m

-28m

D2

① ② ③ ⑯ ⑫ ⑤ ⑥ ④

4.33 Proposed section A-A.

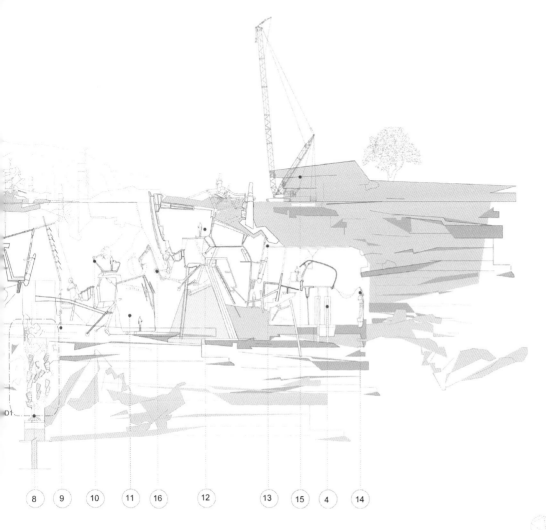

1. The main plaza at the rear of Birzeit church. The plaza is known for having different underground tunnels connecting the village with the surrounding landscape. Israeli setlers have tried many times to occupy the plaza believing that there are jewish archological leftovers there.

2. Heavy-duty vertical lifts connecting to underground quarry and tunnels

3. Pressure monitors and mechanical drilling stations

4. Mechanical slicing of stone using freezing and heating points

5. Water treatment control unit

6. Mechanical lifts for gravel and crushed stone.
Fine gravel is still being imported untill today from Israel with expensive cost, despite the fact that raw materials come from Palestine. A Palestinian investor is recently considering installing new factory near Kalandia to produce gravel as a way of being self-sufficient.

7. Wind flutes and mechnaical drills used as a coding system to stictch the qyuarries around together

8. Water collection using the water sponges and storing it in temporary reservopirs to be directed towards agricultural fields. Water is also injected in machines to cool down the stone cutting process and help cracking the rocks through freezing stations.

9. Water pipes connecting to the sprinklers and temporary reservoirs.

10. Amber injections

11. Horizontal labs to test amber

12. Petrification of amber and stone to accelarate fossilization.

13. Ducts and ventilation units

14. Mixing amber with DNA

15. Cranes to collect treated stone

16. Heat control to accelarate the injection of amber

N   0   4   6   8   10

4.34 Details of proposed section.
Key:
1 Static water squeezed and collected by specially-placed sponges ('water pockets')
2 Fine sand with different grades
3 Coarse sand
4 Gravel.
5 Clean water outlet.
6 Water channels connected to the agricultural lands.
7 Water being collected in the 'water pockets'.
8 'Water pockets' with their manual and automatic collectors, scattered around rocky channels to capture water.
9 Automatic compressors to release the trapped water.
10 Rainwater (with no sewage mixed in) captured and stored for agricultural purposes.
11 Water pipes connected to shallow soak away for the treatment of waste-water for long-term use.

-100m

-150m

-250m

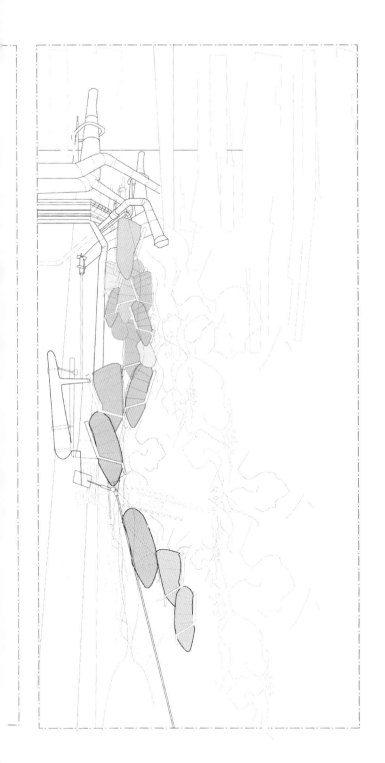
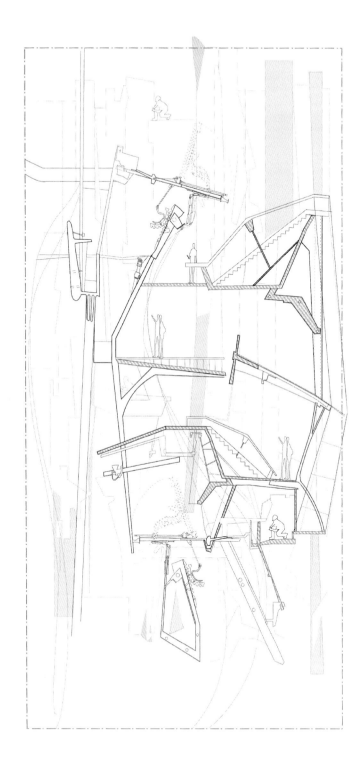

4.35   An imaginary moment underground.
        Injecting the stone with DNA.

4.36 Slicing stone to be relocated.

4.37 Testing out different methods of injecting stone with DNA elements and trapping it in amber.

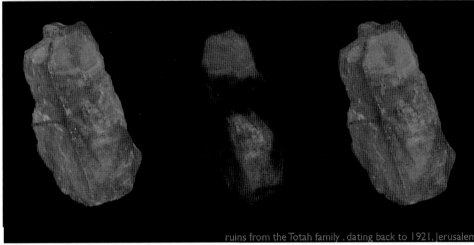

ruins from the Totah family , dating back to 1921, Jerusalem

Further to archaeological excavations, scientists has recently found new traces of land registry documents trapped in amber. The amber also include traces of hair and other DNA contents. After investigation it appears that the family registry document is matching the DNA forensics. Both belong to members of the Totah Family. Contents reveal that the Totah family owned the land back in 1920. In 2003 a new house was built by the family, but was later demolished in 2004 by Israeli army to expand the Israeli settlement of Ramot. This act is part of the 'Big Jerusalem' plan known as E1, which aims to expand Jewish neighbourhoods and erase slowly the Palestinian ones.

Given the fact that these settlements were then considered illegal according to Geneva Convention and international law, the Totah family is now intending to reclaim their stolen land back, now that the Palestinian state has been finally founded.

4.38   An imagined scenario in 2028 showing excavated pieces of stone. The trapped DNA elements reveal the right of a displaced family to reclaim their land. This scenario is inspired from a real story of land confiscation and house demolition that took place in 2004 for the Totah family.

4.39   Underground reclaimed.

4.40   Proposal for Birzeit stone quarry.

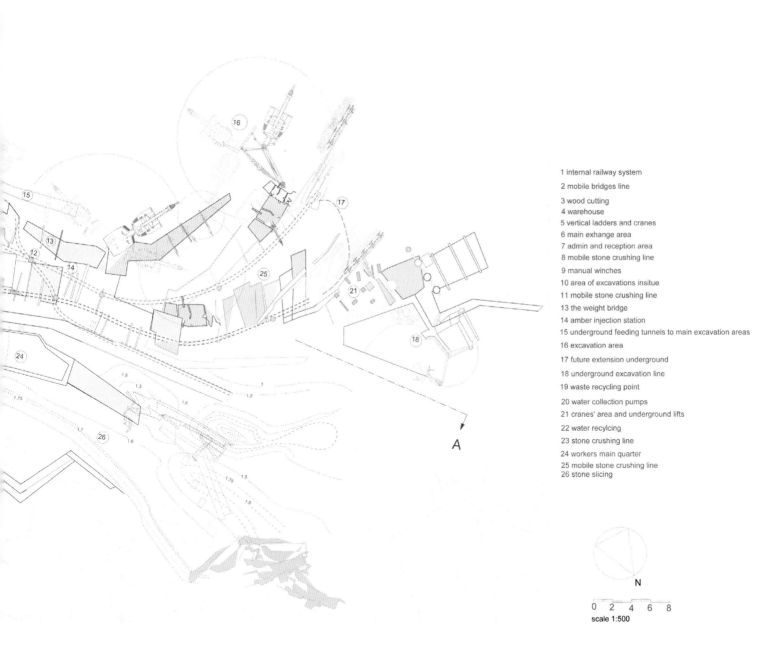

1 internal railway system

2 mobile bridges line

3 wood cutting
4 warehouse
5 vertical ladders and cranes
6 main exhange area
7 admin and reception area
8 mobile stone crushing line
9 manual winches
10 area of excavations insitue
11 mobile stone crushing line
13 the weight bridge
14 amber injection station
15 underground feeding tunnels to main excavation areas
16 excavation area
17 future extension underground
18 underground excavation line
19 waste recycling point
20 water collection pumps
21 cranes' area and underground lifts
22 water recylcing
23 stone crushing line
24 workers main quarter
25 mobile stone crushing line
26 stone slicing

A

N

0 2 4 6 8
scale 1:500

NOTES

1 Weizman, E. (2007) *Hollow Land: Israel's Architecture of Occupation*. London: Verso Books.

2 Ibid.

3 See Weizman, E. (2003) 'The Politics of Verticality: The West Bank as an Architectural Construction', in Franke, A., *Territories: Islands, Camps and Other States of Utopia*. Berlin: Institute for Contemporary Art. 'When the Zionists first arrived in Palestine late in the nineteenth century, the land they found was strangely unfamiliar; different from the one they consumed in texts photographs and etchings. Reaching the map co-ordinates of the site did not bring them there. The search had to continue and thus split in opposite directions along the vertical axis: above, in a metaphysical sense and below as archaeological excavations'.

4 Ben-Gurion, D. (1970) *Memoirs: David Ben-Gurion*. New York: World Pub. Co., p. 70.

5 Golberger, P. 'Passion Set in Stone'. *New York Times*, 10 September 1995. Available at: http://www.nytimes.com/1995/09/10/magazine/passion-set-in-stone.html?sec=&spon=&pagewanted=7 [accessed 12 July 2010]; Hristine, S. 'In Historic District, Synagogue Plans are Criticized', *New York Times*, 9 October 2007. Available at: http://www.nytimes.com/2007/10/09/nyregion/09litchfield.html?_r=1&ref=todayspaper accessed 12 June 2010].

6 Khasawneh, D. (2001) *Memoirs Engraved in Stone: Palestine Urban Mansions*. Ramallah: Riwaq-Centre for Architectural Conservation / Jerusalem: Institute of Jerusalem Studies.

7 Nitzan-Shiftan, A. (2006) 'The Israeli "Place" in East Jerusalem: How Israeli Architects Appropriated the Palestinian Aesthetic after the 67 War', *Jerusalem Quarterly*, No. 27, pp. 15–27.

8 According to the geological survey of Israel, the specifications for limestone to be used for building in Israel is either white, coarse crystalline limestone, originally referred to in Arabic as 'Meleke', or the stone of kings. Cream-coloured micritic limestone, known locally as 'Mizzi Hilu', or sweet rock. Red-coloured limestone known as 'Mizzi Ahmar' meaning the red rock and gray crystalline dolomite which the Israelis has changed its name into 'Mizzi Yehudi', or Jewish rock.

9 Golberger, op. cit.

10 Nitzan-Shiftan, op.cit.

11 See Moshe Safdie's honeycombed box-dwellings, twin-tower 'Gate to Israel' and Zvi Hecker's dodecahedron housing.

12 See Eldar, A. (2010) 'Frank Gehry Steps Down from Museum of Tolerance Project', *Haarez* 15 January 2010. Available at: http://www.haaretz.com/print-edition/news/frank-gehry-steps-down-from-museum-of-tolerance-project-1.261496 [accessed 10 September 2010].

13 Dawson, L. (2005) 'Defining Jewish Identity', *Architectural Review*. Available at: http://findarticles.com/p/articles/mi_m3575/is_1300_217/ai_n14809395/ [accessed 12 July 2010].

14 Prusher, I. 'Palestinians' Stones Cut Both Ways', *The Christian Science Monitor*, 4 January 2000. Available at: http://www.csmonitor.com/2000/0104/p6s1.html [accessed 10 September 2010].

15 Anon. (1994) 'Starting from the North to the South to Build Israeli Quarries: Confiscation of 16,733 Dunums from the West Bank', *Al-Nahar* (September) [Arabic newspaper].

16 According to *Palestine–Israel Journal of Politics Economics and Culture*, 'In the Ramallah district, an Israeli quarry is located near Kufr Malik village, on a 2,523-dunum area. Israel plans to construct another quarry in the Ramallah district on land belonging to the villages of Rantis and Shuqba. In the Hebron district the following areas have been confiscated for quarries: 1,744 dunums between Dura and Al-Thahiriya; approximately 2,677 dunums from Tarqumiya, Dura and Khirbet Jamroura villages; and 2,077 dunums of land belonging to the village of Surif. Lastly, a quarry is located on land which belongs to Majdal Bani Fadel village in the Nablus district'. Available at Qumsieh, V. (1998) 'The Environmental Impact of Jewish Settlements in the West Bank', *The Palestine–Israel Journal of Politics Economics and Culture*, Vol. 5 (1). Available at: http://www.pij.org/details.php?id=427 [accessed 13 May 2010].

17 Bronner, E. (2009) 'Desert's Sand and Rocks Become Precious Resources in West Bank Dispute', *The New York Times*, 7 March 2009, p. 5. Available at: http://www.nytimes.com/2009/03/07/world/middleeast/07westbank.html?ref=world [accessed 4 September 2010].

18 Anon. 'Convention (IV) respecting the Laws and Customs of War on Land and its Annex: Regulations Concerning the Laws and Customs of War on Land. The Hague, 18 October 1907', *International Humanitarian Law – Treaties & Documents* (ICRC). Available at: http://www.icrc.org/ihl.nsf/FULL/195 [accessed 3 September 2010].

19 Jeffay, N. (2009) 'Bibi's "Economic Peace" Faces Key Test at Quarries', *The Jewish Daily Forward*, 24 April 2009. Available at: http://www.forward.com/articles/104861/ [accessed 11 May 2010].

20 Frykberg, M. 'Israel Stripping West Bank Quarries', *ZNET*, 11 May 2009. Available at: http://www.zcommunications.org/israel-stripping-west-bank-quarries-by-mel-frykberg [accessed 2 April 2010].

21 Ibid.

22 Jeffay, op. cit.

23 See Memford's commentary on the changes in economy from farm estate to real estate: Mumford, L. (1961) *The City in History: Its Origins, its Transformations, and its Prospects*. New York: Harcourt, p. 481.

24 Kryss, T. (2004) 'Iraq: Why Did USA Want "Regime Change?"' Available at: http://webcache.googleusercontent.com/search?q=cache:J6F9RDBFQ0kJ:www.krysstal.com/democracy_whyusa_iraq.html+how+does+americans+deal+with+Iraq+natural+resources+oil+do+they+respect+hague+convention&cd=1&hl=en&ct=clnk&gl=uk&client=firefox-a [accessed 3 September 2010].

25 Ibid.

26 According to Tal's report Benjamin Netanyahu the current Israeli prime minister – who is calling for 'economic Peace with the Palestinian Authority to 'help' them build the Palestinian economy and institutions in the West Bank and increase the chances of successful Palestinian self-rule – was asked about the exploitation of quarries issue. Netanyahu's aide, Ron Dermer replied that: 'The new government is going to take a very pragmatic approach to these issues to figure out what will advance the Palestinian economy'.

27 Adiv, A. (2007) 'Palestinian Quarry Workers Organize', *Challenge* (104) (July/August). Available at: http://www.challenge-mag.com/en/article__121 [accessed 15 March 2010].

28 Ibid.

29 For further details about the condition of Palestinian workers, see Anon. 'Wrong Side of the Wall', *Palestine Monitor*, 11 May 2010. Available at: http://www.palestinemonitor.org/spip/spip.php?article1393 [accessed 20 November 2010].

30 See also the records of the Union of Marble and Stone Industry in Palestine (USM). Available at: http://webcache.googleusercontent.com/search?q=cache:ejL7e3xqCqMJ:usm-pal.ps/etemplate.php%3Fid%3D9+stone+industry+in+Palestine+%254+of+the+world's+total+stone+production+making+it+The+12th+largest+stone+producer+in+the+world.&cd=4&hl=en&ct=clnk&gl=uk&client=safari [accessed 21 November 2010].

31 Hammami, R. (2010) 'Qalandiya: Jerusalem's Tora Bora and the Frontiers of Global Inequality', *Jerusalem Quarterly*, No. 41 (Spring), pp. 29–51.

32 Interview with Ghaleb, A., 20 July 2008.

33 See Jerusalem Stone UK. Available at: http://www.jerusalemstoneuk.co.uk [accessed 17 October 2010].

34 Weizman, E. (2003) 'The Politics of Verticality: The West Bank as an Architectural Construction', in Franke, A., *Territories: Islands, Camps and Other States of Utopia*. Berlin: Institute for Contemporary Art.

35 Abu El-Haj, N. (2001) *Facts on the Ground: Archaeological Practice and Territorial Self-fashioning in Israeli Society*. London and Chicago, IL: University of Chicago Press.

36 Ibid.

37 Said, E. (2003) *Freud and the Non-European*. London: Verso Books, p. 47.

38 Weizman, op. cit.

39 Weizman, op. cit.

40 Anon. 'Troubled Waters – Palestinians Denied Fair Access to Water', *Amnesty International*, 27 October 2009. Available at: http://www.reliefweb.int/rw/rwb.nsf/db900SID/MYAI-7X87U6?OpenDocument [accessed 15 April 2010].

41 See the hydro geologic cross-section of the mountain aquifer.

42 Hilal, J. and Ashhab, S. (2006) 'The H2O Factor', in Messelwitz, P. and Rieniets, T. (eds), *City of Collision*. Basel and London: Birkhauser, pp. 184–92.

43 Lein, Y. (July, 2000) Thirsty for a Solution: The Water Crisis in the Occupied Territories and its Resolution in the Final-Status Agreement. Jerusalem, *B'tselem*, p. 42. Available at: http://webcache.googleusercontent.com/search?q=cache:o1TRJAcKdhYJ:www.btselem.org/Download/200007_Thirsty_for_a_Solution_Eng.doc+B'Tselem+The+Israeli+Information+Center+for+Human+Rights+in+the+Occupied+Territories,+Thirsty+for+a+Solution+42+(2000)&cd=1&hl=en&ct=clnk&gl=-uk&client=safari [accessed 23 September 2010].

44 Ibid., p. 43.

45 Amnesty International, 'Troubled Waters – Palestinians Denied Fair Access to Water', *Relief Web*, 27 October 2009. Available at: http://www.reliefweb.int/rw/rwb.nsf/db900SID/MYAI-7X87U6?OpenDocument [accessed 1 November 2010].

46 According to B'tselem's report, the achievement of the Oslo Agreement is seen from the perspective of Palestinian water needs is the increase of water supply to the Occupied Territories by some 30 percent during the interim period, i.e., from September 1995 to May 1999. As for June 2000, a year after the interim period ended according to the agreement, only half of the promised additional quantity was produced and supplied to the Palestinians. Ibid., p. 5.

47 Lein, op. cit.

48 Hilal and Ashhab, op. cit.

49 Swirski, S. (2005) *The Price of Occupation*. Tel Aviv: Mapa Publishers, p. 28 [Hebrew]. According to a B'Tselem report, 40 percent of the Palestinian water gets lost in the leaking pipes and infrastructure inherited to them from Israel. See also Anon. 'The Water Crisis', *B'tselem*. Available at: http://www.btselem.org/English/Water/index.asp [accessed 20 November 2010]; Marble and Stone Centre, http://www.marblecenter-ppu.ps/en/homepage.aspx [accessed 16 September 2010].

50 Taamallah, F. (2006) 'A Thirst for West Bank Water', *The Nation*, 26 June 2006. Available at: http://www.thenation.com/article/thirst-west-bank-water [accessed 8 November 2010].

51 'Wadi Qana is a place almost as soothing as it is beautiful: a fertile valley with seven main natural springs and nine smaller ones, and the endless Wadi Qana river running through it. The river meanders from Huwara, south of Nablus, to Jaljuliye, south of Qalqilya, and then flows into the Yarqon, or Naher el Ooja River. Wadi Qana is between two ranges of hills, making it very suitable for citrus plantations. Indeed, the orange trees and lemon trees spread along the river and shine in the morning sun'. Anon. (2007) 'Water in Salfit, Sewage from Israeli Settlements', 31 December 2007. Available at: http://webcache.googleusercontent.com/search?q=cache:8R5T3hkAhksJ:skipschiel.

wordpress.com/2007/12/31/water-in-salfit-sewage-from-israeli-settle ments/+A+Sleeping+Time+Bomb:+Pollution+of+the+Mountain+ Aquifer+by+Solid+Waste&cd=2&hl=en&ct=clnk&gl=uk&client= safari [accessed 12 June 2011].

52 Shehadeh, R. (2008) *Palestinian Walks: Forays into a Vanishing Landscape*. New York: Scribner, p. xviii.

53 Zecharya, T., Tamar, K. and Gidon, B. (2006) *A Sleeping Time Bomb: Pollution of the Mountain Aquifer by Solid Waste*. Tel Aviv: Friends of the Earth Middle East.

54 Frykberg, M. (2009) 'West Bank Becomes Waste Land', *IPS*, 15 May 2009. Available at: http://ipsnews.net/news.asp?idnews=46858 [accessed 3 November 2010].

55 Ratner, D. (2005) 'Israel's Plan to Dump Tons of Garbage in the West Bank', *Haaretz*, 3 April 2005. Available at: http://www.haaretz.com/ news/israel-plans-to-dump-tons-of-garbage-in-west-bank-1.154867 [accessed 24 July 2010].

56 Taamallah, F. 'A Thirst for West Bank Water', *The Nation*, 26 June 2006. Available at: http://www.thenation.com/article/thirst-west-bank-water [accessed 8 November 2010].

57 Weizman, E. (2007) *Hollow Land: Israel's Architecture of Occupation*. London: Verso, p. 20.

58 As mentioned in earlier chapters, Palestinians holding a Jerusalem identity card have to prove that they are residents in Jerusalem. After the erection of the separation wall, commuters from Jerusalem to the West Bank moved towards the edges of Jerusalem to maintain their right of citizenship with easy access. However, with the changes in the wall boundaries some of these villages were annexed to Jerusalem, like half of Beit Hanina, while others were excluded like Al Ram. Paradoxically, the village of Kofor Aqab – even though it is outside the wall boundaries and closer to Ramallah – is still annexed to Jerusalem municipality. Analysts and critics of the Israeli urban strategies of division believe this could be a time-bomb to push all the Palestinians towards Qufur Aqab, and later exclude the village from the Jerusalem map, so that they lose their identity card.

59 See artist Khaled Jarrar short film, capturing people commuting along the sewage tunnel 'Journey 110'. Anon. (2009) 'A Muddy Journey: Sewage Tunnel becomes Transit Point to Jerusalem', *Reuters*, 2 November 2009. Available at: http://blogs.reuters.com/axismundi/2009/11/02/ a-muddy-journey-sewage-tunnel-becomes-transit-point-to-jerusalem/ [accessed 11 November 2010].

60 Shehadeh, op. cit., p. xv.

61 Weizman, op. cit.

62 Amiry, S. (2010) *Nothing to Lose but Your Life*. Doha: Bloomsbury Qatar Foundation.

63 Gramsci, A., Quintin, H., and Geoffrey, N. (1971) *Selections from the Prison Notebooks of Antonio Gramsci*. London: Lawrence and Wishart.

64 See 'Greenwashing Apartheid: The Jewish National Fund's Environmental Cover Up', JNF ebook, 15 May 2011. Available at: http://jnfebook.net/JNFeBookVol4.pdf [accessed 20 March 2010].

65 This is well reflected in a famous Palestinian folk song narrated by the women who use their subversive language to communicate between each other while collecting water. It has been apparently a common practice between women to add the letter 'L' at the beginning of each word so whichever enemy wouldn't understand their conversation; this has also been a successful tool in communicating between men in prison by choosing different letters and word compositions.

66 According to the local narratives, Birzeit is known for its secret tunnels, which expand from the historic centre of Birzeit to connect with the surrounding terraced olive groves; thus the town was associated with many well-known freedom fighters who used these secret tunnels in their resistance of 1941.

AIR

It is a well-known fact that Palestine/Israel contains a great wealth of biodiversity in terms of the number of species, ecosystems and landscapes. A country, which is only one tenth the size of the UK, is home to a far higher number of species, because of its location at the junction of three continents Africa, Europe and Asia, each with a unique combination of birds, plants and mammals. Not only that, all birds migrating from Europe over Lebanon, Jordan, Palestine/Israel and Egypt to Africa, and vice versa, pass by the land to add to its magic.

> Very few countries can simultaneously boast skies filled with raptors, storks and pelicans, wetlands heaving with egrets, herons, wildfowl and shorebirds, hillsides alive with the songs of warblers, wheatears and bunting.[1]

Palestine/Israel has all of these. Simply it hosts half a billion birds each year to be one of the busiest corridors for bird migration in the whole world.

However, just as the land below has been broken apart with walls and boundaries, the airspace – with its unique routes for birds – is also experiencing its share of complications. The obsession of Israel to control, isolate and 'secure' their existence in the territory, has reached the airspace, such that the 'sky is no longer the limit'. Israel is trying its best to hold control over the whole airspace of the region under its well-used slogan of 'security', stripping Palestinians even from their sovereignty over their airspace. Today, every individual, spot and corner in the West Bank and the Gaza Strip, is being monitored with satellite cameras, just as every radio and TV station is being controlled by Israel. The sky has become a new battle fought over by Israel. Nevertheless, it still remains out of reach and has not yet been exploited as much as the surface of the land has. Luckily enough, boundaries and solid walls cannot as yet divide the airspace, and so Israel still can't fully get hold of it, or control those living species who inhabit it.

I will therefore use this chapter to put an emphasis on the need to step above the exhausted surface of the land as a mean to find other spaces of possibility. In doing so, the aim is to shed light on the issue of airspace, the electromagnetic spectrum, the struggle of Israel to dominate this zone and the challenges they are facing. I will try to uncover another degree of weakness Israel is still concealing, another prospect for a new (aerial) map drawn by Palestinians with the airspace being the 'new ground' or 'space of possibility' that Palestinians could share with the birds that break all boundaries. Maybe one could start to see the sky with its inhabitants as a new tool to connect the fractured territory of Palestine.

AIRSPACE: THE ABSENT MAP OF SURVEILLANCE

According to basic principles of international air laws, any country should enjoy complete and exclusive sovereignty over the airspace above its territory as a continuous link from the surface of the ground to the sky. The 1919 Paris Convention, followed by the 1944 Chicago Convention on International Civil Aviation, affirmed this fundamental principle, stating that it is a breach of international law for any state to violate the airspace of another state.[2] In the case of Palestine/Israel, the rules have had to be changed simply to respond to Israeli's request for full control over the Palestinian airspace.

This demand was manifested during the negotiations for the Oslo Agreement, when Israel insisted on having full control over the Palestinian airspace under the pretext of 'security'. The former head of the IDF strategic planning division and the former head of negotiation unit at that point, Brigader-General Udi Dekel, recommended in his report to the negotiation team enforcing extremely tight regulations on the airspace over the West Bank and the Gaza Strip.

These extreme regulations – including the high restriction of foreign air traffic – were claimed to be related to Israel's vulnerability to 'attacks' through the air, given their location and geography with a 'narrow waist' of about 70 km at the narrowest point of the country, which makes it difficult to track potential air attacks in time. Israel's concern is that any aircraft can fly across its narrow waist in less than four minutes; meanwhile, it takes at least three minutes for any interceptor aircraft to take off. This makes Israel feel threatened, and on that basis they demanded a full unified 'security control' over the airspace above Palestinian territory.[3]

According to the same report, Ben-Gurion International Airport has to be protected as one of the key sensitive spots in Israel. Consequently, this also implies extra control over the West Bank areas and specifically villages overlooking the coastal region, such as Beit Liqia, Kharbatha and Aryeh. This of course means that Israel needs to exercise full aerial sovereignty over these areas, in case any 'possible attack' – as Dekel puts it – might start from there.

In their desperate need for a deal, Palestinians agreed to the enforced Israeli regulations and gave up on their right of sovereignty of their own airspace – as well as their minor requests of having Kalandia airport during 'Oslo' negotiations.[4] Indeed, in the clauses concerning the electromagnetic sphere and airspace, the Oslo Agreement states that:

> All aviation activity or usage of the airspace . . . shall require prior approval of Israel.[5]

To find a way around this problematic issue, a new definition of boundaries in airspace had to be invented for the Palestinian/Israeli situation. Consequently, it was proposed that the sovereign ceiling of the emerging Palestinian state should be significantly lowered, to include only architectural construction and low-flying helicopters. The upper layers of airspace were to remain in Israeli control.[6] This obsession with the sky is increasingly becoming a new form of negotiating power between countries around the world, especially since the last decade, and more specifically after 11 September 2001. Many rumours have spread about demands from the USA to Israel to support them in 'exploring' the neighbouring sky, in order to secure their grounds after the incident of 11 September. Rumours were also spread later about secret agreements between Israel and its neighbouring countries, like Saudi Arabia, Iraq, Kuwait and the UAE, to give Israel 'clear skies' to shorten the distances for attacking Iran and Syria if needed. Although the Arab countries have denied these claims, others have been confirmed. The agreement with Saudi Arabia clearly reveals the Saudi plans to allow a narrow corridor for the use of Israeli air force. According to the *Sunday Times*, a US defense source stated that:

> The Saudis have given their permission for the Israelis to pass over and they will look the other way. They have already done tests to make sure their own jets aren't scrambled and no one gets shot down. This has all been done with the agreement of the [US] State Department.[7]

According to the same report, Saudi officials have confirmed their support stating that both countries share a mutual loathing of the Iranian regime, yet other reports denied it. However, even if other countries deny formal agreements with Israel, they still in effect turn a blind eye against Israeli attempts to 'violate' their airspace, especially when these violations are backed up by the USA. This compact includes not only Saudi Arabia, but also Jordan, Egypt, Iraq and Turkey, which had already several 'visits' from the Israeli air force above its sky before it closed its airspace to Israel after the brutal Israeli raid on the flotilla aid ship on its way to the Gaza Strip on 31 May 2010.

CONTROLLING THE ELECTROMAGNETIC SPECTRUM

The topographical advantages of the West Bank – located on the high ground, and combined with the narrow waste of Palestine/Israel and the overlapping points between Palestinian and Israeli areas – makes it geographically powerful, with a communication system far less vulnerable compared to the Israeli coastal line. According to the aforementioned report prepared by Udi Dekel:

> if a Palestinian transmitter station is located on Eibal Mountain in Nablus as an example, it could virtually jam the entire communication system of Israeli areas broadcasting on the same frequency.[8]

Consequently, Israeli advisers declared clearly that for any negotiation process to proceed with Palestinians, Israel must also have full control over all electromagnetic transmissions. This is seen as essential to prevent any possible 'threat' that might weaken its control over the land. This of course includes radio

and TV stations, since any transmissions with similar frequencies to Israeli ones could lead to disruption in their systems, and most importantly to Ben Gurion International Airport.

Today, however, the control of the airspace and the electromagnetic spectrum enables Israel to monitor actions on the ground and to interfere with radio and TV broadcasts by the Palestinian Authority. Not only that; the Palestinian Authority has also agreed to halt any broadcasting activities if not licensed by Israel. Otherwise, the Israeli Defense Forces would do it themselves by destroying the transmitters. Israel is also able to use the airspace over Palestine as training grounds for its air force,

5.1   A view of Tel Aviv from a village to the west of Ramallah. Photograph by Lana Joudeh.

meaning it can attack and target individual and location anytime and anywhere – a facility which Israel has exercised extremely well in the past decade, especially over the Gazan airspace. In return, Palestinians were given a narrow, low-level aerial corridor, which barely connects the West Bank with the Gaza Strip.[9]

This obsession with control and security has covered the Palestinian/Israeli airspace with an invisible map of exhaustive surveillance, described by Weizman as:

> The most intensively observed and photographed terrain in the world. In a 'vacuum-cleaner' approach to intelligence gathering, sensors aboard unmanned air vehicles (UAVs), aerial reconnaissance jets, early warning Hawkeye planes, and even an Earth-Observation Image Satellite, snatch most signals out of the air. Every floor in every house, every car, every telephone call or radio transmission, even the smallest event that occurs on the terrain, can thus be monitored, policed or destroyed from the air.[10]

BIRDS

From a bird's-eye view over Palestine/Israel, no boundary lines actually exist apart from those seen on the surface of the land. Other than that, all boundaries are dissolved and only freedom is experienced when crossing the blue sky. For that reason, birds have become the language of the Palestinian refugees who are waiting for the day to return to the same freedom as is enjoyed with the birds.

> 'We shall return',
> The nightingale told me,
> When upon a hill we met.
> That nightingale lives on there

> In our dreams.
> Among the hills
> And people, who yearn,
> There is a place for us.
> O heart, how long?
> How long then . . .
> Have we been scattered by the wind? Come,
> We shall return.
> Let us return!
> O heart, do not drop in weariness
> On the path of our return.
> How it wounds our pride to know
> That birds tomorrow will return
> While we still remain here.[11]

This has happened not only because birds are typically associated with freedom, but also because birds have a unique relationship with historic Palestine. As noted, this relatively small area on the world map is known for being one of the busiest corridors for bird's migration in the world. Even though many other species migrate in search for new habitat – including butterflies, fish, whales, deer, zebra, etc. – it is birds that have the longest known non-stop migration of any species, all which adds to their significance:

> Every spring, half a billion birds migrate through Israel and the West Bank from their wintering grounds in Africa to their breeding grounds in Europe, and every autumn they return the same way. Only the Isthmus of Panama, which links North and South America, has heavier traffic, and Panama's airspace doesn't support the same density of military aircraft as Israel's.[12]

This migratory phenomena has added to the magic of the land and has throughout the years attracted

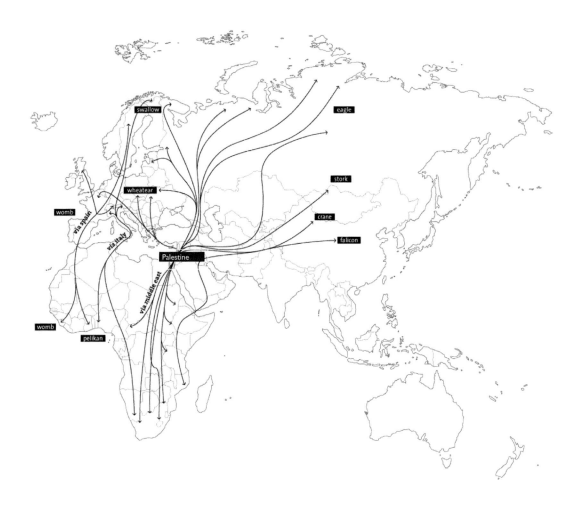

5.2 Bird migration through Palestine.

so many birder watchers and visitors, who come not only to watch the migration of birds, but also to enjoy the variety of resident species which are estimated to exceed those in the UK – even though Palestine/Israel is only one tenth of its size.[13]

INEVITABLE COLLISION
The heavy dependence of Israel on its air force, leading to a high density of military aircraft and the consequent tight security measures, have long been facing a different kind of threat than that being calculated in their negotiations and signed agreements. Indeed, the main challenge to face in the air is actually collision with birds, or what is commonly known as 'bird strike'. The large number of soaring birds that migrate by day, to exploit the thermals rising from the land, in fact is the main political crisis in the air posing a significant threat to Israeli aviation than any other claimed threat. It is reported that Israel has lost more aircraft through

birds collision than by any war or action by so-called 'enemies'. According to the *Birding Israel* website, the Israeli Air Forces (IAF) has suffered greatly in the past three decades, with over 3,400 bird strikes. These bird strikes are highly costly, with three pilots killed and nine aircrafts crashed – causing damage of over $1,000,000 per major accident.[14] According to the IAF, Ben Gurion Airport is at high risk given its location in proximity to the Syria-African Flyway whereby millions of migratory birds – including ducks and geese, storks, pelicans, cranes and egrets, raptors and other types – fly across the region.

Baharav, one of the Israeli army's most significant pilots, who served in the 1967 and 1973 wars has said that the only time his life was threatened was not during wartime, but the day he had to use the ejector seat when hit by a buzzard when traveling at over 700km/h:

> . . . as the bird entered my right jet engine, a huge flame shot out the back. I had only seconds to hit the ejector seat button.[15]

Consequently, Israel has decided to take a close and active interest in the migration of birds. It has built a radar system designed to detect birds through what it calls the 'bird plague zones' above Israel/Palestine's narrow waist.[16] This has taken place through the assistance of Yossi Leshem, who as a PhD student convinced the IAF to fund his doctorate project in 1984 after a severe loss in aircraft were being caused by birds collision, and which remained unpublished.[17]

Today, Leshem is one of the key experts on birds' habits in relation to aircraft safety and one of the academics at Tel Aviv University who teaches in the same field – as well as serving in the Israeli Air Force

as a Lieutenant Colonel.[18] The military airbases have ever since counted on Leshem's special tactics to keep birds away. These defenses include radar systems to track birds, the use of specially trained dogs, sounds and 'scarecrow' images placed in strategic locations to scare the birds away.[19] Leshem – who is also known as the bird chaser – has also produced a series of regulations and guidelines which are still used by the Israeli Air Force; these include the marking of Bird-Plagued Zones (BPZ) in the airspace, according to each migration season. These regulations are used for planning flight paths in order to decrease the chances of bird-plane collisions as much as possible.

RADAR SYSTEM: IT IS ALL ABOUT POLITICS

According to Leshem's mapping of birds, three main routes can be identified through Israel and Palestine: the Rift Valley route; the south west corner route where birds cut across it through the Eilat mountains; and the coastal route where birds fly parallel to the coast to exploit the currents created by offshore winds that are displaced upwards when they hit the hills towards the central highlands. Identifying these three routes of bird movement has thus been the starting point for Leshem to set up his radar system. This work has taken place with the help of a former Soviet general who migrated to Israel, Leonid Dinevitch, who was in charge of weather radar facilities throughout the former USSR. Dinevitch is known for his expertise in weather forecasting and in his joint civilian–military project employing 47 radar stations and three aircraft that generated artificial rain. With his help, camouflaged onion-shaped bird radar device is strategically located at the Latrun hilltop overlooking the road between Jerusalem and Tel Aviv on one of the main routes of the birds' migration. However, choosing the location of the radar point had many other tactical reasons other than birds. It is a very significant point politically and historically, as it witnessed so many battles and was one of the key spots the Israelis were desperate to take, as they could not capture it during the 1948 occupation. Latrun has also been an important international crossroads throughout history, situated near the main roads from Jaffa to Jerusalem and from Gaza to Ramallah and on to Damascus.

After the British withdrew from Palestine in 1948, in order to hand it over to the new Israeli state, Latrun remained under the control of the Arab Legion, who used it to enforce a military siege on Jerusalem by blocking water and food from reaching the city. David Ben-Gurion, the first prime minister of Israel, on his very first day, stressed on the urgency to control the road to Jerusalem; consequently, he ordered repeated attempts to capture Latrun, but Israel could not get hold of until the Six Day War in 1967.

Latrun as an area however did not really have any significant characteristics to mark it until 1982, when it was decided that it would host a 'memorial museum' named as the Latrun Armored Corps Memorial. As Edward Platt reported:

> Leshem wanted to combine his radar with a 'living museum' documenting the coexistence of birds and aircraft, but he knew the migration alone wouldn't generate the kind of audiences he wanted, and so he approached the general of the Armored Corps: 'You are telling the story of the bloodshed, the heritage, the conflict . . . this is the story of the past. And I am coming with the story of the future: bird migration, environment, high-tech, radar, Internet, satellites. Give me a piece of land, about eight acres, on your site, and I will build a museum, an auditorium and a scientific centre'.[20]

Today, therefore, the road from Tel Aviv to Jerusalem is 'decorated' with a few tanks and fragments of aircrafts which throughout my childhood I used to think were the remnants of the 1967 war. But in fact, as I realized very recently these aircraft happen to be the fragments of F-15 Falcon fighters which have been destroyed in collision with storks.

It is estimated by the IAF that the early-warning radar system has been so effective that it has saved them – in addition to lives – over $800 million damage. Yet, another bird expert has denied this claim, stating in a conversation with a *Granata* reporter that:

> Yossi Leshem's network of radar stations is not infallible. Israel is so small that if someone burps in the north, you'll hear it on the border with Egypt, and sometimes southbound birds are over the centre of the country before the radar can pick them up.[21]

THE NARROW PARADISE

> It was astonishing to think how far – and how fast – they had traveled. They had left southern Africa while I was still in England and flying for an average of nine hours a day, at forty kilometres per hour, they had pushed through eastern Africa to their pre-wintering grounds in Sudan and Chad. From there, they turned north-west towards Egypt, following the Nile from Aswan to Qina, before crossing the Sinai peninsula and entering southern Israel. Only this morning, they had been in the vast expanse of the Negev Desert and now they were passing our station on the slopes of Mount Gilboa.[22]

During the peak period between 10 March and 20 April, the residents of Palestine are used to waking up to the sound of wings of the 500 million birds migrating over the Great Syrian-African Valley. The rich and complicated ecosystem, the diversity within the Mediterranean climate, and the location as a bottleneck between three different continents, all add to its uniqueness hosting over 500 different species, in one of the busiest air corridors in the world. Yet, we can't really talk about birds without also talking about their relationship with the surface of the land. Birds generally prefer traveling over land to water when flying long distances, since the former offers them a chance to rest, soar, eat, drink and breed.

In the case of historic Palestine, the key significant locations for birds are associated with the Palestinian coast, Jerusalem mountains, eastern slopes of the West Bank and the Jordan valley. Each one of these zones has distinct environmental characteristics with a different climate and bio-geographical location with a rich variety of habitats. The areas also vary from semi-natural, urban and rural areas, and many of them are rich agricultural areas with high agro-biodiversity.[23]

> I say Palestine and you may say Israel, but for the birds it is the same place. The birds can land everywhere, but every species has its own special place where they land – the pelicans, the cranes, raptors, song birds they each have their own place – like people, I guess.[24]

The West Bank itself is blessed with many water sources originating from its underground springs, as mentioned in previous chapters. The water flows bursting between the lime rocky mountains down to the valleys also attract a great number of birds species, especially the small songbirds who gather there to eat, breed and rest. The desert to the south, which is known in Arabic as *Sahara en-Naqab*, and the Jordan Valley also attract many migratory species.

This is due to the low barometric pressure and air thermals, which make it easy for birds to glide for long distances at high speed and using minimum energy.[25]

The distinct topography of the hilly West Bank, in contrast to the Jordan Valley with its sudden drop below sea level, and the coastal western edge, allow for good variation of uneven heating of the air due to the difference in terrain. This again results in strong thermals for soaring birds, particularly near the hills, which helps them make very little effort when riding the air. The benefits of thermal currents are not only limited to the birds, as pilots also take advantage of them to gain altitude. Thus it is crucial for pilots to be aware of the thermals and the location of soaring birds to avoid any possible collision.

The Palestine Wildlife Society has identified 13 'Important Bird Areas' in Palestine.[26] Jericho district and in particular Mar Saba Monastery near the Dead Sea are considered as key locations for attracting birds, given they lie within the boundaries of the Jerusalem Wilderness Area. Most of that area is classified under the Irano-Turanian climate with a mountainous habitat. The steep slopes of the Jerusalem Wilderness Area and the abundant springs that lead to the Dead Sea thus hold unique geological and topographical phenomena which make this an area of exceptional natural beauty as well as a suitable host for different kinds of species of fauna and flora.

The migration of white storks is particularly remarkable in the region as the narrow corridor of Palestine/Israel is on the migratory route of 85 percent of the world's stork population.[27] Yet, the region also attracts pelicans and other raptors. As Atrash – a Palestinian wildlife expert – explains, this list of birds includes:

5.3   The high cliffs of the Mount of
Temptation, Jericho, which are a natural habitat
for different kinds of birds.

5.4   Wadi al Quilt.

5.5   Walking through the Mount of
Temptation, Jericho.

5.6   Jordan Valley with its desert monasteries.

the Lesser Kestrel, Honey Buzzard, Lesser Spotted Eagle, and Egyptian Vulture, all in which use the Jordan Valley, Jericho, and Jerusalem mountain routes.[28]

Of course, all kinds of songbirds are also a rich asset the region enjoys especially, the famous Bulbul, *Abu Alhenna*, and the equally well-known Palestine Sunbird.

> Most of the hundreds of thousands of white storks that pass through the Beit She'an Valley [referring to Bisan Valley] stop to drink, but these birds wouldn't: with the wind driving them on, they would keep going until dark. They would roost in trees or on a cliff face, and feed on anything they could find – dead frogs, fish and insects. Sometimes, Eran said, they arrive in Israel with blackened legs and bodies, having scavenged through burnt undergrowth to feed on corpses barbecued in bush fires. By tomorrow, they would be over Lebanon and Syria, where they would turn north-west, cutting the corner of the Mediterranean and flying above the Turkish port of Iskenderum. They would cross the Bosphorus at Istanbul, or the west side of the Sea of Marmara, and in Bulgaria, they would reach a turning point: some flocks would keep going into Central and Southern Europe and others would turn east, towards.[29]

On one of my journeys in Palestine I joined Sami Backleh in bird watching. Backleh is a well-known twitcher and an expert on wildlife in Palestine, and he helped me to trace birds and taught me how to monitor and observe their behaviour. Sami also ran an environmental awareness program for the team at Riwaq when I used to work there. What was remarkable about the experience is to learn how much human beings can influence birds habitat; on one hand, we can nourish the habitat around by simply installing a basic feeding station with water and nuts to attract small birds as in the case with small songbirds, and yet we can easily confuse their natural patterns and disturb their behaviour by cutting them off from the natural diversity around. The journey with Backleh gave me a new insight into what eco-activism could be in a region where birds can cross the Separation Wall, while humans cannot. Even without its politics, in the case of Palestine it is not only global warming that the country is worried about – it's the physical boundaries and separation that is also causing major gaps by cutting the ecological greenbelt that connect the species and the natural cycles together.

Backleh and I started our route along the monasteries in the Wadi Al Qilt and Jericho area, this being one of the major pathways during migration times – as well as an important spot to watch resident breeding birds. We observed the soaring birds riding the air and making the best out of the air thermals. Apparently, one of the common ways to locate thermals is by observing the location of clouds, which we did. The result of cooling air inside a rising thermal can cause water to evaporate within the air mass, which in turn causes condensation and accumulates cloud. A cumulus cloud that is still growing and in the process of forming is a good indication that an air thermal is present and thus birds will soon be soaring.[30] We watched different kinds of solitary birds like eagles and hawks, which often take advantage of thermals to extend their flight time as they search for food.

We then also visited Ein Qinia near Ramallah; it is one of the unique spots for birds, since Ein Qinia is rich with its fresh water springs. It has its seasonal streams and wetlands which create a great habitat for different kind of wildlife species. Ein Qinia used to

5.7   Ein Qinia water spring. Photograph
by Majdi Hadid.

5.8   Deer crossing a bypass road in Ein Qinia
opposite an Israeli settlement. Photograph
by Majdi Hadid.

be one of the key picnic spots and a resting point for Palestinians picking olives, as well as for bird species during their autumn and spring migration. Today, with the expansion of the Separation Wall and the new Israeli settlements around it, a bypass road has been constructed cutting across the valley and water route to connect the Israeli settlements directly with roads to Tel Aviv. This cut has also created another form of 'green gap' which is threatening nature and causing major environmental and ecological loss.

We followed birds across the disconnected greenbelt of the territory we viewed. Luckily enough, there isn't much required for birds to nest and hence we saw all different kinds of bird colonies. Each species has its own natural behaviour and pattern of life, plus every bird species has its own particular way to build its nest. Many just use the ground on which to lay their eggs, like the desert species; others use cliffs or holes in walls, like the case near the monasteries in the Jordan Valley; a significant colony for falcons and eagles. Other soaring birds nest mostly in high points such as roofs tops or chimneys.

Behind the Separation Wall, lies another paradise that is currently invisible to Palestinians. It stretches from the southern coast of the Red Sea all the way up to the Mediterranean coast and the Haula Valley. Of course, the distinct characteristics of the environmental zones differ across the map, and thus they host different species in each zone. I have never managed to watch the birds from this other side, especially along the coastal line. This area includes Wadi Gaza, which despite its major disastrous pollution caused by sewage mixing with water; it hosts a tremendous variety of birds, as it is located right along the migratory routes.

THE INVISIBLE NET CAPTURING NATURE

Nothing seems to escape the militarized and political nature of life in Israel, with every little detail – even the birds which traverse its skies – falling into the invisible net of its security's apparatus. The radar system devised by Leshen became a political agenda for the IAF and a mean for further power and control. Latrun, like many other locations is a great spot for birds, but there also cannot be a better spot for a radar system. What could be better than making the dream of David Ben-Gurion – one of the leading Zionists who established the Jewish state – come true?

Fortunately, Israel is unable to hijack birds in the same way it has hijacked other natural resources. What is left of the natural reserves in the West Bank is being confiscated on a military basis, such as the national park of Umm Safa near to Birzeit, which on its own hosts more species than the whole city of London does. With the erection of the Separation Wall, and the consequent borderlines, nature in Palestine is being affected tremendously; the water springs in which birds and species count on are now dried out, or mixed with sewage. Areas for birds to nest, eat, or rest are being separated off in such a way that the natural food cycle is being disrupted and unbalanced, causing the degradation of local and migratory wildlife.

The only remaining natural forest that is known to host a great number of breeding birds in Palestinian area – known as Um al Rihan forest, to the north of Jenin – has also been divided by the wall into two parts. The pine forest of Jabal Abu Ghneim to the north of Bethlehem was also completely flattened to install the illegal Israeli settlement of Har Homa. According to a report by Palestine Wildlife director, Mr. Atrash, this forest was the only greenbelt in the north:

> The natural habitat for mammals, such as wolves and foxes, was destroyed and the natural balance of life was ruined.[31]

Unfortunately, until today very little research has been carried out into the effect of these military boundaries on the species, flora and fauna of Palestine. In addition, there is no Palestinian legislation to protect the natural resources within its territorial area. As a result, the damage is being doubled up by the lack of environmental awareness, which in itself is causing a major threat to the cultural landscape in the West Bank, Gaza Strip and all the undefined leftover spaces emerging from the erection of physical boundaries.

Given the heavy fortification of the Separation Wall, no mammals can cross over to the other side; their habitats have been cut in two. Vegetation has also been affected because of the disruption of pollination patterns. Unfortunately, nature is located everywhere and cannot exist according to the strategic location of Israeli settlements, military walls and the 'security' map of Israel. Wildlife and birds simply don't understand borders. Hence, if the greenbelts connecting the natural cycle are disconnected from below, the region will gradually lose its migratory

birds above just as it is losing local inhabitants on the surface. When there is less diversity in nature, ecosystems will gradually become less productive.

PALESTINE SUNBIRD HIJACKED

Even though the physical capturing of birds is still difficult, Israel is nonetheless doing its best to formalize its own symbolic identity, even with birds. For Israel's 60th anniversary celebrations – yet, for Palestinians it marks 60 years of *Nakba* meaning catastrophe – Israel wanted to choose a bird to become their national symbol, one they could call its own. Various birds were suggested and nominated, such as *bulbul* in Arabic or Pycnonotidae, which is a songbird common in areas like Wadi El Bathan near Nablus and Wadi Al Qilt near Jericho and Ein Qinia, near to the Ramallah area. The other choice was the Palestine Sunbird, a small black bird with glittering colours on his head and neck, very common all over Palestine. Luckily enough, the scientific English name for the bird kept the latter out of the nomination process – that stretched over six months – as the Israeli newspaper *Ha'aretz* reported.[32] Instead, the Israeli president Shimon Peres announced the Hoopoe bird would become the symbol for Israel:

It's a bird that takes good care of its children and uses creative tactics to defend itself.[33]

Uzi Paz, a veteran birdwatcher and former head of the Israel Nature and Parks Authority said in praise of this bird:

It is not a songbird, but chirps when it wants to take over territory. There is no external difference between male and female hoopoes.[34]

So there were good reasons to choose the Hoopoe, even though Peres preferred the dove as being a 'true Zionist' as he puts it, when asked about his personal choice:

The dove is equipped with a homing system, which can lead it home from anywhere it may be – and despite limitations and long distances it is a true Zionist.[35]

Even though Israel is currently selling itself through their famous slogan – Migrating Birds Know no Boundaries – the reality is actually trying to ensure that its airspace is nothing but boundaries militarized by nature, as a further attempt to isolate Palestine and its areas from the natural map.[36] Even when

5.9   Palestine Sunbird. Photograph by Haitham Khatib.

5.10   Hoppoe Bird known in Palestine as *Hudhud*. Photograph by Majdi Hadid.

selecting a bird for an identity symbol, Israel seems to need to strongly support the Zionist state and its original dream. The dove – which as far as I know has always been the symbol of hope and peace to followers of Christianity, Judaism and Islam – is suddenly represented as a Zionist ambassador that will eventually come back to the 'land of Israel', while the Hoopoe represents their creative tactical defense system. It is bizarre, to say the least.

Looking at the other side of the Separation Wall, Palestine is not a state and as such has yet to select its own national symbol. However, local and cultural institutions never hesitate to celebrate the beauty of the sunbirds hovering above the land. The international film festival in Palestine in 2010, indeed chose the Palestine Sunbird as their permanent symbol. The enticement is:

> To build the festival's nest, to reproduce and grow, so that we see flocks of birds of Palestine, carrying the depth and

5.11   Re-imagining Kalandia Checkpoint.

174

sweetness of the experience in their wings . . . For five years, we've been building the words to tell about every new feature of this city [Ramallah] and about any dress and jewelry it wears to look better. This city never changes its dress, as it is woven from joy and delight, with a rose planted behind its ears and the Palestinian sunbird on its shoulder, the bird that the city took as its symbol. This bird, decorated with the colors of the spectrum, was known by the world here in this land, and has taken this land's name, then flew to all parts of this world, just like us, we fly and fly, but always return to our first place.[37]

LEAVE IT FOR THE BIRDS

This magic reality bounding the airspace over Palestine/Israel is perhaps the only sign for a roaming freedom and a dream for return. Apart from the broken lines at the ground currently controlled and exercised by Israel, all other boundaries are dissolved with the freedom that birds possess. However, in order to observe bird migration in Palestine, we also need to keep in the military attempts to monitor it. These so-called Israeli 'security measures', in a country based on fear, are actually trying to isolate the territory from the world outside. Indeed, Israel is imprisoning itself within its own boundaries by thinking that it is keeping the 'other' out. Israel is only fencing itself in. If Israelis want to waste their life drawing lines, Palestinians should spend their time enjoying crossing them with all possible means.

The slogan initiated by the IAF – 'take care we share the air' – might have missed a third partner in this scheme. It is not only IAF and the birds which occupy the sky; Palestinians do too. After all, a simple station on the top of Eibal Mountain in Nablus can capture the whole airspace of Israel, and a bird roaming around the sky can also be the most effective flying machine for crossing all boundaries. Therefore, this might be the time for Palestinians to step back, leaving it for the free birds to draw their own quiet map of possibility. Only they can currently soar and glide above the complicated boundaries. Only they can signify the very thing that Palestinians find so hard to capture. Birds are the freedom encapsulated within this thin corridor, and the poetic force that fills the layers of the sky with grace and power.

Let us hope that the day will come where birds will be taking over all physical boundaries, and instead of the concrete wall separating Palestine from Israel, it will be birds nesting on its remaining traces that will draw the absent map and remind us of a past that will hopefully never come back. Hopefully by then, the Palestinian refugees – who became one of the oldest and largest refugee community in the world today – will also be able to come back, and

birds will no longer be needed as the symbol for their return, rather the means by which they can reclaim the land. Not only do both birds and refugees refuse to accept the logic of boundaries, and the inequality and the repression it involves, but they both also share the search for the means in which freedom can be created.

Therefore, any geography, which emerges from oppression, should be made possible for these birds to occupy, nest, breed, grow and multiply. Eventually, they will accumulate the necessary power to break the solid lines on the surface of the land, and mark new ones yet to come as a product of collective ideology born from the sky. Birds are the ambassadors of freedom in the troubled territory of Palestine/Israel.

MOMENTS OF POSSIBILITY
THE FLYING MACHINE INHABITING THE SKY

Where should we go after the last frontiers, where should the birds fly after the last sky? Where should the plants sleep after the last breath of air? (Mahmoud Darwish).

Away from the complex borderlines on the surface of the West Bank, birds quietly inhabit a space that cannot be reached by mere humans. A series of 'bird machines' thus aims to create a new kind of confrontation between freedom of movement and solid boundaries, in effect by making the Separation Wall a new habitat for birds.

The envisaged 'bird machines' will work alongside the existing invisible networks on the ground of the West Bank. Indeed, these hidden local networks are to decide where and when

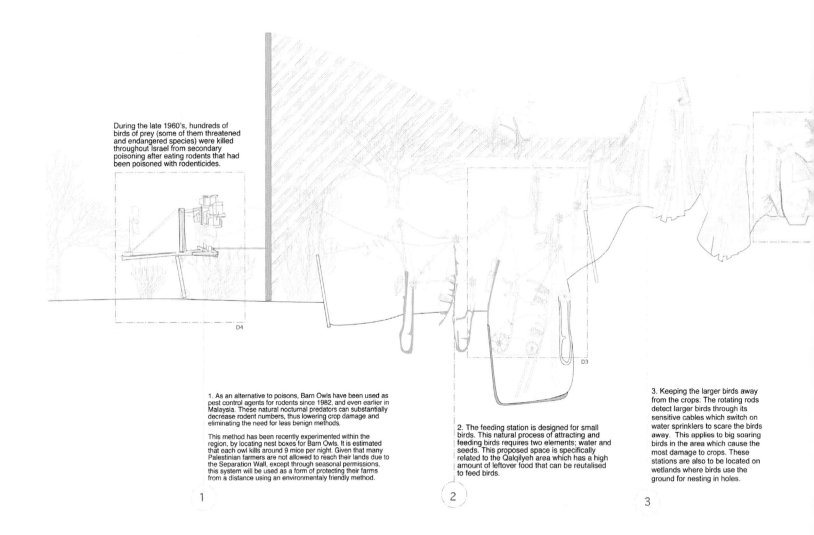

During the late 1960's, hundreds of
birds of prey (some of them threatened
and endangered species) were killed
throughout Israel from secondary
poisoning after eating rodents that had
been poisoned with rodenticides.

D4

D3

1. As an alternative to poisons, Barn Owls have been used as
pest control agents for rodents since 1982, and even earlier in
Malaysia. These natural nocturnal predators can substantially
decrease rodent numbers, thus lowering crop damage and
eliminating the need for less benign methods.

This method has been recently experimented within the
region, by locating nest boxes for Barn Owls. It is estimated
that each owl kills around 9 mice per night. Given that many
Palestinian farmers are not allowed to reach their lands due to
the Separation Wall, except through seasonal permissions,
this system will be used as a form of protecting their farms
from a distance using an environmentaly friendly method.

2. The feeding station is designed for small
birds. This natural process of attracting and
feeding birds requires two elements; water and
seeds. This proposed space is specifically
related to the Qalqilyeh area which has a high
amount of leftover food that can be reutalised
to feed birds.

3. Keeping the larger birds away
from the crops: The rotating rods
detect larger birds through its
sensitive cables which switch on
water sprinklers to scare the birds
away. This applies to big soaring
birds in the area which cause the
most damage to crops. These
stations are also to be located on
wetlands where birds use the
ground for nesting in holes.

1

2

3

5.12   The Bird Machines, section AA.

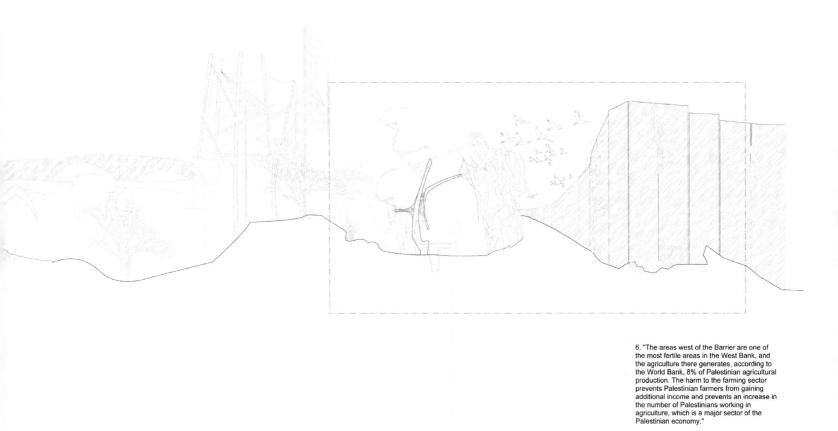

6. "The areas west of the Barrier are one of the most fertile areas in the West Bank, and the agriculture there generates, according to the World Bank, 8% of Palestinian agricultural production. The harm to the farming sector prevents Palestinian farmers from gaining additional income and prevents an increase in the number of Palestinians working in agriculture, which is a major sector of the Palestinian economy."

[B'Tselem - Israeli Information Center for Human Rights in the Occupied Territories]

4. 'The kettle'
(see D2 for details)
The aim of this machine is to create artificial clouds that can help birds in soaring and gliding, as well as directing them towards certain heights in the sky

5. 'The bird machine'.
(see D1 for details)

5

6

The Bird Machine
Section A-A

0   1   2

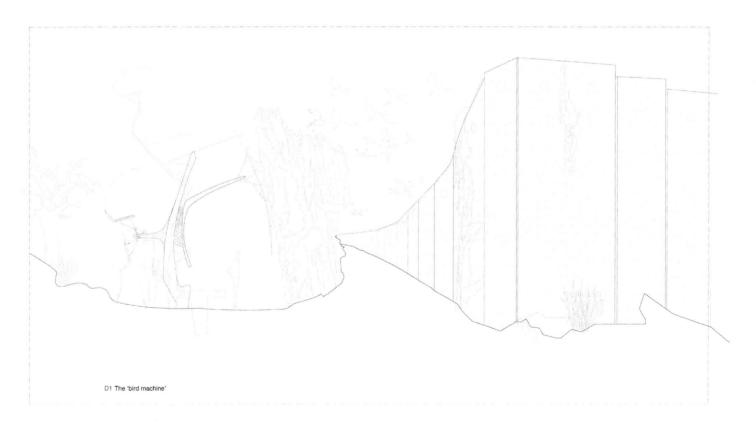

D1 The 'bird machine'

5.13   When the birds take over.

5.14   D1: The Bird Machine.

Birds redefining the West
Bank's aerial map

5.15   Birds re-drawing the Palestinian map.

The Fabric Wall

1 Collective bag-making room for commuters.

2 Main steel structure holding the 'bird machine'.

3 Feeding station: the bags of seeds.

4 Main area for public interaction.

5 'Fabric wall' located on the Palestinian side to provide a habitat for birds to nest and breed.

6 The Separation Wall stretching across the West Bank to isolate Palestinian neighbourhoods and expand Jerusalem on its eastern side.

7 Agricultural lands which belong to the Palestinian villages yet have been expropriated by Israel.

8 'Greenbelt' as a habitat for species to make up for the deserted areas behind the wall. The greenbelt station contains pumps, detectors and different tools to measure water level and detect migration routes.

9 Main access to the maintenance station.

10 Mobile workshop room.

11 Communal space leading to the bird-watching stations.

12 Adabtable mobile tracks for 'greenbelts'.

13 Water trench connected to the 'fabric wall' bird habitat to collect surface water and direct it towards the 'greenbelts'.

14 Bird-watch station to detect migratory birds.

D3
scale 1:250

5.16   The fabric wall.

D2 The Kettle

Soaring migratory birds – such as large birds of prey - glide between areas of rising hot air to aid their long-distance passage. This method, which cannot be used over large bodies of water or on high mountains, concentrates birds into corridors and through tight bottlenecks. 'The kettle' is a term that birdwatchers use to describe a group of migrating birds, that are circling and soaring upward on rising air currents. These thermal currents are mainly caused as a result of warm air moving upward while cold air is displaced, dropping down from higher levels in the atmosphere.

1. Solar panels located on the outerskin of 'the kettle'. The aim is to absorb heat for the internal water pipes, which in returnheats the water wells which in return heats the water well and radiates steam into the air.

2. The neck of 'the kettle'. An openable fan to control the extent of heated air and redirect it towards the targeted areas.

3. Mobile fans to control and direct the heat in the air.

4. Insulated water reservoir containing heated water.

5. Radiation panels to heat the atmosphere and cause air movement.

6. Internal insulated pipes to generate steam

7. Pressure valve.

8. 'Green pockets' located on the outer skin of 'the kettle' to improve internal insulation and provide an additional habitat for animals. It is also a way to camouflage 'the kettles' and integrate them within their context.

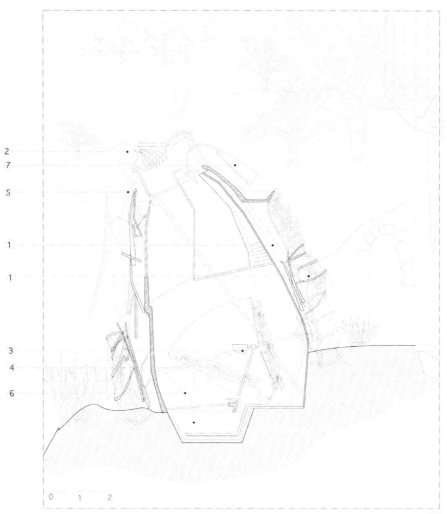

D2

5.17   The Kettle.

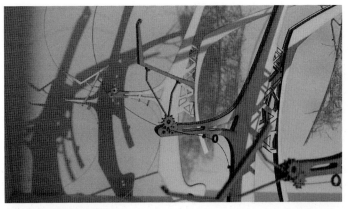
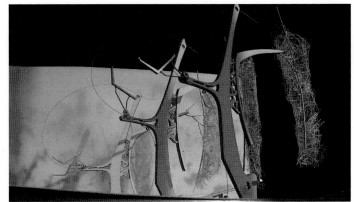

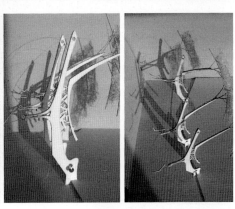

5.18　Making the machines.

5.19   The 'sewing machine'.

5.20   The barn owl nest boxes.

to accumulate their 'aerial forces'. Palestinian commuters are to nurture the machines by spreading their sticky pockets. These are in essence fabric pockets filled in with seeds and other natural elements, such as twigs for nests, which can help to create a habitat for birds when stuck onto rigid elements like the thick concrete slabs of the Separation Wall. Over time, as more and more of the sticky pockets have been surreptitiously accumulated, birds will start to occupy the rigid walls. This process is hence seen as an ongoing strategy to gradually amass power by using birds as collaborators.

The structure for each 'bird machine' ends with a series of spiral curtains which are also attached to one another. As such, they wrap around to hide the networks inside and keep them hidden away from the extensive Israeli CCTV via barbed wire connected to the wall. These spiral curtains are also the place where the sticky pockets are initially located before being picked up and moved towards their final destination higher up the Separation Wall. The curtains are thus a kind of 'sewing machine' run by the birds since they are composed of the main raw materials needed for nesting; layers of fibre, fabric and bird feeding points. When the pockets are located in this initial position, they will become naturally inhabited by birds and their nesting materials (mainly dried grass, hair, fabric and string collected from the inserted curtains as well as from the surrounding context). The process of gathering together the nesting elements will take the birds up to few weeks. Hence, and before reaching a point where the sticky pockets are 'ripe' enough to be used, they need to be collected by local Palestinians, fixed onto elastic cables, and released up towards the Separation Wall, thereby directing the birds towards it. The free natural movement of birds towards the wall acts as a new technique to distract and get beyond with the systems of motion sensors and CCTV cameras which currently pick up any human presence at the moment.

This process of 'quiet encroachment' should be seen as a collective ideology born from the sky; birds are in control, they soar, glide, breed and nest wherever necessary. Furthermore, boundaries are exposed and blurred by the act of birds 'shaking' the assumed solidity of the Separation Wall. When the wall eventually falls – and it will – the birds will always be there to mark the traces of what has been left behind.

The proposed 'bird machines' not only surround the Separation Wall and other physical boundaries of Israeli occupation. They are also to be located in strategic points across the West Bank to act as meeting stations for the invisible networks of Palestinian resistance, providing them with ephemeral coordinate points as an 'invisible' coding system. These points will be mainly generated by creating temporary artificial clouds which connect the detached 'greenbelt' while also setting up thermals to help the birds to soar. This is done primarily through the use of a device which I term the 'kettle', with these being invisibly embedded into the topography of the central highlands of the West Bank to overcome variations in uneven natural heating of the air. This in return results in new thermals which will attract soaring birds in their efforts to gain altitude. The skin of the 'kettle' itself has solar panels fixed to it to create heat variations in the air. Additionally, these solar panels will heat a water reservoir at the bottom of the 'kettle' which will initiate instant clouds whenever needed through the process of water evaporation. Each 'kettle' will be camouflaged into the landscape by having a green skin for its outer panel, which also offers an additional habitat for animals around it.

The 'kettles' will not only be located in the lands of Area B and Area C to assist Palestinians in their journeys while seeking work; their clouds will be also directed above all illegal Israeli settlements hosting birds to glide. They will thus draw a different aerial map of 'alive' points and lines that can then be reconnected at some point in a strategy of resistance. This will hopefully remind the Israeli occupier that they too are being watched, and the Palestinians have not forgotten the seized land, as David Ben Gurion had hoped would happen over time.[38]

BARN OWL NEST BOXES

A whole series of Barn Owl nest boxes are used to be as an agricultural pest controller. They are proposed as a natural way to create 'flying mousetraps' for Palestinian farmers who cannot reach their fields regularly in order to prevent their crops being damaged before harvesting. These 'flying mousetraps' are envisaged as a substitute for the chemicals and poisons which are costly and greatly endanger birds, as happened in Israel in 1997 when a large number of raptors where killed after accidently eating these unnatural pesticides. The new owl nests are to be located either in the inner skin of the 'kettle' devices or installed in clusters across the fields. The boxes themselves will be made from the leftovers of wooden boxes and other furniture currently being used by farmers. Given that Barn Owls are not interested in the nature of the box itself, but rather the size of the access holes, the diameter of the holes in the new boxes will vary, yet will be regulated to a 100 mm maximum diameter to allow only smaller owls to occupy them.

NOTES

1 Quote from Israeli Ministry of Tourism website. Available at: http://www.goisrael.com/tourism_eng [accessed 8 January 2011].

2 See Article 1 of the 1919 Paris Convention, and the 1944 Chicago Convention on international civil aviation.

3 See report by Udi Dekel. Available at: http://jcpa.org/control_of_territorial_airspace/ [accessed 4 December 2010].

4 The Palestinian request to have their own airport in the West Bank, and specifically to regain Kalandia Airport, was rejected given its close location to Jerusalem. Thus, within the Oslo Agreement it was stated that any Palestinian airport should be located far from any Israeli populated area. Subsequently, the Palestinian airport has ended up being located in Rafah. The airport has been closed since 2000 after the *Second Intifada*, and it was later bombed by Israel in 2001.

5 See the Oslo Interim Agreement, annex 1, article xiii.

6 Weizman, E. 'Control in the Air', *Open Democracy*, 1 May 2002. Available at: http://www.opendemocracy.net/ecology-politicsverticality/article_810.jsp%23%3Caccessed [accessed 5 December 2010].

7 Tomlinson, H. (2010) 'Saudi Arabia Gives Israel Clear Skies to Attack Iranian Nuclear Sites', *The Sunday Times*, 12 June 2010. Available at: http://www.timesonline.co.uk/tol/news/world/middle_east/article7148555.ece [accessed 12 January 2011].

8 Dekel, U. 'Control of the Territorial Airspace and the Electromagnetic Spectrum', *Airspace*. Available at: http://www.jcpa.org/text/security/dekel.pdf [accessed 29 November 2010]. See also Diker, D. (2010) *Israel's Critical Security Needs for a Viable Peace*. Jerusalem: Jerusalem Centre for Public Affairs. Available at: http://www.europe-israel.org/download/israel_security.pdf [accessed 8 December 2010].

9 Weizman, op. cit.

10 Ibid.

11 The words of a well-known political song by a Lebanese singer, Fairouz, about the Palestinian refugees in Lebanon and their dream of return.

12 Platt, E. (2008) 'The Migration', *Granata*, 7 July 2008. Available at: http://www.granta.com/Magazine/102/The-Migration [accessed 16 December 2010].

13 Ibid.

14 Anon. 'Birds and Airplanes: The Conflict', *Birding Israel*. Available at: http://www.birds.org.il/740-en/Birding-Israel.aspx [accessed 16 December 2010].

15 Donnison, J. (2010) 'Bird Watchers Find Heaven in "Superhighway" Israel', *BBC News*, 1 December 2010. Available at: http://www.bbc.co.uk/news/world-middle-east-11877873 [accessed 11 December 2010].

16 Platt, op. cit.

17 See also Anon. 'Birds and Airplanes: The Conflict', *Birding Israel*. Available at: http://www.birds.org.il/740-en/Birding-Israel.aspx [accessed 16 December 2010].

18 Leshem has also developed an educational and scientific website on the Internet, called 'Migrating Birds Know No Boundaries'. It includes a series of guidelines and regulations under the name of 'Take care. We share the air', which became the motto of present-day Israeli Defence Force courses on nature protection. See http:www.birds.org.il

19 Picow, M. (2009) 'Yossi Leshem Works to Save Birds and Pilots in the Middle East', *Green Prophet*, 15 March 2009. Available at: http://www.greenprophet.com/2009/03/leshem-hudson-plane-crash-birds/ [accessed 27 November 2010].

20 Platt, op. cit.

21 Ibid.

22 Ibid.

23 This data is based on the records of Palestine Wildlife Society and the register for Important Bird Areas in Palestine (IBA's).

24 Prince-Gibson, E. (2006) ' A Day in the Life of Imad Atrash: Protecting Wildlife in Palestine', *Bridges*, Vol. 2 (6) (October–December). Available at: http://webcache.googleusercontent.com/search?q=cache:Ek03b4KPE6kJ:portal.wildlife-pal.org/php/modules.php%3Fname%3DNews%26file%3Darticle%26sid%3D13+where+do+storks+fly+over+palestine&cd=7&hl=en&ct=clnk&gl=uk&client=safari [accessed 18 December 2010].

25 The sight of dozens or hundreds of birds riding a thermal resembles the water boiling in a kettle – hence the terms 'kettle' or 'boil' are sometimes used to represent a flock of birds circling in a thermal updraft.
See Anon. 'Birds, Thermals and Soaring Flight', *Aerospace*, Available at: http://www.aerospaceweb.org/question/nature/q0253.shtml [accessed 13 November 2010].

26 Important Birds Areas (IBA) data by Palestine Wildlife Society.

27 See *Alternative Tourism Group (ANON)*, www.atg.ps (accessed 11.2.10).

28 Atrash, I. (2008) 'Forests as Important Bird Areas in Palestine', *This Week in Palestine*, No. 118 (February), pp. 28–30.

29 Platt, op. cit.

30 What was also interesting during our tour was watching the natural 'flying mouse-traps' along the fields of Jericho, created by the Palestinian farmers to control their agricultural pests. Instead of using chemicals, Palestinians, Israelis and many other countries around the world, count on barn owls and kestrels – common raptors in the region – to naturally capture pests that might harm their products. The farmers have created simple nest boxes which host owls during the night and kestrels during the day. These are now becoming common features which decorate the agricultural fields on both sides.

31 Prince-Gibson, op. cit.

32 Jabr, S. (2007) 'Don't Hijack the Birds of Palestine', *Jerusalem Journal*, (July), pp. 12–35. Available at: http://www.wrmea.com/archives/July_2007/0707012.html [accessed 28 September 2010].

33 Erlichman, E. 'Hoopoe Israel's New National Bird', *Y Net News*, 30 May 2008. Available at: http://www.ynetnews.com/articles/0,7340,L-3549637,00.html [accessed 19 December 2010].

34 Rinat, Z. (2008) 'Hoopoe Crowned Nat'l Bird', *Haaretz*, 30 May 2008. Available at: http://www.haaretz.com/print-edition/news/hoopoe-crowned-nat-l-bird-1.246885 [accessed 16 June 2010].

35 Erlichman, op. cit.

36 Anon. (2003) 'Migrating Birds Know No Boundaries', *Israeli Ministry of Foreign Affairs*, 19 November 2003. Available at: http://www.mfa.gov.il/mfa/mfa%20publications/photo%20exhibits/migrating%20birds%20know%20no%20boundaries [accessed 12 December 2010].

37 Anon. (2010) 'Al-Kasaba Festival Letter', *Al-Kasaba Theatre and Cinematheque*, 18 October 2010. Available at: http://webcache.googleusercontent.com/search?q=cache:qFm-MmqwN6oJ:www.alkasaba.org/festival2010/details.php%3Fid%3Dgj43v6a215ytocjqrzuv+symbol+palestine+sunbird+festiva%3B&cd=4&hl=en&ct=clnk&gl=uk&client=safari [accessed 4 July 2010].

38 As mentioned by the first Israeli Prime Minister, David Ben Gurion, after the first clearances of Palestinians took place in 1948. He predicted that, over time, 'The old will die and the young will forget'.

Lying between dream and realism, the series of design proposals need to be seen as moments of slow change for those who are currently unable to fit into the distorted Palestinian map, and who have been forcefully removed from the front line of debate due to political realities. These moments are not meant to enforce themselves onto the map, or onto Palestinian people. Instead, they must be seen as possibilities that are inspired and nourished by everyday social and political events, and which, if taken into account, can help change to happen.

The design interventions in the project for Birzeit's historic centre are intended to be subtle and indeed invisible. They are very much embedded within local practices and everyday life to create the social and spatial conditions which will allow local citizens to take over. Birzeit's regeneration is seen as a moment of reality that I started from and always returned to. On the other hand, the 'Underground' and 'Air' chapters offer a tactical critique of the current strategies of Israeli occupation, and indeed offer a sort of ironic and subversive form of reclamation.

By going underground, the design language is a form of confrontation. It addresses the 'other' while by capturing, crushing and excavating their underground territory. This is why the existing machinery that is viciously taking over the Palestinian landscape – cranes, bulldozers, trucks, lifts, etc. – are deliberately retained for my proposed interventions. Their familiar dystopian face is kept as a fake moment of normality, and is then masked by invisible tactics for healing. While the machines add a dramatic countenance on the surface, underneath they are used to 'stitch' spaces together across the whole map. Despite their seeming anger, when touching the earth, these giant machines inject memories, absorb rainwater and release what can bring life back to the dying earth. The moments of possibility in the 'Air' chapter hold more of dreamlike and surreal character. They propose possibilities above the surface and its confined boundaries, emphasizing on the need to shake up the seeming solidity of lines on the ground. Meanwhile, the devices are in a process of organic accumulation, and as such cultivate hope. The 'machine' in this context challenges the norm by promoting bird habitats with all their delicacy and fragility, in order to capture what is still left in the air to breath.

Despite the different design languages, they complement one another in that they share the common aim of accumulating power while offering varying registers of possibilities. Some tackle straightforward points of confrontation, while others have a broader scope that penetrates everywhere below ground or up in the air. None of my interventions are meant to impose themselves on the land, even the speculative interventions which might be misread as 'bold' monumental objects. In reality, they work discreetly underground and in the air to assist local agencies. The real challenge is to see where and how these moments can overlap to become integrated within a silent network of resistance. Can a stone quarry, a cluster of bird nests, and a worker and commuter waiting to cross a checkpoint, act to inform one another? I believe it is possible.

Collectiveness, time and patience can work to alter realities in the West Bank; together they represent a form of invisible tracing in which the effect can show up on a longer timescale – exactly when it will be too late to stop. Nonetheless, everything is ephemeral, temporary, movable and reversible. In summary, the proposed resistance tactics are about searching for and weaving together a series of invisible networks that can overlap. It is the accumulation and scale of these hidden networks that matters, as they have always existed, and will continue to do so. These moments are thus the meeting points between the inner and outer world inhabited today by Palestinians; they take their place in the dialogue of the real and the imagined, the personal with the social, and the individual with the collective. Out of these simple interventions, one can change the 'facts on the ground'.

SEEING LESS
AND LESS
OF THE OTHER

Despite the possibilities cited in this book, one needs to keep in mind Dovey's category of 'concealed power' in shaping the Palestinian socio-political map.[1] Under the shadows of confining Palestinians into specific geographical boundaries – whether physically or psychologically – lie so many layers of internal occupation.

Indeed, the fact that Palestinians are today seeing less and less of the 'other' has its own long-term impact. I believe that the less one encounters the 'other', the more possible we forget they exist – and the more possible that Palestinians forget the cause of having to travel through the 'no-drive' zones and alternative routes. At that point, creative forms of spatial resistance might lose their weight and become

just another way to normalize the Israeli oppression. Therefore, Palestinians need to be able to challenge being passive audience members in what is in reality a battle.

'Breathing bubbles' injected between the (Israeli-drawn) map to avoid the eruption of a new revolution in Palestine, is what Ramallah and many other urban pockets currently represent. As mentioned in earlier chapters, Ramallah is seen by some urban analysts as a deliberate site for consumption and 'social liberty' facilitated by Israel to release the pressure amongst the wealthiest of the oppressed: 'A fantasy of a co-existence of occupation and freedom',[2] which in turn nourishes passiveness. The troubled economic forces, combined with the leftovers of the

6.1 Abu Dis trapped behind the Separation Wall. Photograph by Majdi Hadid.

189

Oslo Agreement, are accelerating social and spatial disorders, and as such are playing a key role in pulling attention away from the occupier. All of this is taking place behind a fake mask of economic livelihood and modernity.

Looking at the problem from a slightly different angle, *Wadi al Nar* – the famous informal route known as the 'Valley of Fire', connecting the northern part of the West Bank with Bethlehem and the south – is another reminder of how creative daily alterations can be 'hijacked' as a tool to reinforce and normalize the borderlines.[3] With Israeli forces asphalting this route and widening it, it seems that they have managed to release the pressure vessel, which otherwise could have erupted in revolution. Now, Palestinians seem to have forgotten that this site was never meant to be the formal way of communication. Suddenly, the one-time ephemeral spot of creativity has been turned into a permanent checkpoint on the map, creating even deeper nodes of occupation through adaptation.

This process of 'occupation from within', which Israel has been enforcing over the past decade, has also been exercised spatially through the torture of waiting, movement and chaos that I referred to in earlier chapters. Some critics argue that this is being consciously done as a strategy of 'learned helplessness'[4] in which actions driven by fear have formed a key part of the Israeli occupation.[5] The conditions of waiting, immobility and constant chaos for Palestinians at Israeli checkpoints has over time forced many Palestinians – who might otherwise wish to travel – to decide not to do so in order to avoid the humiliation of having to face spatial tools which convey in them a sense of helplessness and despair.[6]

Moreover, the invisible force of Israeli power is best manifested through the tactics of occupation by 'remote control', as many Palestinians refer to it. This was definitely exercised to its extreme in the Oslo Peace Agreement, as explained in this book. When Israel withdrew from the Palestinian areas after the Oslo Agreement, they handed them over to a non-sovereign Palestinian regime appointed to act on their behalf. This, in effect, created conditions for population and economic control from a distance, through techniques such as surveillance, checkpoints, bypass roads, administrative and natural resources control.[7] But it also meant that there is no 'physical' confrontation with the excluded 'other', as explained in the first and second chapter of this volume. And thus the strategies for defiance, resistance and mass civil disobedience, which characterized the *First Intifada*, became almost impossible (apart from the military checkpoints and zones marking the borderlines).[8] The Oslo Peace Agreement meant that the people who led the *First Intifada* were suddenly alienated from any political role. This, I believe, has caused a major shift in Palestinian lifestyles and the ways in which its people negotiate its space and politics. The successful tools that existed prior to the Oslo Peace Agreement are currently missing: lack of ownership, leadership, sense of community, and above all, economic sovereignty.

The *First Intifada* is therefore a very crucial event to keep in mind for its spatial context, rather than its political achievements. That period led to a relatively sustainable economy compared to later in the 1990s, in the sense that during that period one could at least see the seeds for economic prosperity, which then became almost absent after the Oslo Agreement. The small-scale local and collective initiatives – mainly in agriculture – which spread across the whole West Bank and the Gaza Strip after the *First Intifada* have now unfortunately become dominated by a very specific, and indeed small sector of society.

According to a recent documentary by two film directors, Mariam Shaheen and George Azar, Palestinians were substantially more economically sufficient in the 1970s and 1980s and even used to export fruit and vegetables throughout the Arab world.[9] Following the Oslo Peace Agreement, agriculture and farming stopped being a priority. On the one hand, agricultural lands were mostly located in Areas B and C according to the new zoning, which lay out of the Palestinians' sovereignty, and on the other hand, water and other natural resources fell under full Israeli control. Furthermore, after the Oslo Agreement the Palestinian economic planners favoured costly new industrial schemes over agricultural development, which proved to be problematic. According to the Bisan Centre for Research and Development, the agricultural lands of Marj Bin Amer, considered to be the 'bread basket' of the Palestinians, were selected as the new industrial zone by the Palestinian Authority. This was largely due to Israeli insistence and pressure. Furthermore, Israel insisted that no water reservoirs or electricity plants could be built by Palestinians, which automatically means that all resources have to be provide and purchased through Israel.[10]

Today, in the area for this new industrial zone of Al Jalameh, Israel exerts complete control over water, electricity and infrastructure. The project has now been discussed for over 16 years but nothing has been implemented, apart from destroying all the agricultural lands in Al Jalameh to build one long gravel road which sits unused and leads to nowhere.[11]

Unfortunately the donors – the German Development Bank – now realize that the project cannot ever be feasible while Israel controls the borders and natural resources. But what were the Palestinian officials thinking about when they agreed to the plan?

In other words, the 1980s seems to have offered a more prosperous society for Palestinians. It was the only time when all agencies were working horizontally rather than vertically. However, I would like to stress here that I'm not calling for another *Intifada* to take place: instead I'm simply pointing out the continued absence of a credible body that might lift Palestinians back up again. It seems to me that it is now far more important to revive the social relationships and collective processes that managed – even if silently – to empower every individual during the *First Intifada*. Indeed, no initiative can work in isolation from the other components of power, and so 'bottom-up' movements in the case of Palestine need to be celebrated and work in parallel with 'top-down' organized political movements. Above all, ordinary Palestinians need to be able to recognize their own independent autonomy, which is an aspect I tried to touch upon with the design for Birzeit's historic centre.

Despite the above points, what still exists today, or at least is slowly being reborn, is an ad-hoc social mobilization which is crystallizing to become collective in certain contexts. It might not yet be fully rooted in popular committees, as the case of the 1970s and 1980s, but the early signs are there. Some, like Tamari, argue that no alternative resistance strategy has evolved ever since the *First Intifada*, which in many ways is true in a conventional sense.[12] However, I don't think the informal and passive movements of resilience that have been evolving

6.2 Flooding the exhausted surface.

recently are to be ignored, or undermined, as they are initiating tactical forms of 'horizontal' resistance, spreading in different scales across the map, while also trying to formulate a sense of leadership within its cores.

Therefore, the Separation Wall and other physical boundaries are the least of the problem from a Palestinian perspective. What is far more dangerous are the invisible forms of occupation which seem to be penetrating through and are causing a severe decay

within Palestinian daily life. Occupation through imagination, time, immobility and remote control, is thus more critical than the Separation Wall and other parts of the 'tsunami of concrete' and borderlines found on the surface of the land today.

TOWARDS A MORE CREATIVE POLITICS IN PALESTINE

Ian McEwan, the well-known British author, accepted the Israeli 'Jerusalem International Book Fair' Prize for 2011. While trying 'shyly' to criticize Israeli occupation, amidst critical views about his visit, and despite my own disagreement with some statements he made in support of Israel and against the elected Hamas government, McEwan stressed the need for a new era of political creativity that could allow for a different kind of space:

> There are some similarities between a novel and a city. A novel, of course, is not merely a book, a physical object of pages and covers, but a particular kind of mental space, a place of exploration, of investigation into human nature. Likewise, a city is not only an agglomeration of buildings and streets. It is also a mental space, a field of dreams and contention. Within both entities, people, individuals, imaginary or real, struggle for their 'right to self-realisation'.[13]

I would argue that the 'field of dreams' mentioned by McEwan is currently in a state of rebirth in Palestine. Unfortunately, it might not have all the ingredients required to keep it nourished, but it has the will and persistence of people who go far beyond looking at buildings to discover what lies in-between. The subtle new spaces emerging – despite their chaotic nature – are indeed challenging the rhetorical question of planning without sovereignty or full power over urban space. Unlike the imposed planning policies that have been enforced on Palestine to date, this book shows that design should be about cultivating possibilities by reversing the current map and starting from its voids. It is about resilience that creates collectiveness, which in turn can initiate change. The new social spaces in Palestine – though not yet as visible on the world-stage as a mass protest or full-scale revolution – seem to be gradually destroying the linearity of the conventional ones imposed by Israel.

OTHER POSSIBLE MOMENTS

Because the territorial logic of Israeli occupation has created a Palestinian 'Thirdspace' which is emerging in response to oppression, Palestine is no longer just the city or the village – it is also the in-between, the dead spaces, and the margins. Therefore, it seems that any design interventions to stitch the land have to lead to a more elastic space born from the will to connect – a space of resistance that keeps on changing with the conditions. Design interventions need to respond to this instability through the tactics of an emergent architecture, which might seem ephemeral in its nature, yet is quick in its effects. What is needed today is a responsive architecture, which multiplies surfaces with boundaries to create new virtual dimensions. It might seem confusing to the viewer, but is very familiar to Palestinians since it addresses those leftover spots which have been left to decline. Invisibility, subversion and silence – on and below the surface – can be put to work three-dimensionally to reclaim the land. For that reason, these kinds of residual spaces have formed a key component in all of my design interventions in order to back up social networks and break down any lines, solid walls or thick boundaries imposed with an unwanted spatial system of codes.

The design interventions – or more correctly, the moments of possibility proposed in this book – may not hold the full answer or the solution for the Palestinian/Israeli conflict. However, they do illustrate how one could begin to pick up on a very simple detail from daily life and celebrate it, and then turn what might seem a very normal observation into a subversive concept, and then after that turn this concept into a tool, and that tool into a design proposal. Indeed, my wish is to argue that resilience as a way of life is not necessarily a form of giving up or accepting facts on the ground, as many might argue. Instead, it can be a creative tool of resistance when backed up with a clear strategy, such as can be provided – as shown here – by innovative architectural design proposals.

Hence, these design possibilities bring an alternative voice to Palestine by seeking possibilities in the spatial gaps rather than the imposed maps. Nevertheless, other agencies that refuse to accept inequality and try to find the means to resist it also exist in these gaps, especially in terms of the new 'security' measures against possible 'imagined' threats which seem to dominate around the world today. Indeed, with the forces of power exercising hegemony over the framing of spaces and the shaping of the built environment, a process of fragmentation can clearly be seen to be taking place globally, cutting away existing communities on the one hand and connecting them together in new ways on another.[14] Such processes might be at their most visible and brutal in Palestine, yet the forces of neo-imperialism, globalization and inequality are emblematically reshaping contemporary cities everywhere. Blurred border lines are being solidified, restructuring the ways in which people can move and act, creating a network of undermined and suppressed societies who have been left behind and are then engaged in struggles to overcome the hidden forces of state power. For that reason, we must always keep Edward Said's lines in the back of our minds in order to sustain the process of resistance, which we can only do by 'reaffirming the power of culture over the culture of power'.

NOTES

1 See Dovey, K. (1999) *Framing Places: Mediating Power in Built Form.* London: Routledge.

2 See Ramallah Syndrome. Available at: http://ramallahsyndrome.blogspot.com/2009_10_01_archive.html [accessed 11 April 2011].

3 Following the isolation of Jerusalem from the rest of the West Bank, the direct routes through Jerusalem were blocked and thus an informal alternative route had to be born as the only mean to reconnect Bethlehem and Hebron with the north. This route was named by the Palestinians as the 'Valley of Fire'. Later, one Palestinian initiated his mobile grocery shop in a container for the commuters along the route. This spot was taken over by Israel and became a permanent checkpoint, known today as the 'container checkpoint', with a watchtower and an iron gate.

4 For more information about the theory of Pavlov and Seligman on human actions driven by fear, see 'Learned Helplessness', Wikipedia. Available at: http://en.wikipedia.org/wiki/Learned_helplessness [accessed 20 April 2012]. 'As a technical term, it means a condition of a human being or an animal in which it has learned to behave helplessly, even when the opportunity is restored for it to help itself by avoiding an unpleasant or harmful circumstance to which it has been subjected. Learned helplessness theory may result from a perceived absence of control over the outcome of a situation'.

5 Yazid Anani, a Palestinian landscape architect, has talked about this subject in the Ramallah Lectures series. See 'Learned Helplessness', Ramallah Lecture. Available at: http://theramallahlecture.blogspot.com/2008/07/learned-helplessness.html [accessed 13 February 2011].

6 Overmier, J.B. and Seligman, M.E.P. (1967). 'Effects of Inescapable Shock Upon Subsequent Escape and Avoidance Responding', *Journal of Comparative and Physiological Psychology*, Vol. 63, pp. 28–33.

7 As has been noted in earlier chapters, this applies only to areas A and B, as area C and East Jerusalem has always been in full control of the Israeli Forces.

8 See also Tamari's reflection on Weizman's Hollow Land. Tamari, S. (2009) 'Architectural Laboratory of the Extreme? Reflections on Weizman's Hollow Land', *Jerusalem Quarterly*, Vol. 38, pp. 21–3.

9 See the documentary, *Donor Opium*, directed by Mariam Shaheen and George Azar. Available at: http://www.youtube.com/watch?v=wVTYyRLMljc [accessed 22 December 2011].

10 Ibid.

11 Ibid.

12 Tamari, op. cit.

13 McEwan, I. (2011) 'Ian McEwan on Winning the Jerusalem Prize', *The Guardian*, 24 February 2011.

14 Dovey, op. cit.

Bibliography

Abu El-Haj, N. (2001) *Facts on the Ground: Archaeological Practice and Territorial Self-fashioning in Israeli Society*. London and Chicago, IL: University of Chicago Press.

Abu-Zahra, N. (2008) 'Identity Cards and Coercion in Palestine', in Rachel, P. and Susan, J.S. (eds), *Fear: Critical Geopolitics and Everyday Life*. Burlington, VT: Ashgate, pp. 175–91.

Abunimah, A. (2011) 'Egypt's Uprising and its Implications for Palestine', *Electronic Intifada*, 29 January 2011. Available at: http://electronicintifada.net/content/egypts-uprising-and-its-implications-palestine/9203 [accessed 14 May 2011].

Adiv, A. (2007) 'Palestinian Quarry Workers Organize', *Challenge*, No. 104 (July/August). Available at: http://www.challenge-mag.com/en/article__121 [accessed 15 March 2010].

Agamben, G. (2005) *State of Exception*. Chicago, IL: University of Chicago Press.

Agamben, G. (1998) *Homo Sacer: Sovereign Power and Bare Life*. Stanford, CA: Stanford University Press.

Al Sayyad, N. (2004) *The End of Tradition?* London: Routledge.

Amiry, S. (2004) *Sharon and My Mother-in-law: Ramallah Diaries*. New York: Pantheon Books.

Amiry, S. (2010) *Nothing to Lose but Your Life*. Doha: Bloomsbury Qatar Foundation.

Amiry, S. (2010) *Menopausal Palestine: Women at the Edge*. New Delhi: Women Unlimited (an associate of Kali for Women).

Amiry, S., Tamari, V. (1989) *The Palestinian Village Home*. London: British Museum.

Amiry, S. (2003) *Throne Villages Architecture: Palestinian Rural Mansions*. Ramallah: Riwaq [Arabic text].

Amiry, S. (2002) 'Getting There', in Amiry, S. and Hadid, M., *Earthquake in April*. Ramallah and Jerusalem: Riwaq, Centre for Architectural Conservation and Institute of Jerusalem Studies, pp. xii–xiix.

Amiry, S. (2009) 'Third Riwaq Biennale 2009, Venice-Palestine', in *Geography 101* (catalogue published for the 3rd Riwaq Biennale). Ramallah: Riwaq, Vol. 1.

Amnesty International (2009) 'Troubled Waters – Palestinians Denied Fair Access to Water', *Relief Web*, 27 October 2009. Available at: http://www.reliefweb.int/rw/rwb.nsf/db900SID/MYAI-7X87U6?OpenDocument [accessed 1 November 2010].

Anderson, B. (1993) *Imagined Communities: Reflections on the Origin and Spread of Nationalism*. London: Verso.

Anani, Y. (2010) 'Interview with Yazid Anani by Shuriq Harb', *ArtTerritories*, 7 September 2010. Available at: http://webcache.googleusercontent.com/search?q=cache:krLo_OHvTtUJ:www.artterritories.net/%3Fpage_id%3D889+ramallah+for+rent+ngos+only+artterritories&cd=1&hl=en&ct=clnk&gl=uk&client=safari&source=www.google.co.uk [accessed 9 June 2011].

Anani, Y. and Tamari, V. (2010) 'Ramallah – The Fairest of Them All?', *Nafas*, August 2010. Available at: http://universes-in-universe.org/eng/nafas/articles/2010/ramallah [accessed 2 June 2010].

Anon. 'Birds and Airplanes: The Conflict', *Birding Israel*. Available at: http://www.birds.org.il/740-en/Birding-Israel.aspx [accessed 16 December 2010].

Anon. 'Birds of Palestine', *Gazelle – The Palestinian Biological Bulletin*. Available at: http://www.gazelle.8m.net/photo.html [accessed 20 June 2011].

Anon. 'Birds, Thermals and Soaring Flight', *Aerospace*. Available at: http://www.aerospaceweb.org/question/nature/q0253.shtml [accessed 13 November 2010].

Anon. 'Convention (IV) respecting the Laws and Customs of War on Land and its annex: Regulations concerning the Laws and Customs of War on Land. The Hague, 18 October 1907', *International Humanitarian Law – Treaties & Documents (ICRC)*. Available at: http://www.icrc.org/ihl.nsf/FULL/195 [accessed 3 September 2010].

Anon. 'Estudio Teddy Cruz', *California-Architects.com*. Available at: http://www.california-architects.com/estudio/ [accessed 11 May 2011].

Anon. 'Learned Helplessness', *Wikipedia*. Available at: http://en.wikipedia.org/wiki/Learned_helplessness [accessed 20 April 2012].

Anon. 'Statistics on Unemployment and Poverty', *B'tselem*. Available at: http://webcache.googleusercontent.com/search?q=cache:-sUjodPNUT8J:www.btselem.org/english/freedom_of_movement/unemployment_statistics.asp+unemployment+in+palestine+btselem&cd=1&hl=en&ct=clnk&gl=uk&client=safari&source=www.google.co.uk [accessed 8 June 2011].

Anon. 'The Water Crisis', *B'tselem*. Available at: http://www.btselem.org/English/Water/index.asp [accessed 20 November 2010].

Anon. 'Water in Salfit, Sewage from Israeli Settlements', 31 December 2007. Available at: http://webcache.googleusercontent.com/search?q=cache:8R5T3hkAhksJ:skipschiel.wordpress.com/2007/12/31/water-in-salfit-sewage-from-israeli-settlements/+A+Sleeping+Time+Bomb:+Pollution+of+the+Mountain+Aquifer+by+Solid+Waste&cd=2&hl=en&ct=clnk&gl=uk&client=safari [accessed 12.6.11).

Anon. 'Workers from the Occupied Territories', *B'tselem*. Available at: http://webcache.googleusercontent.com/search?q=cache:zwHWCgbQWAgJ:www.btselem.org/english/Workers/+low+wages+of+palestinian+workers+in+ISrael+btselem&cd=1&hl=en&ct=clnk&gl=uk&client=safari&source=www.google.co.uk [accessed 21 May 2011].

Anon. (1976) 'Recommendation Concerning the Safeguarding and Contemporary Role of Historic Areas', *UNESCO*, 26 November 1976. Available at: http://portal.unesco.org/en/ev.php-URL_ID=13133&URL_DO=DO_TOPIC&URL_SECTION=201.html [accessed 13 January 2010].

Anon. (1994) 'Starting from the North to the South to Build Israeli Quarries: Confiscation of 16,733 Dunums from the West Bank', *Al-Nahar*, September 1994 [Arabic newspaper].

Anon. (1995) 'The Israeli-Palestinian Interim Agreement (Oslo II): Israeli-Palestinian Interim Agreement on the West Bank and the Gaza Strip', 28 September 1995. Available at: http://www.acpr.org.il/publications/books/44-Zero-isr-pal-interim-agreement.pdf [accessed 2 June 2010].

Anon. (2003) 'Migrating Birds Know No Boundaries', *Israeli Ministry of Foreign Affairs*, 19 November 2003. Available at: http://www.mfa.gov.il/mfa/mfa%20publications/photo%20exhibits/migrating%20birds%20know%20no%20boundaries [accessed 12 December 2010].

Anon. (2009) 'A Muddy Journey: Sewage Tunnel Becomes Transit Point to Jerusalem', Reuters, 2 November 2009. Available at: http://blogs.reuters.com/axismundi/2009/11/02/a-muddy-journey-sewage-tunnel-becomes-transit-point-to-jerusalem/ [accessed 11 November 2010).

Anon. (2009) 'Israeli Settlements in the West Bank', *The Big Picture*, 17 June 2009. Available at: http://www.boston.com/bigpicture/2009/06/israeli_settlements_in_the_wes.html [accessed 27 June 2011].

Anon. (2009) 'Reflect and Resist', Guardian.co.uk, 13 June 2009. Available at: http://www.guardian.co.uk/artanddesign/2009/jun/13/art-theatre [accessed 27 October 2009].

Anon. (2010) 'Al-Kasaba Festival Letter', *Al-Kasaba Theatre and Cinematheque*, 18 October 2010. Available at: http://webcache.googleusercontent.com/search?q=cache:qFm-MmqwN6oJ:www.alkasaba.org/festival2010/details.php%3Fid%3Dgj43v6a215ytocjqrzuv+symbol+palestine+sunbird+festiva%3B&cd=4&hl=en&ct=clnk&gl=uk&client=safari [accessed 4 October 2010].

Anon. (2011) 'Egyptian Workers form New Union', *TUC Press Release*, 30 January 2011. Available at: http://www.tuc.org.uk/international/tuc-19067-f0.cfm [accessed 28 February 2011].

Anon. (2011) 'Facebook Removes Page Calling for a "Third Palestinian Intifada"', *Haaretz*, 29 March 2011. Available at: http://www.haaretz.com/news/diplomacy-defense/facebook-removes-page-calling-for-a-third-palestinian-intifada-1.352623 [accessed 10 April 2011].

Architects and Planners for Justice in Palestine (APJP). Available at: www.http://apjp.org/ [accessed 4 June 2011].

Atrash, I. (2008) 'Forests as Important Bird Areas in Palestine', *This Week in Palestine*, No. 118 (February), pp. 28–30.

Augé, M. (2000) *Non-Places: Introduction to Anthropology of Supermodernity*. New York: Verso.

Barclay, A. (2010) 'Resisting Spaciocide: Notes on the Spatial Struggle in Israel-Palestine', MA thesis, Cardiff University, 2010. Available at: http://www.scribd.com/doc/51342175/Resisting-Spaciocide-in-Palestine-by-A-Barclay [accessed 2 April 2011].

Baumann, Z. (1998) *Globalization: The Human Consequences*. Cambridge: Polity Press.

Bayat, A. (2010) *Life as Politics. How Ordinary People Change the Middle East*. Amsterdam: Amsterdam University Press.

Bayat, A. (1997) *Street Politics: Poor People's Movements in Iran*. New York: Columbia University Press.

Bayat, A. (1987) *Workers and Revolution in Iran: A Third World Experience of Workers' Control*. London: Zed Books.

Bayat, A. (1991) *Work, Politics, and Power: An International Perspective on Workers' Control and Self-management*. New York: Monthly Review Press.

Bayat, A. (1997) 'Un-civil Society: The politics of the "informal people"', *Third World Quarterly*, Vol. 18 (1), pp. 53–72. Available at: http://abahlali.org/files/Iran.pdf [accessed 26 May 2011].

BBC News (2009) 'Dye-job Donkeys Wow Gaza Children', *BBC News*, 9 October 2009. Available at: http://news.bbc.co.uk/1/hi/8297812.stm [accessed 17 May 2010].

Beckett, K. and Western, B. (2000) 'Governing Social Marginality: Welfare, Incarceration and the Transformation of State Policy', *Punishment and Society*, Vol. 3 (1), pp. 43–59.

Ben-Gurion, D. (1970) *Memoirs: David Ben-Gurion*. New York: World Pub. Co.

Benvenisti, M. (2000) *Sacred Landscape: The Buried History of the Holy Land Since 1948*. Berkeley, CA: University of California Press.

Benvenisti, M. (1996) *City of Stone: The Hidden History of Jerusalem*. Berkeley and Los Angeles, CA: University of California Press.

Benvenisti, M. (1986) *Conflicts and Contradictions*. New York: Villard Books.

Benvenisti, M. (1972) *The Crusaders in the Holy Land*. New York: Macmillan.

Benvenisti, M. (1976) *Jerusalem, the Torn City*. Minneapolis, MN: University of Minnesota Press.

Benvenisti, M. (1984) *The West Bank Data Project: A Survey of Israel's Policies (AEI Studies)*. Washington, DC: American Enterprise Institute for Public Policy Research.

Benvenisti, D. (1946) *Our Land* (in Hebrew). Jerusalem: Kiriyat Sefer.

Bergman, S. and Tore, S. (eds) (2008). *The Ethics of Mobilities: Rethinking Place, Exclusion, Freedom and Environment*. Burlington, VT: Ashgate.

Bevan, R. (2006) *The Destruction of Memory: Architecture at War*. London: Reaktion Books.

Bhabha, Homi K. (1994) *The Location of Culture*. London and New York: Routledge.

Bhabha, Homi K. (2011) *Our Neighbours, Ourselves: Contemporary Reflections on Survival* (Hegel-lectures). Berlin and New York: De Gruyter.

Bishara, A. (2006) *Checkpoints: Fragments of a Story.* Translated by M. Goggenheimer. Tel Aviv: Babel.

Brown, A. (2004) 'The Immobile Mass: Movement Restrictions in the West Bank', *Social & Legal Studies*, Vol. 13 (4), pp. 501–21.

Bronner, E. (2009) 'Desert's Sand and Rocks Become Precious Resources in West Bank Dispute', *The New York Times*, 7 March 2009, p. 5. Available at: http://www.nytimes.com/2009/03/07/world/middleeast/07westbank.html?ref=world [accessed 4 September 2010].

Bshara, K. (2009) 'Preserving the Contemporary: Palestine Refugee Camps – From Destiny to Destinations', in *Geography 101* (catalogue published for the 3rd Riwaq Biennale). Ramallah: Riwaq, Vol. 1, p. 39.

B'tselem: The Israeli Information Center for Human Rights in the Occupied Territories. Available at: http://www.btselem.org/english/ [accessed 31 January 2010].

Cantarow, E. (2009) 'Living by the Gate From Hell', *Sabbah Report*, 9 December 2009. Available at: http://sabbah.biz/mt/archives/2009/12/09/living-by-the-gate-from-hell/ [accessed 12 May 2010].

Carmel, H. (2010) 'Jaba's Bare Ground', *Panoramio*, 9 April 2010. Available at: http://www.panoramio.com/photo/34165521 [accessed 13 June 2011].

Castells, M. (1996) *The Rise of the Network Society*. Malden, MA: Blackwell.

Cohen, A. (2005) 'Eitam Prohibits Palestinians from Drilling for Water in West Bank', *Haaretz*, 10 February 2005.

Coon, A. (1992) *Town Planning Under Military Occupation: An Examination of the Law and Practice of Town Planning in the Occupied West Bank*. Aldershot: Dartmouth.

Cope, M. (1996) 'Weaving the Everyday: Identity, Space, and Power in Lawrence, Massachusetts, 1920–1939', *Urban Geography*, Vol. 17 (2), pp. 179–204.

Cresswell, T. (2006) *On the Move: Mobility in the Modern Western World*. New York: Routledge.

Cupers, K., Meissen, M. and James, W. (2002) *Spaces of Uncertainty*. Wuppertal: Muller und Busmann.

Davis, M. (2007) *Planet of Slums*. London: Verso.

Davis, M. (2007) *In Praise of Barbarians: Essays Against Empire*. Chicago, IL: Haymarket Books.

Davis, U. (1989) *Israel: An Apartheid State*. New York: Zed Books.

David, R. (2005). 'Israel Plans to Dump Tons of Garbage in the West Bank', *Haaretz*, 4 April 2005.

Dawson, L. (2005) 'Defining Jewish Identity', *Architectural Review*, June 2005. Available at: http://findarticles.com/p/articles/mi_m3575/is_1300_217/ai_n14809395/ [accessed July 2010].

De Certeau, M. (1984) *The Practice of Everyday Life*. Berkeley, CA: University of California Press.

Decolonizing Architecture. Available at: http://www.decolonizing.ps/site/?page_id=11 [accessed 20 November 2008).

Dekel, U. 'Control of the Territorial Airspace and the Electromagnetic Spectrum', *Airspace*. Available at: http://www.jcpa.org/text/security/dekel.pdf [accessed 29 November 2010].

Derfner, L. (2011) 'People Get Ready – There's a Train Coming', *The Jerusalem Post*, 23 February 2011.

Derrida, J. (1973) *'Speech and Phenomena' and other essays on Husserl's Theory of Signs*, (translated by David B. Allison). Evanston: Northwestern University Press.

Diker, D. (ed.) (2010) *Israel's Critical Security Needs for a Viable Peace*. Jerusalem: Jerusalem Centre for Public Affairs. Available at: http://www.europe-israel.org/download/israel_security.pdf [accessed 8 December 2010].

Donnison, J. (2010) 'Bird Watchers Find Heaven in "Superhighway" Israel', *BBC News*, 1 December 2010. Available at: http://www.bbc.co.uk/news/world-middle-east-11877873 [accessed 11 December 2010].

Dovey, K. (1999) *Framing Places: Mediating Power in Built Form*. London: Routledge.

Edlund, L. (2004) *Cultural Heritage for the Future: An Evaluation Report of Nine Years' Work by Riwaq for the Palestinian Heritage 1995–2004*. Stockholm: Swedish International Development Cooperation Agency.

Efrat, E. (2006) *The West Bank and the Gaza Strip: A Geography of Occupation and Disengagement*. London: Routledge.

Etienne, B. (2001) 'Outlines of a Topography of Cruelty: Citizenship and Civility in the ERA of Global Violence', *Constellations*, Vol. 8 (1).

Erlichman, E. (2008) 'Hoopoe Israel's New National Bird', *Y Net News*, 30 May 2008. Available at: http://www.ynetnews.com/articles/0,7340,L-3549637,00.html [accessed 19 December 2010].

Falah, G.-W. (2003) 'Dynamics and Patterns of the Shrinking Arab Lands in Palestine', *Political Geography*, Vol. 22, pp. 179–209.

Falah, G.-W. (2005) 'The Geopolitics of "Enclavisation" and the Demise of a Two-State Solution to the Israeli – Palestinian Conflict', *Third World Quarterly*, Vol. 26 (8), pp. 1341–72.

Feitelson, E. and Haddad, M. (eds) (2000) *Management of Shared Groundwater Resources: The Israeli-Palestinian Case with an International Perspective*. Boston, MA: Dordrecht and London: Kluwer Academic Publishers.

Fisher, S. and Kathy, D. (1993) *Negotiating at the Margins: The Gendered Discourses of Power and Resistance*. New Brunswick, NJ: Rutgers University Press.

Foucault, M. (1972) *The Archeology of Knowledge* (translated by Sheridan Smith, A.M.). London: Tavistock Publications.

Foucault, M. (1986) 'Of Other Spaces', *Diacritics*, Vol. 16 (1), pp. 22–7. Available at: http://www.foucault.info/documents/heteroTopia/foucault.heteroTopia.en.html [accessed 20 April 2011].

Foucault, M. (1990) *The History of Sexuality: An Introduction*. New York: Vintage Books.

Foucault, M. (1997) 'Michel Foucault: Of Other Spaces (1967), Heterotopias'. *Focault.info*, 1997. Available at: http://www.foucault.info/documents/heteroTopia/foucault.heteroTopia.en.html [accessed 12 November 2010).

Franke, A. (ed.) (2003) *Territories: Islands, Camps and Other States of Utopia*. Berlin: KW Berlin und Verlag der Buchhandlung.

Fraser, M. (2007) 'Beyond Koolhaas', in Rendell, J., Hill, J., Fraser, M. and Dorrian, M. (eds), *Critical Architecture*. London: Routledge, pp. 32–9.

Fraser, M. (2007) 'Introduction: The Cultural Context of Critical Architecture', in Rendell, J., Hill, J., Fraser, M. and Dorrian, M. (eds), *Critical Architecture*. London: Routledge, pp. 249–51.

Frykberg, M. (2009) 'West Bank Becomes Waste Land', *IPS*, 15 May 2009. Available at: http://ipsnews.net/news.asp?idnews=46858 [accessed 3 November 2010].

Frykberg, M. (2009) 'Israel Stripping West Bank Quarries', *ZNET*, 11 May 2009. Available at: http://www.zcommunications.org/israel-stripping-west-bank-quarries-by-mel-frykberg [accessed 2 April 2010].

Garb, Y. (2006) 'The Softer Side of Collision', in Rieniets, T. and Misselwitz, P. (eds), *City of Collision: Jerusalem and the Principles of Conflict Urbanism*. Basel: Publishers for Architecture, pp. 286–93.

Gazit, S. (1995) *The Carrot and the Stick: Israel's Policy in Judea and Samaria, 1967–68*. New York: B'nai B'rith Book Service.

Golberger, P. (1995) 'Passion Set in Stone'. *New York Times*, 10 September 1995, p. 7. Available at: http://www.nytimes.com/1995/09/10/magazine/passion-set-in-stone.html?sec=&spon=&pagewanted=7 [accessed 12 July 2010].

Golzari, N. and Sharif, Y. (2011) 'Reclaiming Space and Identity: Heritage-led Regeneration in Palestine', *The Journal of Architecture*, Vol. 16 (1), pp. 121–44.

Graham, S. (2003) 'Lessons in Urbicide', *New Left Review*, Vol. 19, pp. 63–77.

GUST (2002) *Post Ex Sub Dis: Urban Fragmentations and Constructions*. Rotterdam: 010 Publishers.

Hamdi, N. (2010) *The Placemaker's Guide to Building Community*. London: Earthscan.

Hamdi, N. (2004) *Small Change: The Art of Practice and the Limits of Planning in Cities*. London: Earthscan.

Hammami, R. (2006) *Human Agency at the Frontiers of Global Inequality: An Ethnography of Hope in Extreme Places*. The Hague: Institute of Social Studies.

Hammami, R. (2004) 'On the Importance of Thugs: The moral economy of a checkpoint', *Middle East Report*, Vol. 231 (Summer), pp.26–34.

Hammami, R. (2004) 'Two-State Dis/Solution – On the Importance of Thugs: The Moral Economy of a Checkpoint', *Middle East Report*, Vol. 34 (2), p. 26.

Hammami, R. (2010) 'Qalandiya: Jerusalem's Tora Bora and the Frontiers of Global Inequality', *Jerusalem Quarterly*, No. 41 (Spring), pp. 29–51.

Hanafi, S. (2009) 'Spacio-cide: Colonial Politics, Invisibility and Rezoning in Palestinian Territory', *Contemporary Arab Affairs*, Vol. 2 (1), pp. 106–21.

Hannam, K., Sheller, M. and Urry, J. (2006) 'Editorial: Mobilities, Immobilities and Moorings', *Mobilities*, Vol. 1 (1), pp. 1–22.

Harel, A. 'Palestinians Abandon 1,000 Hebron Homes Under IDF, Settler Pressure', *Jerusalemites*. Available at: http://www.jerusalemites.org/reports/87.htm [accessed 20 November 2008].

Harker, C. (2009) 'Student Im/mobility in Birzeit, Palestine', *Mobilities*, Vol. 4 (1), pp. 11–35.

Harvey, D., Cunningham, D. and Goodbun, J. (2002) 'Reviews – Spaces of Capital: Towards a Critical Geography', *Radical Philosophy*, Vol. 114 (38).

Hass, A. (2002) 'Israel's Closure Policy: An Ineffective Strategy of Containment and Repression', *Journal of Palestine Studies*, Vol. 31 (3), pp. 5–20.

Hass, A. (2010) 'Israel Withholding NGO Employees' Work Permits', *Haaretz*, 20 January 2010. Available at: http://www.haaretz.com/hasen/spages/1143854.html [accessed 21 January 2009].

Hayden, D. (1995) *The Power of Place: Urban Landscapes as Public History*. Cambridge, MA: MIT Press.

Hilal, J. and Ashhab, S. (2006) 'The H2O Factor', in Messelwitz, P. and Rieniets, T. (eds), *City of Collision*. Basel and London: Birkhauser, pp. 184–92.

Hristine, S. (2007) 'In Historic District, Synagogue Plans are Criticized', *New York Times*, 9 October 2007. Available at: http://www.nytimes.com/2007/10/09/nyregion/09litchfield.html?_r=1&ref=todayspaper [accessed 12 June 2010].

Issacharoff, A. and Haaretz Correspondent (2008) '"VIP Tunnel" Smuggling Wealthy Gazans into Egypt', *Haaretz*, 25 December 2008. Available at: http://www.haaretz.com/print-edition/news/vip-tunnel-smuggling-wealthy-gazans-into-egypt-1.260177 [accessed 2 June 2011].

Jabr, S. (2007) 'Don't Hijack the Birds of Palestine', *Jerusalem Journal*, (July), pp. 12–35. Available at: http://www.wrmea.com/archives/July_2007/0707012.html [accessed 28 September 2010].

Jackobson, J. (2008) 'Learned Helplessness', *The Ramallah Lecture*, 11 July 2008. Available at: http://theramallahlecture.blogspot.com/2008/07/learned-helplessness.html [accessed 13 February 2011].

Jakobson, J. (2008) 'Ramallahisation', *The Ramallah Lecture*, 14 July 2008. Available at: http://theramallahlecture.blogspot.com/2008/07/ramallahisation.html [accessed 2 January 2010].

Jerusalem Stone. Available at: http://www.jerusalemstoneuk.co.uk [accessed 17 October 2010].

Jeffay, N. (2009) 'Bibi's "Economic Peace" Faces Key Test at Quarries', *The Jewish Daily Forward*, 24 April 2009. Available at: http://www.forward.com/articles/104861/ [accessed 11 May 2010].

Jokilehto, J. (1999) *A History of Architectural Conservation*. Oxford: Butterworth-Heinemann.

Jubeh, N. (2009) 'Fifty Villages and more: The protection of rural Palestine, in *Geography 101* (catalogue published for the 3rd Riwaq Biennale). Ramallah: Riwaq, Vol. 1.

Jubeh, N. and Bshara, K. (2002). *Ramallah: Architecture and History*. Ramallah and Jerusalem: Riwaq, and Institute of Jerusalem Studies [Arabic text].

Karkar, S. (2007) 'The First Intifada, 20 Years Later', *The Electronic Intifada*, 10 December 2007. Available at: http://electronicintifada.net/v2/article9155.shtml [accessed 12 September 2009].

Kemp, A. (2000) 'Border Space and National Identity in Israel', *Theory and Criticism, Space, Land, Home on the Normalization of a 'New Discourse'*, Vol. 16, p. 282. [Hebrew].

Khalidi, W. (1992) *All that Remains: The Palestinian Villages Occupied and Depopulated by Israel in 1948*. Washington, DC: Institute for Palestine Studies.

Khalili, L. (2009) *Politics of the Modern Arab World: Critical Issues in Modern Politics*. London: Routledge.

Khamaisi, R. (1995) 'Land Ownership as a Determinant in the Formation of Residential Areas in Arab Localities', *Geoforum*, Vol. 26 (2), p. 211.

Khamaisi, R. (2006) 'Villages Under Siege', in Misselwitz, P. and Rieniets, T. (eds), *City of Collision: Jerusalem and the Principles of Conflict Urbanism*. Basel: Birkhäuser, p. 121.

Khasawneh, D. (2001) *Memoirs Engraved in Stone: Palestine Urban Mansions*. Ramallah: Riwaq, Centre for Architectural Conservation and Jerusalem: Institute of Jerusalem Studies.

Kossak, F. (2010) *Agency: Working with Uncertain Architectures*. London: Routledge.

Kryss, T. (2004) 'Iraq: Why did USA want Regime Change?'. Available at: http://webcache.googleusercontent.com/search?q=cache:J6F9RDBFQ0kJ:www.krysstal.com/democracy_whyusa_iraq.html+how+does+americans+deal+with+Iraq+natural+resources+oil+do+they+respect+hague+convention&cd=1&hl=en&ct=clnk&gl=uk&client=firefox-a [accessed 3 September 2010].

Leary, C. (1999) *Mind the Gap: Berlin-London*. Berlin: The British Council.

Lefebvre, H. (1991) *The Production of Space*. Oxford: Basil Blackwell.

Lefebvre, H. (2004) *The Production of Space* (translated by Donald Nicholson, S.). Malden, MA: Blackwell.

Lefebvre, H. (1991) *Critique of Everyday Life* (translated by Moore, J.). London: Verso.

Lein, Y. (July, 2000) *Thirsty for a Solution: The Water Crisis in the Occupied Territories and its Resolution in the Final-Status Agreement*. Jerusalem, B'tselem, p. 42. Available at: http://webcache.googleusercontent.com/search?q=cache:o1TRJAcKdhYJ:www.btselem.org/Download/200007_Thirsty_for_a_Solution_Eng.doc+B'Tselem+The+Israeli+Information+Center+for+Human+Rights+in+the+Occupied+Territories,+Thirsty+for+a+Solution+42+(2000)&cd=1&hl=en&ct=clnk&gl=uk&client=safari [accessed 23 September 2010].

Libeskind, D. (2000) *Daniel Libeskind: The Space of Encounter*. New York: Universe.

Lobe, J. (2002) 'Israeli Settlements Control Nearly Half of West Bank', *CommonDreams.org*, 14 May 2002. Available at: http://www.commondreams.org/headlines02/0514–04.htm [accessed 22 November 2008].

Manzo Kathryn, A. (1992) *Domination, Resistance and Social Change in South Africa: The Local Effects of Global Power*. Westport, CT: Praeger.

Massey, D. (1994) *Space, Place, and Gender*. Minneapolis, MN: University of Minnesota Press.

McCarthy, R. (2009) 'Rawabi, the New Palestinian City That Could Rise on the West Bank', *Guardian.co.uk*, 8 September 2009. http://www.guardian.co.uk/world/2009/sep/08/new-palestinian-city-west-bank [accessed 28 October 2009].

McEwan, I. (2011) 'Ian McEwan on Winning the Jerusalem Prize', *The Guardian*, 24 February 2001.

Miessen, M. and Basar, S. (2006) *Did Someone Say Participate? An Atlas of Spatial Practice – A Report from the Front Lines of Cultural Activism Looks at Spatial Practitioners Who Actively Trespass into Neighbouring or Alien Fields of Knowledge*. Cambridge, MA: MIT Press.

Misselwitz, P. and Rieniets, T. (eds) (2006) *City of Collision: Jerusalem and the Principles of Conflict Urbanism*. Basel: Birkhäuser.

Mitchell, M. (2003) *Rebuilding Community in Kosovo*. Powys: Centre for Alternative Technology Publications.

Mualem, M. (2011) 'After Obama Speech, Netanyahu Rejects Withdrawal to "indefensible" 1967 Borders', *Haarez*, 19 May 2011. Available at: http://www.haaretz.com/news/diplomacy-defense/after-obama-speech-netanyahu-rejects-withdrawal-to-indefensible-1967-borders-1.362869 [accessed 24 May 2011].

Muhawi, F. (2001) 'The Politics of Land Use and Zoning Under the Oslo Accords', MA thesis, State University of Buffalo.

Mumford, L. (1961) *The City in History: Its Origins, its Transformations, and its Prospects*. New York: Harcourt.

Nassar, I. (2006) 'Colonization by Imagination', in Misselwitz, P. and Rieniets, T. (eds), *City of Collision*. New York: Birkhauser, pp. 222–6.

Nevins, J. (2002) *Operation Gatekeeper: The Rise of the Illegal Alien and the Making of the US-Mexico Boundary*. New York: Routledge.

Nitzan-Shiftan, A., Kassif Mayslits, G. and Kassif, U. (2007) 'Neuland', in Rendell, J., Hill, J., Fraser, M. and Dorrian, M. (eds), *Critical Architecture*. London: Routledge, pp. 325–31.

Nitzan-Shiftan, A. (2004) 'Seizing Locality in Jerusalem', in Alsayyed, N. (ed.), *The End of Tradition?* London and New York: Routledge, pp. 231–55.

Nitzan-Shiftan, A. (2006) 'The Israeli "Place" in East Jerusalem: How Israeli Architects Appropriated the Palestinian Aesthetic After the 67 War', *Jerusalem Quarterly*, No. 27, pp. 15–27.

OCHA (United Nations Office for the Coordination of Human Affairs) (2007) 'West Bank and Gaza Strip Closure Maps: December 2007', *OCHA*. Available at: http://unispal.un.org/pdfs/WB-G_ClosureMaps.pdf [accessed 15 February 2010].

Overmier, J.B. and Seligman, M.E.P. (1967) 'Effects of Inescapable Shock Upon Subsequent Escape and Avoidance Responding', *Journal of Comparative and Physiological Psychology*, Vol. 63, pp. 28–33.

Palestine Monitor (2010) 'Wrong side of the wall', *Palestine Monitor*, 11 May 2010. Available at: http://www.palestinemonitor.org/spip/spip.php?article1393 [accessed 20 November 2010].

PASSIA: The Palestinian Academic Society for the Study of International Affairs. Available at: http://www.passia.org [accessed 4 June 2011].

Picow, M. (2009) 'Yossi Leshem Works to Save Birds and Pilots in the Middle East', *Green Prophet*, 15 March 2009. Available at: http://www.greenprophet.com/2009/03/leshem-hudson-plane-crash-birds/ [accessed 27 November 2010].

Pile, S. and Keith, M. (1997) *Geographies of Resistance*. London: Routledge.

Platt, E. (2008) 'The Migration', *Granata*, 7 July 2008. Available at: http://www.granta.com/Magazine/102/The-Migration [accessed 16 December 2010].

Powell, H. (2005) 'Recycling Junkspace: Finding space for 'playtime' in the city', *Journal of Architecture*, Vol.10 (2), pp. 201–22.

Pullan, W. (2006) 'Locating the Civic in the Frontier: Damascus Gate', in Miessen, M. and Basar, S. (eds), *Did Someone Say Participate? An Atlas of Spatial Practice*. London and Cambridge, MA: MIT Press and Frankfurt Revolver, pp. 109–22.

Pullan, W. (2007) 'Contested Mobilities and the Spatial Topography of Jerusalem', in Purbrick, L., Aulich, J. and Dawson, G. (eds), *Contested Spaces: Sites, Representations and Histories of Conflict*. London: Palgrave Macmillan.

Prince-Gibson, E. (2006) 'A Day in the Life of Imad Atrash: Protecting Wildlife in Palestine', *Bridges*, Vol. 2 (6) (October–December). Available at: http://webcache.googleusercontent.com/search?q=cache:Ek03b4KPE6kJ:portal.wildlife-pal.org/php/modules.php%3Fname%3DNews%26file%3Darticle%26sid%3D13+where+do+storks+fly+over+palestine&cd=7&hl=en&ct=clnk&gl=uk&client=safari [accessed 18 December 2010].

Prince-Gibson, E. (2006) 'A Day in the life Imad Atrash – Protecting Wildlife in Palestine', *Bridge Magazine*, Vol. 2 (6).

Prusher, I. (2000) 'Palestinians' Stones Cut Both Ways', *The Christian Science Monitor*, 4 January 2000. Available at: http://www.csmonitor.com/2000/0104/p6s1.html [accessed 10 September 2010].

Qumsieh, V. (1998) 'The Environmental Impact of Jewish Settlements in the West Bank', *The Palestine–Israel Journal of Politics Economics and Culture*, Vol. 5 (1). Available at: http://www.pij.org/details.php?id=427 [accessed May 13 2010].

Ramallah Syndrome. Available at: http://ramallahsyndrome.blogspot.com/2009_10_01_archive.html [accessed 11 April 2011].

Ratner, D. (2005), 'Israel's Plan to Dump Tons of Garbage in the West Bank', *Haaretz*, 3 April 2005. Available at: http://www.haaretz.com/news/israel-plans-to-dump-tons-of-garbage-in-west-bank-1.154867 [accessed 24 July 2010].

Rendell, J. Hill, J., Fraser, M. and Dorrian, M. (eds) (2007) *Critical Architecture*. London: Routledge.

Rinat, Z. (2008) 'Hoopoe Crowned Nat'l Bird', *Haaretz*, 30 May 2008. Available at: http://www.haaretz.com/print-edition/news/hoopoe-crowned-nat-l-bird-1.246885 [accessed 16 June 2010].

RIWAQ. Available at: http://www.riwaq.org [accessed 27 March 2009].

Riwaq Biennale (2009) *A Geography: 50 Villages*. Ramallah: Riwaq – Centre for Architectural Conservation.

Roy, S. (2001) 'Palestinian Society and Economy: The Continued Denial of Possibility', *Journal of Palestine Studies*, Vol. 30 (4), pp. 5–20.

Sadler, S. (1998) *The Situationist City*. Cambridge, MA: MIT Press.

Said, E. (1978) *Orientalism*. London: Routledge and Kegan Paul.

Said, E. (1994) *The Politics of Dispossession: The Struggle for Palestinian Self-determination, 1969–1994*. New York: Pantheon Books.

Said, E. (1995) *The Politics of Dispossession: The Struggle for Palestinian Self-determination, 1969–1994*. London: Vintage Books.

Said, E. (1996) *Peace and its Discontents: Essays on Palestine in the Middle East Peace Process*. New York: Vintage

Said, E. (2000) *The End of the Peace Process: Oslo and After*. New York: Pantheon Books.

Said, E. (2003) *Freud and the Non-European*. London: Verso Books

Said, E. and Jean, M. (1986) *After the Last Sky: Palestinian Lives*. New York: Pantheon Books.

Sassen, S. (2000) 'A New Geography of Centers and Margins: Summary and Implications', in Legates, R. and Stout, F. (eds), *The City Reader*. London: Routledge.

Schiff, Z. and Ya'ari, E. (1990) *The Intifada*. Jerusalem: Schocken.

Schoenfeld, S. (2005) *Palestinian and Israeli Environmental Narratives: Proceedings of a Conference Held in Association with the Middle East Environmental Futures Project*. Toronto: Centre for International and Security Studies, York University.

Schouten, P. (2008) 'Theory Talks #20: David Harvey on the Geography of Capitalism: Understanding Cities as Polities and Shifting Imperialisms', *Theory Talks*, 9 October 2008. Available at: http://www.theory-talks.org/2008/10/theory-talk-20-david-harvey.html [accessed 20 October 2009].

Scott, J.C. (1985) *Weapons of the Weak: Everyday Forms of Peasant Resistance*. New Haven, CT: Yale University Press.

Scott, J.C. (1990) *Hidden Transcripts: Domination and the Arts of Resistance*. New Haven, CT: Yale University Press.

Segal, R. and Weizman, E. (eds) (2003) *A Civilian Occupation: The Politics of Israeli Architecture*. Tel Aviv: Babel.

Shabi, R. (2011) 'Israel's Government Raises Alarm at Events in Egypt', *The Guardian*, 4 February 2011.

Available at: http://www.guardian.co.uk/world/2011/feb/04/israel-government-egypt-jerusalem-post [accessed 12 May 2011).

Shalev, N. and Cohen-Lifshitz, A. (2008) *The Prohibited Zone: Israeli Planning Policies in the Palestinian Villages in Area C*. Jerusalem: BIMKOM. Available at: http://sandbox.rebuildingalliance.org/wp-content/uploads/2011/04/23ProhibitedZone.pdf [accessed 8 June 2011].

Shamir, R. (2005) 'Without Borders? Notes on Globalization as a Mobility Regime', *Sociological Theory*, Vol. 23 (2).

Sharon, A. (1998) 'Zionist Quotes', *Scribd*, 15 November 1998. Available at: http://www.scribd.com/doc/6200102/zionist-quotes [accessed 18 November 2008].

Shehadeh, R. (2008) *Palestinian Walks: Forays into a Vanishing Landscape*. New York: Scribner.

Shenker, J. (2011) 'Cairo's Biggest Protest Yet Demands Mubarak's Immediate Departure', *The Guardian*, 5 February 2011. Available at: http://www.guardian.co.uk/profile/jackshenker [accessed 13 February 2011].

Shibli, A. (2006) 'Al-Manara Square: Monumental Architecture and Power', *Jerusalem Quarterly*, Vol. 26 (Spring), pp. 52–64.

Simons, J. (1995) *Foucault and the Political*. London: Routledge.

Soja, Edward W. (1996) *Third Space*. Oxford and Cambridge, MA: Blackwell Publishers.

Sorkin, M. (2005) *Against the Wall: Israel's Barrier to Peace*. New York: New Press.

Sorkin, M. (2002) *The Next Jerusalem: Sharing the Divided City*. New York: Monacelli Press.

Stefano, P. (1996) 'Economic Analysis of Investments in Cultural Heritage: Insights from Environmental Economics', *Elaw*, June 1996. Available at: http://www.elaw.org/system/files/Economic.Analysis.Investments.Cultural.Heritage.pdf [accessed 10 January 2010].

Steinberg, G. (2004) 'Abusing the Legacy of the Holocaust: The Role of NGOs in Exploiting Human Rights to Demonize Israel', *Jewish Political Studies Review*, Vol. 16, pp. 3–4. Available at: http://209.85.229.132/search?q=cache:YU4xd36PZtAJ:www.jcpa.org/phas/phas-steinberg-f04.htm+role+of+ngos+in+palestine+political+agendas&cd=2&hl=en&ct=clnk&client=safari [accessed 20 January 2010].

Sufian, Sandra M. and Mark, L. (2007) *Reapproaching Borders: New Perspectives on the Study of Israel-Palestine*. Lanham, MD: Rowman & Littlefield Publishers.

Swirski, S. (2005) *The Price of Occupation*. Tel Aviv: Mapa Publishers [Hebrew text].

Taamallah, F. (2006) 'A Thirst for West Bank Water', *The Nation*, 26 June 2006. Available at: http://www.thenation.com/doc/20060626/Taamallah [accessed 24 July 2010].

Tamari, S. (2009) 'Architectural Laboratory of the Extreme? Reflections on Weizman's Hollow Land', *Jerusalem Quarterly*, No. 38 (Summer), pp. 21–3.

Taraki, L. (2006) *Living Palestine: Family Survival, Resistance, and Mobility Under Occupation*. Syracuse, NY: Syracuse University Press.

Tawil-Souri, H. (2010) 'Orange, Green, and Blue: Palestinian Identity Cards as Media and Material Artifacts', in Lyon, D., Zureik, E. and Abu-Laban, Y. (eds), *Surveillance and State of Exception: The Case of Israel/Palestine*. New York: Routledge.

Taylor, A. (2011) 'Catching Zebra', *The Guardian*. Available at: http://www.catchingzebra.com/post/223406020/world-animal-day-2009-a-gaza-made-zebra-a [accessed 20 March 2011].

Tomlinson, H. (2010) 'Saudi Arabia Gives Israel Clear Skies to Attack Iranian "Nuclear Sites"', *The Sunday Times*, 12 June 2010. Available at: http://www.timesonline.co.uk/tol/news/world/middle_east/article7148555.ece (accessed 12 January 2011].

Tomlinson, J. (1999) *Globalization and Culture*. Chicago, IL: University of Chicago Press.

UNESCO. Available at: http://whc.unesco.org/en/nominations [accessed 28 December 2010].

Usher, G. (2005) 'Unmaking Palestine: On Israel, the Palestinians and the Wall', *Journal of Palestine Studies*, Vol. 35 (1), pp. 25–43.

Waked, S. (2005) 'Sharif Waked: Chic Point – Fashion for Israeli Checkpoints', *Nafas Art Magazine*, March 2005. Available at: http://universes-in-universe.org/eng/nafas/articles/2005/waked [accessed 21 May 2011].

Weaver, M. and Frank, M. (1997) *Conserving Buildings: A Manual of Techniques and Materials*. New York: John Wiley & Sons.

Weizman, E. (2002) 'Control in the Air', *Open Democracy*, 1 May 2002. Available at: http://www.opendemocracy.net/ecology-politicsverticality/article_810.jsp%23%3Caccessed [accessed 5 December 2010].

Weizman, E. (2002) '10. Roads, Over and Under', *Open Democracy*, 30 April 2002. Available at: http://www.opendemocracy.net/ecology-politicsverticality/article_809.jsp [accessed 8 June 2011].

Weizman, E. (2003) 'The Politics of Verticality: The West Bank as an Architectural Construction', in Franke, A., *Territories: Islands, Camps and Other States of Utopia*. Berlin: Institute for Contemporary Art.

Weizman, E. (2007) *Hollow Land: Israel's Architecture of Occupation*. London: Verso.

Winstanley, A. (2011) 'The World Turned Upside Down: Is Egypt Heading for a Social Revolution?', *The New Left Project*, 16 February 2011. http://www.winstanleys.org/2011/02/turned-upside-down/ [accessed 23 May 2011).

Yacobi, H. (2004) *Constructing a Sense of Place: Architecture and the Zionist Discourse*. Aldershot: Ashgate.

Yiftachel, O. (2002) 'Territory as the Kernel of the Nation: Space, Time and Nationalism in Israel/Palestine', *Geopolitics*, Vol. 7 (2), pp. 215–48.

Yiftachel, O. (2006) *Ethnocracy: Land and Identity Politics in Israel/Palestine*. Philadelphia, PA: University of Pennsylvania Press.

Ze'ev, S. and Ehud, Y. (1990) *The Intifada*. Jerusalem: Schocken.

Zhu, L. and Goethert, R. (2009) 'Upgrading Historic Cities by Integrated and Innovative Solutions', *Proceedings of the Institution of Civil Engineers. Municipal Engineer*, Vol. 162 (2), pp. 87–94.

Zecharya, T., Tamar, K. and Gidon, B. (2006) *A Sleeping Time Bomb: Pollution of the Mountain Aaquifer by Solid Waste*. Tel Aviv: Friends of the Earth Middle East.

Index